IMPACT

Short Stories for Pleasure

edited by

DONALD L. STANSBURY

Bakersfield College

PRENTICE-HALL, INC., Englewood Cliffs, N.J.

To my daughter Julia

13–451724–5

Library of Congress Catalog Card No. 77-148493

Current printing (last digit): 10 9 8 7 6 5 4 3 2 1

Printed in the United States of America
Prentice-Hall International, Inc., London
Prentice-Hall of Australia, Pty. Ltd., Sydney
Prentice-Hall of Canada, Ltd., Toronto
Prentice-Hall of India Private Limited, New Delhi
Prentice-Hall of Japan, Inc., Tokyo

Grateful acknowledgment is made for permission to reprint the following selections:
THE SUPERMEN: Reprinted by permission of the author's agent, Lurton Blassingame. Copyright © 1960, HMH Publishing Co., Inc. MARIHUANA AND A PISTOL: First published in *Esquire Magazine* in March, 1940. Story is now reprinted by permission of author's literary agent, Roslyn Targ Literary Agency, Inc. THE SNIPER: From Spring Sowing by Liam O'Flaherty. Reprinted by permission of Harcourt, Brace & World, Inc. JUST LATHER, THAT'S ALL: © 1962 by Angel Flores. From *Great Spanish Short Stories*, edited by Angel Flores. N. Y.: Dell, 1962. THE SEA DEVIL: First published by *The Saturday Evening Post*. Copyright 1953 by The Curtis Publishing Company. Reprinted by permission of Brandt & Brandt. THE TIGER'S HEART: Reprinted by permission of *Esquire Magazine*. © 1951 by Esquire, Inc. THE RAIN HORSE: From *WODWO* by Ted Hughes. Copyright © 1959 by Ted Hughes. Reprinted by permission of Harper & Row, Publishers. Reprinted from the January 1960 issue of *Harper's Magazine* by permission of the author. Also reprinted by permission of Faber and Faber Ltd. THE NEW DEAL: Reprinted by permission of the author's agent, Lurton Blassingame. Copyright © 1963 HMH Publishing Co., Inc. HOW MR. HOGAN ROBBED A BANK: Copyright © 1956 by John Steinbeck. Appeared originally in *The Atlantic Monthly*. Reprinted by permission of McIntosh and Otis, Inc. THE CATBIRD SEAT: Copyright © 1945 by James Thurber. From *The Thurber Carnival*, published by Harper & Row. Originally printed in *The New Yorker*. THE BIG IT: Copyright © 1960 by A. B. Guthrie, Jr. Reprinted by permission of the publisher, Houghton Mifflin Company. WET SATURDAY: Copyright 1938, 1965 by John Collier. Originally appeared in *The New Yorker*. Reprinted by permission of Harold Matson Co., Inc. THE SNAKE: Reprinted from *Prairie Schooner* by permission of the University of Nebraska Press. Copyright 1961 by the University of Nebraska Press. DE MORTUIS: Copyright 1942 by John Collier. Originally appeared in *The New Yorker*. Reprinted by permission of Harold Matson Co., Inc. BARGAIN: Copyright © 1960 by A. B. Guthrie, Jr. Reprinted by permission of the publisher, Houghton Mifflin Company. A & P: © Copyright 1962 by John Updike. Reprinted from *Pigeon Feathers and Other Stories*, by John Updike, by permission of Alfred A. Knopf, Inc. Originally published in *The New Yorker*. DEBUT: Copyright 1968 by Kristin Hunter. Reprinted by permission of Harold Matson Co., Inc. SUCKER: Copyright © 1963 by Carson McCullers. Reprinted by permission of Robert Lantz-Candida Donadio Literary Agency, Inc. ON THE ROAD: Reprinted by permission of Harold Ober Associates Incorporated. Copyright 1935, 1952 by Langston Hughes. THE BITTER BREAD: Copyright © 1966 by Jesse Hill Ford; and Sarah Davis Ford and Katherine Kieffer Musgrove, trustees, from *Fishes, Birds, and Songs of Men* by Jesse Hill Ford, by permission of Atlantic, Little, Brown and Co. KING OF THE BINGO GAME: Reprinted by permission of William Morris Agency, Inc. Copyright © 1944 by Ralph Ellison. POISON: Copyright 1950 by Roald Dahl. Reprinted from *Someone Like You*, by Roald Dahl, by permission of Alfred A. Knopf, Inc. THE BURNING: © 1965 Atlantic Monthly Co., assigned to Jack Cady, c/o Broome Agency, Columbus, Montana 59019. THE LEDGE: Reprinted by permission of Lawrence Sargent Hall. Copyright 1960 by Lawrence Sargent Hall. First published in *The Hudson Review*, Volume XI, No. 4, Winter 1958-1959. A GOOD MAN IS HARD TO FIND: Copyright, 1953, by Flannery O'Connor. Reprinted from her volume *A Good Man Is Hard To Find and Other Stories* by permission of Harcourt, Brace, Jovanovich, Inc. THE WATCHERS: Copyright © 1965 by *Harper's Magazine*, Inc. Reprinted by permission of the author and her agent, Theron Raines. THE CROWD: Copyright 1950 by Ray Bradbury. Reprinted by permission of Harold Matson Co., Inc. FREEWAY TO WHEREVER: © 1959 Southern Methodist University Press. Originally appeared in *The Southwest Review*. NIGHT IN FUNLAND: From *Night in Funland and Other Stories* by William Peden. Reprinted by permission of the Louisiana State University Press.

CONTENTS

PREFACE

IMPACT: Short Stories For Pleasure is dedicated not to analysis, but to the pleasure that comes from reading short fiction. The book came into being because I like to read fiction very much myself—particularly short stories—and because I wanted to give students, their teachers, and the general reader a collection of stories that would be exciting, interesting, and fun to read. It seemed to me that far too many of the existing short story anthologies are overly concerned with the modern "literary" story and its analysis, rather than with the presentation of stories that will keep the reader excitedly turning the pages. My feeling is that a story's ultimate value is the pleasure it gives a reader. After he has learned to enjoy reading fiction, perhaps the reader can develop techniques of analysis for greater understanding—but the thrill and the delight of reading must come first, or analysis is merely an empty exercise.

Unfortunately, the students who most need to experience pleasurable reading—those who are relatively inexperienced or unsophisticated in the ways of literature—are often subjected to analysis before they learn to like reading fiction. No wonder that they leave school hating literature and refusing to read a novel or a short story ever again.

With such students in mind, I have selected thirty-three stories that seem to me to provide some kind of impact for the general reader. The stories come from acknowledged masters of fiction who represent a number of nationalities and racial backgrounds. All of the stories were selected according to the following criteria: (1) each had to have a strong story line or suspenseful plot; (2) each had to be relatively short—ten to twelve pages or less; and (3) each had to be simply written with an easily understandable vocabulary and a straightforward presentation and style. While literary merit was not one of the major requirements, most of the stories nevertheless have enough literary value to compete with the best short fiction.

The stories are arranged in groups of three and, overall, from shortest to longest and from easiest to most difficult. Each group of three stories may seem to have similarities in subject, character, or theme, but no "thematic" arrangement as such was intended; therefore, they may be read in any order. In general, those stories at the beginning of the book are more suspenseful and realistic, and consequently easier to read, while those toward the end—several bordering on the grotesque or fantastic—are more complex.

The teaching apparatus connected with the stories has been kept simple and short. The bulk of it appears in the back of the anthology so as not to intimidate the reader. There are, however, pre-reading stimulator questions or statements at the beginning of each story and a short biography of the author at the end. The Study Guide at the back of the book may be ignored entirely or used selectively, as the reader wishes. The Study Guide includes the following items for each story: (1) a set of ten objective comprehension questions with multiple-choice answers, of which eight questions deal with the facts in the story ("What Facts Do You Remember?") and two concern the ideas ("What Ideas Did You Find?"); (2) a composition exercise with two highly specific writing assignments; and (3) a language or vocabulary exercise ("Study Exercise—Language") presenting a variety of language activities—vocabulary building, word and usage problems and curiosities, word etymologies, etc. The intent in all the exercises is to be as relevant as possible to the concerns of today's students and to make the exercises simple, specific, and interesting.

I am indebted to many people who have offered criticisms, suggestions, and help in preparing the book. Of these I would especially like to thank Paul O'Connell, William H. Oliver, and Robert Carle of Prentice-Hall for their encouragement, understanding, and patience throughout the long process of putting the book together. And to my wife, Beverly, I extend my appreciation for her wifely patience, perseverance, and typing skill under pressure in preparing the manuscript. I would further like to thank the authors, publishers, and agents listed in the Acknowledgments for permission to reprint their stories.

Donald L. Stansbury

William M. Clark

Why do some robbers kill their victims after a theft?

Should a man protect his property—and his life—in any way he can?

See how one store owner handles some young thugs who think they have become a new breed of

THE
SUPERMEN

George Summers was late in closing up. The Friday-night footfalls of the trading farmers had died away while he wiped the counter in his small lunchroom. It was a soft night with a small mist and his motion was not hurried as he started for the door to snap the latch before his final act of cashing up.

There was a light shudder of brakes and the slam of a car door. He checked his movement toward the front, in anticipation of possible further business.

When the three young men strode in, he regretted his lateness and his waiting. They were of a type for whom he desired to do no favors, a breed that he feared because they were not of his age and he had given up trying to understand whatever he had read about them.

It was only through reading that he knew them for what they were. Center Brayton had never nurtured any such people.

1

Center Brayton was too old in its fear of God and its stable employment. It had never felt the impact of the bursting of the disciplinary dam.

The three young men had an air of matured evil. They looked past the point of return. There was no boyishness in their manner, no joy in their walk. They were not excited about the misty lateness in which they were abroad. They were not excited about anything.

Two of them walked in step toward the far corner by the register. One, tall and pimpled, flung a coarse-voiced summons at George.

"Cigarettes," he said.

George had a momentary ray of hope and then he saw the third youngster reach over and snap the catch on the night latch and take up an indolent position where he could watch the street. After that, there was no more hope, and his spine tingled a little as he faced the two.

He stood and waited for them to declare themselves. That was all he could do. The telephone was too slow to be of use. The blows would be quicker. He never doubted the coming of the blows. He felt very tired.

The old wall clock ticked solidly and the boy at the door shuffled his feet, grating the introdden sand.

George wondered what paralysis had gripped humanity that humanity had not been able to wipe out this creeping menace before it became a threat to the hinterlands around the city cradle from which it had sprung.

George knew how vulnerable the hinterlands were. Center Brayton had never known hoodlums or crime even in the days of Dutch Schultz. It had been too small for even minor gangsters.

It was not too small for this new breed, these cold-faced, old-young spawn of neglected schools of vice. Nothing was too small for them because the rewards of vice were not the reason for their acts. They sought only pain and savagery and once they had discovered the weakness of the small towns, they would be back, again and again, menacing the streets even in their absence.

They were beginning to discover the small towns. An old man with an empty cash register and a ravished store had been found dead at Turner Corners just last week. The scouts were out from the cities and it was going to take a strong shock to hold the evil to its old locale.

George noted the earmarks of the age, the long haircuts and the pseudo-Mexican sideburns, the black jacket on the one and the combat coat on the other. They showed no weapons even when they made their move. Their stance and their sneers seemed weapon enough. Their presence alone was a promise of violence.

"All right, man, this is it," suddenly said the tall invader. "You stand back against the wall and stay nice and still. You got things we want."

George backed up. He backed up tight against the shelves that lined the wall, the shelves packed with the familiar merchandise that had been his life since he had come home to find peace after the guns had gone quiet in Europe in 1945. He had gone a long way and seen much death to keep America from such as this. The thrust from abroad had been stopped but the creed had seeped silently in.

He backed up tight to the shelves and he said nothing, but his soul cried out because he did not like what was coming. He resented the need and he felt that, somewhere, there was much to be blamed.

"Hit the register, Joe," said the tall one.

The companion eased past George with a heedless push that seemed to have measured the actions to be expected from the merchant and to have found them wanting in hazard or even in bother. He punched the "No Sale" key and the drawer opened wide. He scooped bills and change into his hand and so to his pockets.

"Sixty bucks, maybe," he stated.

The tall one spat on the floor. "Big Deal," he said.

Joe brushed past George again, carelessly, as he had done before. He almost seemed to be inviting challenge and George wondered if, somewhere in the twists of his mind, he needed some kind of justification for his already planned acts, some childish symbol like the knocking of a chip from a shoulder. George would have liked to have explored the thought but there was no longer time. Things seemed to be moving faster. The clock ticked again.

Joe had reached the end of the counter when the tall leader spoke once more.

"Wait a minute, Joe," he said. He turned his voice to George. "Where's the rest of it?"

"That's all there is," said George.

"Nuts."

He turned to the watcher at the door. "How's the street?" he asked.

"Quiet," said the watcher. "The whole town's asleep. Christ, what a burg."

"Tear the telephone, Joe," said the tall one.

Wires were snapped from the wall. The instrument was hurled across the room. The leader took a piece of lead pipe from his pocket.

"Hit him a couple, Joe," he said, unemotionally. "He's got more dough than that."

Joe put his hand into his pocket and brought out a similar, unimaginative weapon. He slapped it into his other palm. He licked his lips and took a step along the counter toward where George stood, still backed against the shelves, one hand in front of him, the other resting in back, for support.

George sighed. There was just so much in living that was so hard to explain. There were so many sides to this thing that he wished he had time to consider them all, to weigh them, to moderate his needs, to offer mercy or opportunity or a guide to other paths. There wasn't time. These things had been tried by wiser men than he. These boys had probably been lectured to and prayed over and paroled and pleaded with.

He only wished that he was sure that they were the same probers who had done the brutal job at Turner Corners.

Joe took another step.

"Why don't you just take what you have and leave?" asked George, his voice rising despite his weariness and his reluctant acceptance of their denial.

Again the clock was loud.

"Hurry up, Joe," said the tall one. "Do you need some help with the man?" He laughed and, in the stillness, the laugh rang clear and brutal and cold.

That was when George, hating the need and the waste and the recrimination that he would launch tomorrow on the lacks that had forced this ugly end, brought up the hand that had rested behind him. It was typical of the stupid arrogance of the three hoodlums that they had not noticed this hand. It showed a lack in their education, a flaw in their quick course in crime, because in that hand was their undoing. The hand held a blue-steel Luger, and their overlooking it was an error that it was now too late to remedy, and yet a natural error because they had never before encountered any semblance of resistance in their pitiful victims.

It was a fitting weapon to confront them because it was a relic of the days when hoodlumism in the black uniforms of the crooked cross had threatened the peace of the entire world. George had picked it up from the dead hand of a disillusioned superman.

For a moment, as Joe paused in mid-stride, as the tall one raised his arm for a savage throw, George thought idly of mere threats or words, but the hopelessness of any appeal save force was so clear to his inner being that he was discarding the thought even as he thumbed off the safety and ducked the flying pipe and squeezed the trigger. The Luger bucked once and he swung it to the other near target and squeezed again. There was a gurgled something from Joe as he clutched at his belly and went down, but there was no sound from the tall one as he, in turn, collapsed.

The watcher at the door was yelling in full volume as he loosed the latch, but the gun spoke once more and he grabbed his shoulder and raised the other arm aloft in surrender.

"Was it you boys at Turner Corners?" asked George, probing for the last remnant of defense, reaching for the denial that would serve to turn him from his task.

The boy nodded. He nodded twice and then his face contorted and he opened his mouth to scream, and George set his lips and shot again and the scream was cut off and the boy spun around and fell, face down, arms spread out like a fallen scarecrow, the fiery dragon on his coat stretched taut and strangely still.

Then the store was quiet except for the tick of the clock and the long drawn sigh for the terrible need.

WILLIAM M. CLARK writes almost exclusively about the subject he knows and loves best—his home state of Maine. Most of his fiction is set in that locale. His books include *Maine Is in My Heart*, *Tales of Cedar River*, and *More Tales of Cedar River*. He has also contributed short stories to many magazines.

Chester B. Himes

When a person is on a marihuana "high," how are his mental faculties affected?

Can someone under the influence of a drug commit murder and not even know it?

Observe what happens to one man caught in a combination of

MARIHUANA AND A PISTOL

"Red" Caldwell bought two "weeds" and went to the room where he lived and where he kept his pearl handled blue-steel .38 revolver in the dresser drawer and smoked them. Red was despondent because his girl friend had quit him when he didn't have any more money to spend on her. But at the height of his jag, despondency became solid to the touch and attained weight which rested so heavily upon his head and shoulders that he forgot his girl friend in the feeling of the weight.

As night came on it grew dark in the room; but the darkness was filled with colors of dazzling hue and grotesque pattern in which he abruptly lost his despondency and focused instead on the sudden, brilliant idea of light.

In standing up to turn on the light, his hand gripped the rough back of the chair. He snatched his hand away, receiving

7

the sensation of a bruise. But the light bulb, which needed twist-ing, was cool and smooth and velvety and pleasing to the touch so that he lingered awhile to caress it. He did not turn it on because the idea of turning it on was gone, but he returned slowly to the middle of the floor and stood there absorbed in vacancy until the second idea came to him.

He started giggling and then began to laugh and laugh and laugh until his guts retched because it was such a swell idea, so amazingly simple and logical and perfect that it was excrutiat-ingly funny that he had never thought of it before—he would stick up the main offices of the Cleveland Trust Company at Euclid and Ninth with two beer bottles stuck in his pockets.

His mind was not aware that the thought had come from any desire for money to win back his girl friend. In fact it was an absolutely novel idea and the completely detailed execution of it exploded in his mind like a flare, showing with a stark, livid clarity his every action from the moment of his entrance into the bank until he left it with the money from the vault. But in reviewing it, the detailed plan of execution eluded him so that in the next phase it contained a pistol and the Trust Company had turned into a theater.

Perhaps ten minutes more passed in aimless wanderings about the two-by-four room before he came upon a pistol, a pearl handled blue-steel .38. But it didn't mean anything other than a pistol, cold and sinister to the touch, and he was extremely puzzled by the suggestion it presented that he go out into the street. Already he had lost the thought of committing a robbery.

Walking down the street was difficult because his body was so light, and he became angry and annoyed because he could not get his feet down properly. As he passed the confectionery store his hand was tightly gripping the butt of the pistol and he felt its sinister coldness. All of a sudden the idea came to him complete in every detail—only this time it was a confectionery store. He could remember the idea coming before, but he could not remember it as ever containing anything but the thought of robbing a confectionery store.

He opened the door and went inside, but by that time the idea was gone again and he stood there without knowing what for. The sensation of coldness produced by the gun made him think of his finger on the trigger, and all of a sudden the scope of the fascinating possibilities opened up before him, inspired by the feeling of his finger on the trigger of the pistol. He could shoot a man—or even two, or three, or he could go hunting and kill everybody.

He felt a dread fascination of horror growing on him which attracted him by the very essence of horror. He felt on the brink of a powerful sensation which he kept trying to capture but which kept eluding him. His mind kept returning again and again to his finger on the trigger of the pistol, so that by the time the storekeeper asked him what he wanted, he was frantic and he pulled the trigger five startling times, feeling the pressure on his finger and the kick of the gun and then becoming engulfed with stark, sheer terror at the sound of the shots.

His hands flew up, dropping the pistol on the floor. The pistol made a clanking sound, attracting his attention, and he looked down at it, recognizing it as a pistol and wondering who would leave a pistol on a store floor.

A pistol on a store floor. It was funny and he began to giggle, thinking, *a pistol on a store floor,* and then he began to laugh, louder and louder and harder, abruptly stopping at sight of the long pink and white sticks of peppermint candy behind the showcase.

They looked huge and desirable and delicious beyond expression and he would have died for one; and then he was eating one, and then two, reveling in the sweetish mint taste like a hog in slop, and then he was eating three, and then four, and then he was gorged and the deliciousness was gone and the taste in his mouth was bitter and brackish and sickening. He spat out what he had in his mouth. He felt like vomiting.

In bending over to vomit he saw the body of an old man lying in a puddle of blood and it so shocked him that he jumped up and ran out of the store and down the street.

He was still running when the police caught him but by that time he did not know what he was running for.

CHESTER B. HIMES was born in Jefferson City, Missouri, in 1909. He lived for a time in Cleveland and New York, and he studied briefly at Ohio State University. For many years he has lived in Paris, where he sometimes publishes his novels in French before they appear in English. Among his books are *If He Hollers Let Him Go, Lonely Crusade, Cast the First Stone, The Third Generation, Cotton Comes to Harlem*, and *Pink Toes*.

Liam O'Flaherty

If you were in the army and fighting a war, would you volunteer to be a sniper and kill soldiers and civilians with a high-powered rifle?

If you suddenly found yourself being shot at by an enemy sniper, how would you fight back?

A young soldier in the Irish Republican Army finds he must kill at a distance in

THE SNIPER

The long June twilight faded into night. Dublin lay enveloped in darkness but for the dim light of the moon that shone through fleecy clouds, casting a pale light as of approaching dawn over the streets and the dark waters of the Liffey. Around the beleaguered Four Courts the heavy guns roared. Here and there through the city, machine-guns and rifles broke the silence of the night, spasmodically, like dogs barking on lone farms. Republicans and Free Staters were waging civil war.

On a roof-top near O'Connell Bridge, a Republican sniper lay watching. Beside him lay his rifle and over his shoulders were slung a pair of field glasses. His face was the face of a student, thin and ascetic, but his eyes had the cold gleam of the fanatic. They were deep and thoughtful, the eyes of a man who is used to look at death.

He was eating a sandwich hungrily. He had eaten nothing since morning. He had been too excited to eat. He finished the sandwich, and, taking a flask of whiskey from his pocket, he took a short draught. Then he returned the flask to his pocket. He paused for a moment, considering whether he should risk a smoke. It was dangerous. The flash might be seen in the darkness and there were enemies watching. He decided to take the risk.

Placing a cigarette between his lips, he struck a match. There was a flash and a bullet whizzed over his head. He dropped immediately. He had seen the flash. It came from the opposite side of the street.

He rolled over the roof to a chimney stack in the rear, and slowly drew himself up behind it, until his eyes were level with the top of the parapet. There was nothing to be seen—just the dim outline of the opposite housetop against the blue sky. His enemy was under cover.

Just then an armored car came across the bridge and advanced slowly up the street. It stopped on the opposite of the street, fifty yards ahead. The sniper could hear the dull panting of the motor. His heart beat faster. It was an enemy car. He wanted to fire, but he knew it was useless. His bullets would never pierce the steel that covered the gray monster.

Then round the corner of a side street came an old woman, her head covered by a tattered shawl. She began to talk to the man in the turret of the car. She was pointing to the roof where the sniper lay. An informer.

The turret opened. A man's head and shoulders appeared, looking toward the sniper. The sniper raised his rifle and fired. The head fell heavily on the turret wall. The woman darted toward the side street. The sniper fired again. The woman whirled round and fell with a shriek into the gutter.

Suddenly from the opposite roof a shot rang out and the sniper dropped his rifle with a curse. The rifle clattered to the roof. The sniper thought the noise would wake the dead. He stopped to pick the rifle up. He couldn't lift it. His forearm was dead.

"Christ," he muttered, "I'm hit."

Dropping flat onto the roof, he crawled back to the parapet. With his left hand he felt the injured right forearm. There was no pain—just a deadened sensation, as if the arm had been cut off.

Quickly he drew his knife from his pocket, opened it on the breast-work of the parapet, and ripped open the sleeve. There was a small hole where the bullet had entered. On the other side there was no hole. The bullet had lodged in the bone. It must have fractured it. He bent the arm below the wound. The arm bent back easily. He ground his teeth to overcome the pain.

Then taking out the field dressing, he ripped open the packet with his knife. He broke the neck of the iodine bottle and let the bitter fluid drip into the wound. A paroxysm of pain swept through him. He placed the cotton wadding over the wound and wrapped the dressing over it. He tied the ends with his teeth.

Then he lay against the parapet, and, closing his eyes, he made an effort of will to overcome the pain.

In the street beneath all was still. The armored car had retired speedily over the bridge, with the machine-gunner's head hanging lifelessly over the turret. The woman's corpse lay still in the gutter.

The sniper lay still for a long time nursing his wounded arm and planning escape. Morning must not find him wounded on the roof. The enemy on the opposite roof covered his escape. He must kill that enemy and he could not use his rifle. He had only a revolver to do it. Then he thought of a plan.

Taking off his cap, he placed it over the muzzle of his rifle. Then he pushed the rifle slowly over the parapet, until the cap was visible from the opposite side of the street. Almost immediately there was a report, and a bullet pierced the center of the cap. The sniper slanted the rifle forward. The cap slipped down into the street. Then catching the rifle in the middle, the sniper dropped his left hand over the roof and let it hang, lifelessly. After a few moments he let the rifle drop to the street. Then he sank to the roof, dragging his hand with him.

Crawling quickly to the left, he peered up at the corner of the roof. His ruse had succeeded. The other sniper, seeing the cap and rifle fall, thought he had killed his man. He was now standing before a row of chimney pots, looking across, with his head clearly silhouetted against the western sky.

The Republican sniper smiled and lifted his revolver above the edge of the parapet. The distance was about fifty yards—a hard shot in the dim light, and his right arm was paining him like a thousand devils. He took a steady aim. His hand trembled with eagerness. Pressing his lips together, he took a deep breath through his nostrils and fired. He was almost deafened with the report and his arm shook with the recoil.

Then when the smoke cleared he peered across and uttered a cry of joy. His enemy had been hit. He was reeling over the parapet in his death agony. He struggled to keep his feet, but he was slowly falling forward, as if in a dream. The rifle fell from his grasp, hit the parapet, fell over, bounded off the pole of a barber's shop beneath and then clattered on the pavement.

Then the dying man on the roof crumpled up and fell forward. The body turned over and over in space and hit the ground with a dull thud. Then it lay still.

The sniper looked at his enemy falling and he shuddered. The lust of battle died in him. He became bitten by remorse. The sweat stood out in beads on his forehead. Weakened by his wound and the long summer day of fasting and watching on the roof, he revolted from the sight of the shattered mass of his dead enemy. His teeth chattered, he began to gibber to himself, cursing the war, cursing himself, cursing everybody.

He looked at the smoking revolver in his hand, and with an oath he hurled it to the roof at his feet. The revolver went off with the concussion and the bullet whizzed past the sniper's head. He was frightened back to his senses by the shock. His nerves steadied. The cloud of fear scattered from his mind and he laughed.

Taking the whiskey flask from his pocket, he emptied it at a draught. He felt reckless under the influence of the spirit. He decided to leave the roof now and look for his company commander, to report. Everywhere around was quiet. There was not much danger in going through the streets. He picked up his revolver and put it in his pocket. Then he crawled down through the sky-light to the house underneath.

When the sniper reached the laneway on the street level, he felt a sudden curiosity as to the identity of the enemy sniper whom he had killed. He decided that he was a good shot, whoever he was. He wondered did he know him. Perhaps he had been in his own company before the split in the army. He decided to risk going over to have a look at him. He peered round the corner into O'Connell Street. In the upper part of the street there was heavy firing, but around here all was quiet.

The sniper darted across the street. A machine-gun tore up the ground around him with a hail of bullets, but he escaped. He threw himself face downward beside the corpse. The machine-gun stopped.

Then the sniper turned over the dead body and looked into his brother's face.

LIAM O'FLAHERTY was a man of action who worked at many different jobs—soldier, seaman, lumberjack, laborer—before becoming a writer. As a soldier he fought in France during World War I and ended up a shell-shock victim. Then, after some five years of traveling around the world and working at various jobs, he returned to his native Ireland and joined the Irish Republican Army to help fight for the establishment of the Irish Free State. Some of his famous books include *The Informer, Spring Sowing,* and *Two Lovely Beasts and Other Stories.*

Hernando Téllez

What situations can you think of in which a barber might want to slit a customer's throat with a razor?

Would you deliberately allow an enemy to give you a shave with a straight razor?

Look inside a barbershop south of the border and find

JUST LATHER, THAT'S ALL

He said nothing when he entered. I was passing the best of my razors back and forth on a strop. When I recognized him I started to tremble. But he didn't notice. Hoping to conceal my emotion, I continued sharpening the razor. I tested it on the meat of my thumb, and then held it up to the light. At that moment he took off the bullet-studded belt that his gun holster dangled from. He hung it up on a wall hook and placed his military cap over it. Then he turned to me, loosening the knot of his tie, and said, "It's hot as hell. Give me a shave." He sat in the chair.

I estimated he had a four-day beard. The four days taken up by the latest expedition in search of our troops. His face seemed reddened, burned by the sun. Carefully, I began to prepare the soap. I cut off a few slices, dropped them into the cup, mixed in a bit of warm water, and began to stir with the brush. Immediately the foam began to rise. "The other boys in the group should have this much beard, too." I continued stirring the lather.

"But we did all right, you know. We got the main ones. We brought back some dead, and we've got some others still alive. But pretty soon they'll all be dead."

"How many did you catch?" I asked.

"Fourteen. We had to go pretty deep into the woods to find them. But we'll get even. Not one of them comes out of this alive, not one."

He leaned back on the chair when he saw me with the lather-covered brush in my hand. I still had to put the sheet on him. No doubt about it, I was upset. I took a sheet out of a drawer and knotted it around my customer's neck. He wouldn't stop talking. He probably thought I was in sympathy with his party.

"The town must have learned a lesson from what we did the other day," he said.

"Yes," I replied, securing the knot at the base of his dark, sweaty neck.

"That was a fine show, eh?"

"Very good," I answered, turning back for the brush. The man closed his eyes with a gesture of fatigue and sat waiting for the cool caress of the soap. I had never had him so close to me. The day he ordered the whole town to file into the patio of the school to see the four rebels hanging there, I came face to face with him for an instant. But the sight of the mutilated bodies kept me from noticing the face of the man who had directed it all, the face I was now about to take into my hands. It was not an unpleasant face, certainly. And the beard, which made him seem a bit older than he was, didn't suit him badly at all. His name was Torres. Captain Torres. A man of imagination, because who else would have thought of hanging the naked rebels and then holding target practice on certain parts of their bodies? I began to apply the first layer of soap. With his eyes closed, he continued. "Without any effort I could go straight to sleep," he said, "but there's plenty to do this afternoon." I stopped the lathering and asked with a feigned lack of interest: "A firing squad?" "Something like that, but a little slower." I got on with the job of lathering his beard. My hands started trembling again. The man could not possibly realize it, and this was in my favor. But I would have preferred that he hadn't come. It was likely that many of our faction had seen him enter. And an enemy under one's roof imposes certain conditions. I would be obliged to shave that beard like any other one, carefully, gently, like that of any customer, taking pains to see that no single pore emitted a drop of blood. Being careful to see that the little tufts of hair did not lead the blade astray. Seeing that his skin ended up clean, soft, and healthy, so that passing the back of my hand over it I couldn't feel a hair. Yes, I was secretly a rebel, but I was also a conscientious barber, and proud of the preciseness of my profession. And this four-days' growth of beard was a fitting challenge.

I took the razor, opened up the two protective arms, exposed the blade and began the job, from one of the sideburns downward. The razor responded beautifully. His beard was inflexible and hard, not too long, but thick. Bit by bit the skin emerged. The razor rasped along, making its customary sound as fluffs of lather mixed with bits of hair gathered along the blade. I paused a moment to clean it, then took up the strop again to sharpen the razor, because I'm a barber who does things properly. The man, who had kept his eyes closed, opened them now, removed one of his hands from under the sheet, felt the spot on his face where the soap had been cleared off, and said, "Come to the school today at six o'clock." "The same thing as the other day?" I asked horrified. "It could be better," he replied. "What do you plan to do?" "I don't know yet. But we'll amuse ourselves." Once more he leaned back and closed his eyes. I approached him with the razor poised. "Do you plan to punish them all?" I ventured timidly. "All." The soap was drying on his face. I had to hurry. In the mirror I looked toward the street. It was the same as ever: the grocery store with two or three customers in it. Then I glanced at the clock: two-twenty in the afternoon. The razor continued on its downward stroke. Now from the other sideburn down. A thick, blue beard. He should have let it grow like some poets or priests do. It would suit him well.

A lot of people wouldn't recognize him. Much to his benefit, I thought, as I attempted to cover the neck area smoothly. There, for sure, the razor had to be handled masterfully, since the hair, although softer, grew into little swirls. A curly beard. One of the tiny pores could be opened up and issue forth its pearl of blood. A good barber such as I prides himself on never allowing this to happen to a client. And this was a first-class client. How many of us had he ordered shot? How many of us had he ordered mutilated? It was better not to think about it. Torres did not know that I was his enemy. He did not know it nor did the rest. It was a secret shared by very few, precisely so that I could inform the revolutionaries of what Torres was doing in the town and of what he was planning each time he undertook a rebel-hunting excursion. So it was going to be very difficult to explain that I had him right in my hands and let him go peacefully—alive and shaved.

　　The beard was now almost completely gone. He seemed younger, less burdened by years than when he had arrived. I suppose this always happens with men who visit barber shops. Under the stroke of my razor Torres was being rejuvenated— rejuvenated because I am a good barber, the best in the town, if I may say so. A little more lather here, under his chin, on his Adam's apple, on this big vein. How hot it is getting! Torres must be sweating as much as I. But he is not afraid. He is a calm man, who is not even thinking about what he is going to do with the prisoners this afternoon. On the other hand I, with this razor in my hands, stroking and re-stroking his skin, trying to keep blood from oozing from these pores, can't even think clearly. Damn him for coming, because I'm a revolutionary and not a murderer. And how easy it would be to kill him. And he deserves it. Does he? No! What the devil! No one deserves to have someone else make the sacrifice of becoming a murderer. What do you gain by it? Nothing. Others come along and still others, and the first ones kill the second ones and they the next ones and it goes on like this until everything is a sea of blood. I could cut this throat just so, zip! zip! I wouldn't give him time to complain and since he has his eyes closed he wouldn't see the glistening knife blade or my glistening eyes. But I'm trembling like a real murderer. Out of his neck a gush of blood would spout onto the sheet, on the chair, on my hands, on the floor. I would have to close the door. And the blood would keep inching along the floor, warm, ineradicable, uncontainable, until it reached the street, like a little scarlet stream. I'm sure that one solid stroke, one deep incision, would prevent any pain. He wouldn't suffer. But what would I do with the body? Where would I hide it? I would have to flee, leaving all I have behind, and take refuge far away, far, far away. But they would follow until they found me. "Captain Torres' murderer. He slit his throat while he was shaving him—a coward." And then on the other side. "The avenger of us all. A name to remember. (And here they would mention my name.) He was the town barber. No one knew he was defending our cause."

And what of all this? Murderer or hero? My destiny depends on the edge of this blade. I can turn my hand a bit more, press a little harder on the razor, and sink it in. The skin would give way like silk, like rubber, like the strop. There is nothing more tender than human skin and the blood is always there, ready to pour forth. A blade like this doesn't fail. It is my best. But I don't want to be a murderer, no sir. You came to me for a shave. And I perform my work honorably. . . . I don't want blood on my hands. Just lather, that's all. You are an executioner and I am only a barber. Each person has his own place in the scheme of things. That's right. His own place.

Now his chin had been stroked clean and smooth. The man sat up and looked into the mirror. He rubbed his hands over his skin and felt it fresh, like new.

"Thanks," he said. He went to the hanger for his belt, pistol and cap. I must have been very pale; my shirt felt soaked. Torres finished adjusting the buckle, straightened his pistol in the holster and after automatically smoothing down his hair, he put on the cap. From his pants pocket he took out several coins to pay me for my services. And he began to head toward the door. In the doorway he paused for a moment, and turning to me he said:

"They told me that you'd kill me. I came to find out. But killing isn't easy. You can take my word for it." And he headed on down the street.

HERNANDO TÉLLEZ was born in Bogota, Colombia, in 1908 and received his education there. As a young man he became a journalist and has since been associated with many of Colombia's most popular newspapers. In 1950 he published a volume of short stories, *Cenizas al Viento,* which extended his literary fame as a writer of contemporary tragicomic tales set in his native land.

Stephen Crane

Why do people fear a corpse and dislike touching or handling it?

Why would combat soldiers burying a dead buddy be bothered by having to throw dirt on the friend's face?

In this war story two officers react strangely to

THE UPTURNED FACE

"What will we do now?" said the adjutant, troubled and excited.

"Bury him," said Timothy Lean.

The two officers looked down close to their toes where lay the body of their comrade. The face was chalk-blue; gleaming eyes stared at the sky. Over the two upright figures was a windy sound of bullets, and on top of the hill Lean's prostrate company of Spitzbergen infantry was firing measured volleys.

"Don't you think it would be better—" began the adjutant. "We might leave him until tomorrow."

"No," said Lean. "I can't hold that post an hour longer. I've got to fall back, and we've got to bury old Bill."

"Of course," said the adjutant, at once. "Your men got entrenching tools?"

Lean shouted back to his little line, and two men came

slowly, one with a pick, one with a shovel. They started in the direction of the Rostina sharpshooters. Bullets cracked near their ears. "Dig here," said Lean gruffly. The men, thus caused to lower their glances to the turf, became hurried and frightened, merely because they could not look to see whence the bullets came. The dull beat of the pick striking the earth sounded amid the swift snap of close bullets. Presently the other private began to shovel.

"I suppose," said the adjutant slowly, "we'd better search his clothes for—things."

Lean nodded. Together in curious abstraction they looked at the body. Then Lean stirred his shoulders suddenly, arousing himself.

"Yes," he said, "we'd better see what he's got." He dropped to his knee, and his hands approached the body of the dead officer. But his hands wavered over the buttons of the tunic. The first button was brick-red with drying blood, and he did not seem to dare to touch it.

"Go on," said the adjutant, hoarsely.

Lean stretched his wooden hand, and his fingers fumbled the bloodstained buttons. At last he rose with ghastly face. He had gathered a watch, a whistle, a pipe, a tobacco-pouch, a handkerchief, a little case of cards and papers. He looked at the adjutant. There was a silence. The adjutant was feeling that he had been a coward to make Lean do all the grisly business.

"Well," said Lean, "that's all, I think. You have his sword and revolver?"

"Yes," said the adjutant, his face working, and then he burst out in a sudden strange fury at the two privates. "Why don't you hurry up with that grave? What are you doing, anyhow? Hurry, do you hear? I never saw such stupid—"

Even as he cried out in his passion, the two men were labouring for their lives. Ever overhead the bullets were spitting.

The grave was finished. It was not a masterpiece—a poor little shallow thing. Lean and the adjutant again looked at each other in a curious silent communication.

Suddenly the adjutant croaked out a weird laugh. It was a terrible laugh which had its origin in that part of the mind which is first moved by the singing of the nerves. "Well," he said humorously to Lean, "I suppose we had best tumble him in."

"Yes," said Lean. The two privates stood waiting, bent over their implements. "I suppose," said Lean, "it would be better if we laid him in ourselves."

"Yes," said the adjutant. Then, apparently remembering that he had made Lean search the body, he stooped with great fortitude and took hold of the dead officer's clothing. Lean joined him. Both were particular that their fingers should not feel the corpse. They tugged away; the corpse lifted, heaved, toppled, flopped into the grave, and the two officers, straightening, looked again at each other—they were always looking at each other. They sighed with relief.

The adjutant said, "I suppose we should—we should say something. Do you know the service, Tim?"

"They don't read the service until the grave is filled in," said Lean, pressing his lips to an academic expression.

"Don't they?" said the adjutant, shocked that he had made the mistake. "Oh, well," he cried, suddenly, "let us—let us say something—while he can hear us."

"All right," said Lean. "Do you know the service?"

"I can't remember a line of it," said the adjutant.

Lean was extremely dubious. "I can repeat two lines, but—"

"Well, do it," said the adjutant. "Go as far as you can. That's better than nothing. And the beasts have got our range exactly."

Lean looked at his two men. "Attention," he barked. The privates came to attention with a click, looking much aggrieved. The adjutant lowered his helmet to his knee. Lean, bareheaded, stood over the grave. The Rostina sharpshooters fired briskly.

"O Father, our friend has sunk in the deep waters of death, but his spirit has leaped toward Thee as the bubble arises from the lips of the drowning. Perceive, we beseech, O Father, the little flying bubble, and—"

Lean, although husky and ashamed, had suffered no hesitation up to this point, but he stopped with a hopeless feeling and looked at the corpse.

The adjutant moved uneasily. "And from Thy superb heights," he began, and then he too came to an end.

"And from Thy superb heights," said Lean.

The adjutant suddenly remembered a phrase in the back of the Spitzbergen burial service, and he exploited it with the triumphant manner of a man who has recalled everything, and can go on.

"O God, have mercy—"

"O God, have mercy—" said Lean.

"Mercy," repeated the adjutant, in quick failure.

"Mercy," said Lean. And then he was moved by some violence of feeling, for he turned upon his two men and tigerishly said, "Throw the dirt in."

The fire of the Rostina sharpshooters was accurate and continuous.

One of the aggrieved privates came forward with his shovel. He lifted his first shovel-load of earth, and for a moment of inexplicable hesitation it was held poised above this corpse which from its chalk-blue face looked keenly out from the grave. Then the soldier emptied his shovel on—on the feet.

Timothy Lean felt as if tons had been swiftly lifted from off his forehead. He had felt that perhaps the private might empty the shovel on—on the face. It had been emptied on the feet. There was a great point gained there—ha, ha!—the first shovelful had been emptied on the feet. How satisfactory!

The adjutant began to babble. "Well, of course—a man we've messed with all these years—impossible—you can't, you know, leave your intimate friends rotting on the field. Go on, for God's sake, and shovel, you."

The man with the shovel suddenly ducked, grabbed his left arm with his right hand, and looked at his officer for orders. Lean picked the shovel from the ground. "Go to the rear," he said to the wounded man. He also addressed the other private. "You get under cover, too; I'll finish this business."

The wounded man scrambled hard for the top of the ridge without devoting any glances to the direction from whence the bullets came, and the other man followed at an equal pace; but he was different, in that he looked back anxiously three times.

This is merely the way—often—of the hit and unhit.

Timothy Lean filled the shovel, hesitated, and then, in a

movement which was like a gesture of abhorrence, he flung the dirt into the grave, and as it landed it made a sound—plop. Lean suddenly stopped and mopped his brow—a tired labourer.

"Perhaps we have been wrong," said the adjutant. His glance wavered stupidly. "It might have been better if we hadn't buried him just at this time. Of course, if we advance tomorrow the body would have been—"

"Damn you," said Lean, "shut your mouth." He was not the senior officer.

He again filled the shovel and flung the earth. Always the earth made that sound—plop. For a space, Lean worked frantically, like a man digging himself out of danger.

Soon there was nothing to be seen but the chalk-blue face. Lean filled the shovel. "Good God," he cried to the adjutant. "Why didn't you turn him somehow when you put him in? This—" Then Lean began to stutter.

The adjutant understood. He was pale to the lips. "Go on," he cried, beseechingly, almost in a shout.

Lean swung back the shovel. It went forward in a pendulum curve. When the earth landed it made a sound—plop.

STEPHEN CRANE was born in Newark, New Jersey, in 1871. He became a newspaperman in his youth and financed his college education by working as a correspondent for the New York *Tribune.* Although his first novels, *Maggie: A Girl of the Streets* and *The Red Badge of Courage,* established his fame as a novelist, he earned little money from either book. He went to London in 1898 and married Cora Taylor. Afterward he wrote newspaper reports on the Spanish-American War, suffered from increasingly failing health, and finally died in Germany in 1900, at the age of 29. His most famous short story, "The Open Boat," is considered a classic story of men adrift at sea in a boat.

Stephen Crane

*Would you have the courage to run out in the open
with enemy troops firing at you?*

*Why would a young Civil War soldier risk
death to fill some canteens with drinking water?*

Witness such courage in

A MYSTERY OF HEROISM

The dark uniforms of the men were so coated with dust
from the incessant wrestling of the two armies that the regiment
almost seemed a part of the clay bank which shielded them from
the shells. On the top of the hill a battery was arguing in tremendous roars with some other guns, and to the eye of the infantry,
the artillerymen, the guns, the caissons, the horses, were distinctly
outlined upon the blue sky. When a piece was fired, a red streak
as round as a log flashed low in the heavens, like a monstrous
bolt of lightning. The men of the battery wore white duck trousers, which somehow emphasized their legs; and when they ran
and crowded in little groups at the bidding of the shouting officers,
it was more impressive than usual to the infantry.

Fred Collins, of A Company, was saying: "Thunder! I wisht
I had a drink. Ain't there any water round here?" Then somebody
yelled, "There goes th' bugler!"

As the eyes of half the regiment swept in one machinelike movement there was an instant's picture of a horse in a great convulsive leap of a death wound and a rider leaning back with a crooked arm and spread fingers before his face. On the ground was the crimson terror of an exploding shell, with fibres of flame that seemed like lances. A glittering bugle swung clear of the rider's back as fell headlong the horse and the man. In the air was an odour as from a conflagration.

Sometimes they of the infantry looked down at a fair little meadow which spread at their feet. Its long, green grass was rippling gently in a breeze. Beyond it was the gray form of a house half torn to pieces by shells and by the busy axes of soldiers who had pursued firewood. The line of an old fence was now dimly marked by long weeds and by an occasional post. A shell had blown the well-house to fragments. Little lines of gray smoke ribboning upward from some embers indicated the place where had stood the barn.

From beyond a curtain of green woods there came the sound of some stupendous scuffle, as if two animals of the size of islands were fighting. At a distance there were occasional appearances of swift-moving men, horses, batteries, flags, and, with the crashing of infantry volleys were heard, often, wild and frenzied cheers. In the midst of it all Smith and Ferguson, two privates of A Company, were engaged in a heated discussion, which involved the greatest questions of the national existence.

The battery on the hill presently engaged in a frightful duel. The white legs of the gunners scampered this way and that way, and the officers redoubled their shouts. The guns, with their demeanours of stolidity and courage, were typical of something infinitely self-possessed in this clamour of death that swirled around the hill.

One of a "swing" team was suddenly smitten quivering to the ground, and his maddened brethren dragged his torn body in their struggle to escape from this turmoil and danger. A young soldier astride one of the leaders swore and fumed in his saddle, and furiously jerked at the bridle. An officer screamed out an order so violently that his voice broke and ended the sentence in a falsetto shriek.

The leading company of the infantry regiment was somewhat exposed, and the colonel ordered it moved more fully under the shelter of the hill. There was the clank of steel against steel.

A lieutenant of the battery rode down and passed them, holding his right arm carefully in his left hand. And it was as if this arm was not at all a part of him, but belonged to another man. His sober and reflective charger went slowly. The officer's face was grimy and perspiring, and his uniform was tousled as if he had been in direct grapple with an enemy. He smiled grimly when the men stared at him. He turned his horse toward the meadow.

Collins, of A Company, said: "I wisht I had a drink. I bet there's water in that there ol' well yonder!"

"Yes; but how you goin' to git it?"

For the little meadow which intervened was now suffering a terrible onslaught of shells. Its green and beautiful calm had vanished utterly. Brown earth was being flung in monstrous handfuls. And there was a massacre of the young blades of grass. They were being torn, burned, obliterated. Some curious fortune of the battle had made this gentle little meadow the object of the red hate of the shells, and each one as it exploded seemed like an imprecation in the face of a maiden.

The wounded officer who was riding across this expanse said to himself, "Why, they couldn't shoot any harder if the whole army was massed here!"

A shell struck the gray ruins of the house, and as, after the roar, the shattered wall fell in fragments, there was a noise which resembled the flapping of shutters during a wild gale of winter. Indeed, the infantry paused in the shelter of the bank appeared as men standing upon a shore contemplating a madness of the sea. The angel of calamity had under its glance the battery upon the hill. Fewer white-legged men laboured about the guns. A shell had smitten one of the pieces, and after the flare, the smoke, the dust, the wrath of this blow were gone, it was possible to see white legs stretched horizontally upon the ground. And at that interval to the rear, where it is the business of battery horses to stand with their noses to the fight awaiting the command to drag their guns out of the destruction or into it or wheresoever these incomprehensible humans demanded with whip and spur—in this line of passive and dumb spectators, whose fluttering hearts yet would not let them forget the iron laws of man's control of them—in this rank of brute-soldiers there had been relentless and hideous carnage. From the ruck of bleeding and prostrate horses, the men of the infantry could see one animal raising its stricken body with its fore legs, and turning its nose with mystic and profound eloquence toward the sky.

Some comrades joked Collins about his thirst. "Well, if yeh want a drink so bad, why don't yeh go git it!"

"Well, I will in a minnet, if yeh don't shut up!"

A lieutenant of artillery foundered his horse straight down the hill with as great concern as if it were level ground. As he galloped past the colonel of the infantry, he threw up his hand in swift salute. "We've got to get out of that," he roared angrily. He was a black-bearded officer, and his eyes, which resembled beads, sparkled like those of an insane man. His jumping horse sped along the column of infantry.

The fat major, standing carelessly with his sword held horizontally behind him and with his legs far apart, looked after the receding horseman and laughed. "He wants to get back with orders pretty quick, or there'll be no batt'ry left," he observed.

The wise young captain of the second company hazarded to the lieutenant colonel that the enemy's infantry would probably soon attack the hill, and the lieutenant colonel snubbed him.

A private in one of the rear companies looked out over the meadow, and then turned to a companion and said, "Look there, Jim!" It was the wounded officer from the battery, who some time before had started to ride across the meadow, supporting his right arm carefully with his left hand. This man had encountered a shell apparently at a time when no one perceived him, and he could now be seen lying face downward with a stirruped foot stretched across the body of his dead horse. A leg of the charger extended slantingly upward precisely as stiff as a stake. Around this motionless pair the shells still howled.

There was a quarrel in A Company. Collins was shaking his fist in the faces of some laughing comrades. "Dern yeh! I ain't afraid t' go. If yeh say much, I will go!"

"Of course, yeh will! You'll run through that there medder, won't yeh?"

Collins said, in a terrible voice, "You see now!" At this ominous threat his comrades broke into renewed jeers.

Collins gave them a dark scowl and went to find his captain. The latter was conversing with the colonel of the regiment.

"Captain," said Collins, saluting and standing at attention—in those days all trousers bagged at the knees—"captain, I want t' get permission to go git some water from that there well over yonder!"

The colonel and the captain swung about simultaneously and stared across the meadow. The captain laughed. "You must be pretty thirsty, Collins?"

"Yes sir, I am."

"Well—ah," said the captain. After a moment he asked, "Can't you wait?"

"No, sir."

The colonel was watching Collins's face. "Look here, my lad," he said, in a pious sort of a voice—"look here, my lad"—Collins was not a lad—"don't you think that's taking pretty big risks for a little drink of water?"

"I dunno," said Collins uncomfortably. Some of the resentment toward his companions, which perhaps had forced him into this affair, was beginning to fade. "I dunno wether 'tis."

The colonel and the captain contemplated him for a time.

"Well," said the captain finally.

"Well," said the colonel, "if you want to go, why, go."

Collins saluted. "Much obliged t' yeh."

As he moved away the colonel called after him. "Take some of the other boys' canteens with you an' hurry back now."

"Yes, sir, I will."

The colonel and the captain looked at each other then, for it had suddenly occurred that they could not for the life of them tell whether Collins wanted to go or whether he did not.

They turned to regard Collins, and as they perceived him surrounded by gesticulating comrades, the colonel said: "Well, by thunder! I guess he's going."

Collins appeared as a man dreaming. In the midst of the questions, the advice, the warnings, all the excited talk of his company mates, he maintained a curious silence.

They were very busy in preparing him for his ordeal. When they inspected him carefully it was somewhat like the examination that grooms give a horse before a race; and they were amazed, staggered by the whole affair. Their astonishment found vent in strange repetitions.

"Are yeh sure a-goin'?" they demanded again and again.

"Certainly I am," cried Collins, at last furiously.

He strode sullenly away from them. He was swinging five or six canteens by their cords. It seemed that his cap would not remain firmly on his head, and often he reached and pulled it down over his brow.

There was a general movement in the compact column. The long animal-like thing moved slightly. Its four hundred eyes were turned upon the figure of Collins.

"Well, sir, if that ain't th' derndest thing! I never thought Fred Collins had the blood in him for that kind of business."

"What's he goin' to do, anyhow?"

"He's goin' to that well there after water."

"We ain't dyin' of thirst, are we? That's foolishness."

"Well, somebody put him up to it, an' he's doin' it."

"Say, he must be a desperate cuss."

When Collins faced the meadow and walked away from the regiment, he was vaguely conscious that a chasm, the deep valley of all prides, was suddenly between him and his comrades. It was provisional, but the provision was that he return as a victor. He had blindly been led by quaint emotions, and laid himself under an obligation to walk squarely up to the face of death.

But he was not sure that he wished to make a retraction, even if he could do so without shame. As a matter of truth, he was sure of very little. He was mainly surprised.

It seemed to him supernaturally strange that he had allowed his mind to maneuver his body into such a situation. He understood that it might be called dramatically great.

However, he had no full appreciation of anything, excepting that he was actually conscious of being dazed. He could feel his dulled mind groping after the form and colour of this incident. He wondered why he did not feel some keen agony of fear cutting his sense like a knife. He wondered at this, because human expression had said loudly for centuries that men should feel afraid of certain things, and that all men who did not feel this fear were phenomena—heroes.

He was, then, a hero. He suffered that disappointment which we would all have if we discovered that we were ourselves capable of those deeds which we most admire in history and legend. This, then, was a hero. After all, heroes were not much.

No, it could not be true. He was not a hero. Heroes had no shames in their lives, and, as for him, he remembered borrowing fifteen dollars from a friend and promising to pay it back the next day, and then avoiding that friend for ten months. When at home his mother had aroused him for the early labour of his life on the farm, it had often been his fashion to be irritable, childish, diabolical; and his mother had died since he had come to the war.

He saw that, in this matter of the well, the canteens, the shells, he was an intruder in the land of fine deeds.

He was now about thirty paces from his comrades. The regiment had just turned its many faces toward him.

From the forest of terrific noises there suddenly emerged a little uneven line of men. They fired fiercely and rapidly at distant foliage on which appeared little puffs of white smoke. The spatter of skirmish firing was added to the thunder of the guns on the hill. The little line of men ran forward. A colour sergeant fell flat with his flag as if he had slipped on ice. There was hoarse cheering from this distant field.

Collins suddenly felt that two demon fingers were pressed into his ears. He could see nothing but flying arrows, flaming red. He lurched from the shock of this explosion, but he made a mad rush for the house, which he viewed as a man submerged to the neck in a boiling surf might view the shore. In the air, little pieces of shell howled and the earthquake explosions drove him insane with the menace of their roar. As he ran the canteens knocked together with a rhythmical tinkling.

As he neared the house, each detail of the scene became vivid to him. He was aware of some bricks of the vanished chimney lying on the sod. There was a door which hung by one hinge.

Rifle bullets called forth by the insistent skirmishers came from the far-off bank of foliage. They mingled with the shells and the pieces of shells until the air was torn in all directions by hootings, yells, howls. The sky was full of fiends who directed all their wild rage at his head.

When he came to the well, he flung himself face downward into its darkness. There were furtive silver glintings some feet from the surface. He grabbed one of the canteens and, unfastening its cap, swung it down by the cord. The water flowed slowly in with an indolent gurgle.

And now as he lay with his face turned away he was suddenly smitten with the terror. It came upon his heart like the grasp of claws. All the power faded from his muscles. For an instant he was no more than a dead man.

The canteen filled with a maddening slowness, in the manner of all bottles. Presently he recovered his strength and addressed a screaming oath to it. He leaned over until it seemed as if he intended to try to push water into it with his hands. His eyes as he gazed down into the well shone like two pieces of metal and in their expression was a great appeal and a great curse. The stupid water derided him.

There was the blaring thunder of a shell. Crimson light shone through the swift-boiling smoke and made a pink reflection on part of the wall of the well. Collins jerked out his arm and canteen with the same motion that a man would use in withdrawing his head from a furnace.

He scrambled erect and glared and hesitated. On the ground near him lay the old well bucket, with a length of rusty chain. He lowered it swiftly into the well. The bucket struck the water and then, turning lazily over, sank. When, with hand reaching tremblingly over hand, he hauled it out, it knocked often against the walls of the well and spilled some of its contents.

In running with a filled bucket, a man can adopt but one kind of gait. So through this terrible field over which screamed practical angels of death Collins ran in the manner of a farmer chased out of a dairy by a bull.

His face went staring white with anticipation—anticipation of a blow that would whirl him around and down. He would fall as he had seen other men fall, the life knocked out of them so suddenly that their knees were no more quick to touch the ground than their heads. He saw the long blue line of the regiment, but his comrades were standing looking at him from the edge of an impossible star. He was aware of some deep wheel ruts and hoof-prints in the sod beneath his feet.

The artillery officer who had fallen in this meadow had been making groans in the teeth of the tempest of sound. These futile cries, wrenched from him by his agony, were heard only by shells, bullets. When wild-eyed Collins came running, this officer raised himself. His face contorted and blanched from pain, he was about to utter some great beseeching cry. But suddenly his face straightened and he called: "Say, young man, give me a drink of water, will you?"

Collins had no room amid his emotions for surprise. He was mad from the threats of destruction.

"I can't!" he screamed, and in his reply was a full description of his quaking apprehension. His cap was gone and his hair was riotous. His clothes made it appear that he had been dragged over the ground by the heels. He ran on.

The officer's head sank down and one elbow crooked. His foot in its brass-bound stirrup still stretched over the body of his horse and the other leg was under the steed.

But Collins turned. He came dashing back. His face had now turned gray and in his eyes was all terror. "Here it is! here it is!"

The officer was as a man gone in drink. His arm bent like a twig. His head drooped as if his neck were of willow. He was sinking to the ground, to lie face downward.

Collins grabbed him by the shoulder. "Here it is. Here's your drink. Turn over. Turn over, man, for God's sake!"

With Collins hauling at his shoulder, the officer twisted his body and fell with his face turned toward that region where lived the unspeakable noises of the swirling missiles. There was the faintest shadow of a smile on his lips as he looked at Collins. He gave a sigh, a little primitive breath like that from a child.

Collins tried to hold the bucket steadily, but his shaking hands caused the water to splash all over the face of the dying man. Then he jerked it away and ran on.

The regiment gave him a welcoming roar. The grimed faces were wrinkled in laughter.

His captain waved the bucket away. "Give it to the men!"

The two genial, skylarking young lieutenants were the first to gain possession of it. They played over it in their fashion.

When one tried to drink the other teasingly knocked his elbow. "Don't, Billie! You'll make me spill it," said the one. The other laughed.

Suddenly there was an oath, the thud of wood on the ground, and a swift murmur of astonishment among the ranks. The two lieutenants glared at each other. The bucket lay on the ground empty.

STEPHEN CRANE (For biography, see p. 26.)

Arthur Gordon

What are some of the dangers a man may face when he goes hunting or fishing by himself?

How would you free yourself if you were tied to a fleeing animal by a long, stout rope?

See what happens when a night fisherman encounters

THE SEA DEVIL

The man came out of the house and stood quite still, listening. Behind him, the lights glowed in the cheerful room, the books were neat and orderly in their cases, the radio talked importantly to itself. In front of him, the bay stretched dark and silent, one of the countless lagoons that border the coast where Florida thrusts its great green thumb deep into the tropics.

It was late in September. The night was breathless; summer's dead hand still lay heavy on the land. The man moved forward six paces and stood on the sea wall. He dropped his cigarette and noted where the tiny spark hissed and went out. The tide was beginning to ebb.

Somewhere out in the blackness a mullet jumped and fell back with a sullen splash. Heavy with roe, they were jumping less often, now. They would not take a hook, but a practiced eye could see the swirls they made in the glassy water. In the dark of the moon, a skilled man with a cast net might take half a dozen in an hour's work. And a big mullet makes a meal for a family.

The man turned abruptly and went into the garage, where his cast net hung. He was in his late twenties, wide-shouldered and strong. He did not have to fish for a living, or even for food. He was a man who worked with his head, not with his hands. But he liked to go casting alone at night.

He liked the loneliness and the labor of it. He liked the clean taste of salt when he gripped the edge of the net with his teeth as a cast netter must. He liked the arching flight of sixteen pounds of lead and linen against the starlight, and the weltering crash of the net into the unsuspecting water. He liked the harsh tug of the retrieving rope around his wrist, and the way the net came alive when the cast was true, and the thud of captured fish on the floor boards of the skiff.

He liked all that because he found in it a reality that seemed to be missing from his twentieth-century job and from his daily life. He liked being the hunter, skilled and solitary and elemental. There was no conscious cruelty in the way he felt. It was the way things had been in the beginning.

The man lifted the net down carefully and lowered it into a bucket. He put a paddle beside the bucket. Then he went into the house. When he came out, he was wearing swimming trunks and a pair of old tennis shoes. Nothing else.

The skiff, flat-bottomed, was moored off the sea wall. He would not go far, he told himself. Just to the tumbledown dock half a mile away. Mullet had a way of feeding around old pilings after dark. If he moved quietly, he might pick up two or three in one cast close to the dock. And maybe a couple of others on the way down or back.

He shoved off and stood motionless for a moment, letting his eyes grow accustomed to the dark. Somewhere out in the channel a porpoise blew with a sound like steam escaping. The man smiled a little; porpoises were his friends. Once, fishing in the Gulf he had seen the charter-boat captain reach overside and gaff a baby porpoise through the sinewy part of the tail. He had hoisted it aboard, had dropped it into the bait well, where it thrashed around, puzzled and unhappy. And the mother had swum alongside the boat and under the boat and around the boat, nudging the stout planking with her back, slapping it with her tail, until the man felt sorry for her and made the captain let the baby porpoise go.

He took the net from the bucket, slipped the noose in the retrieving rope over his wrist, pulled the slipknot tight. It was an old net, but still serviceable; he had rewoven the rents made by underwater snags. He coiled the thirty-foot rope carefully, making sure there were no kinks. A tangled rope, he knew, would spoil any cast.

The basic design of the net had not changed in three thousand years. It was a mesh circle with a diameter of fourteen feet. It measured close to fifteen yards around the circumference and could, if thrown perfectly, blanket a hundred and fifty square feet of sea water. In the center of this radial trap was a small iron collar where the retrieving rope met the twenty-three separate drawstrings leading to the outer rim of the net. Along this rim, spaced an inch and a half apart, were the heavy lead sinkers.

The man raised the iron collar until it was a foot above his head. The net hung soft and pliant and deadly. He shook it gently, making sure that the drawstrings were not tangled, that the sinkers were hanging true. Then he eased it down and picked up the paddle.

The night was black as a witch's cat; the stars looked fuzzy and dim. Down to the southward, the lights of a causeway made a yellow necklace across the sky. To the man's left were the tangled roots of a mangrove swamp; to his right, the open waters of the bay. Most of it was fairly shallow, but there were channels eight feet deep. The man could not see the old dock, but he knew where it was. He pulled the paddle quietly through the water, and the phosphorescence glowed and died.

For five minutes he paddled. Then, twenty feet ahead of the skiff, a mullet jumped. A big fish, close to three pounds. For a moment it hung in the still air, gleaming dully. Then it vanished. But the ripples marked the spot, and where there was one there were often others.

The man stood up quickly. He picked up the coiled rope, and with the same hand grasped the net at a point four feet below the iron collar. He raised the skirt to his mouth, gripped it strongly with his teeth. He slid his free hand as far as it would go down

the circumference of the net so that he had three points of contact
with the mass of cordage and metal. He made sure his feet were
planted solidly. Then he waited, feeling the tension that is older
than the human race, the fierce exhilaration of the hunter at the
moment of ambush, the atavistic desire to capture and kill and
ultimately consume.

A mullet swirled, ahead and to the left. The man swung
the heavy net back, twisting his body and bending his knees so as
to get more upward thrust. He shot it forward, letting go simultaneously with rope hand and with teeth, holding a fraction of a
second longer with the other hand so as to give the net the necessary spin, impart the centrifugal force that would make it flare
into a circle. The skiff ducked sideways, but he kept his balance.
The net fell with a splash.

The man waited for five seconds. Then he began to
retrieve it, pulling in a series of sharp jerks so that the drawstrings
would gather the net inward, like a giant fist closing on this seg-
ment of the teeming sea. He felt the net quiver, and knew it was
not empty. He swung it, dripping, over the gunwhale, saw the
broad silver side of the mullet quivering, saw too the gleam of a
smaller fish. He looked closely to make sure no sting ray was hidden in the mesh, then raised the iron collar and shook the net out.
The mullet fell with a thud and flapped wildly. The other victim
was an angel fish, beautifully marked, but too small to keep. The
man picked it up gently and dropped it overboard. He coiled the
rope, took up the paddle. He would cast no more until he came
to the dock.

The skiff moved on. At last, ten feet apart, a pair of stakes
rose up gauntly out of the night. Barnacle encrusted, they once
had marked the approach from the main channel. The man guided
the skiff between them, then put the paddle down softly. He stood
up, reached for the net, tightened the noose around his wrist.
From here he could drift down upon the dock. He could see it
now, a ruined skeleton in the starshine. Beyond it a mullet jumped
and fell back with a flat, liquid sound. The man raised the edge
of the net, put it between his teeth. He would not cast at a single
swirl, he decided; he would wait until he saw two or three close
together. The skiff was barely moving. He felt his muscles tense
themselves, awaiting the signal from the brain.

Behind him in the channel he heard the porpoise blow again, nearer now. He frowned in the darkness. If the porpoise chose to fish this area, the mullet would scatter and vanish. There was no time to lose.

A school of sardines surfaced suddenly, skittering along like drops of mercury. Something, perhaps the shadow of the skiff, had frightened them. The old dock loomed very close. A mullet broke water just too far away; then another, nearer. The man marked the spreading ripples and decided to wait no longer.

He swung back the net, heavier now that it was wet. He had to turn his head, but out of the corner of his eye he saw two swirls in the back water just off the starboard bow. They were about eight feet apart, and they had the sluggish oily look that marks the presence of something big just below the surface. His conscious mind had no time to function, but instinct told him that the net was wide enough to cover both swirls if he could alter the direction of his cast. He could not halt the swing, but he shifted his feet slightly and made the cast off balance. He saw the net shoot forward, flare into an oval, and drop just where he wanted it.

Then the sea exploded in his face. In a frenzy of spray, a great horned thing shot like a huge bat out of the water. The man saw the mesh of his net etched against the mottled blackness of its body and he knew, in the split second in which thought was still possible, that those twin swirls had been made not by two mullet, but by the wing tips of the giant ray of the Gulf Coast, *Manta birostris,* also known as clam cracker, devil ray, sea devil.

The man gave a hoarse cry. He tried to claw the slipknot off his wrist, but there was no time. The quarter-inch line snapped taut. He shot over the side of the skiff as if he had roped a runaway locomotive. He hit the water head first and seemed to bounce once. He plowed a blinding furrow for perhaps ten yards. Then the line went slack as the sea devil jumped again. It was not the full-grown manta of the deep Gulf, but it was close to nine feet from tip to tip and it weighed over a thousand pounds. Up into the air it went, pearl-colored underbelly gleaming as it twisted in a frantic effort to dislodge the clinging thing that had fallen upon it. Up into the starlight, a monstrous survival from the dawn of time.

The water was less than four feet deep. Sobbing and choking, the man struggled for a foothold on the slimy bottom. Sucking in great gulps of air, he fought to free himself from the rope. But the slipknot was jammed deep into his wrist; he might as well have tried to loosen a circle of steel.

The ray came down with a thunderous splash and drove forward again. The flexible net followed every movement, impeding it hardly at all. The man weighed a hundred and seventy-five pounds, and he was braced for the shock, and he had the desperate strength that comes from looking into the blank eyes of death. It was useless. His arm straightened out with a jerk that seemed to dislocate his shoulder; his feet shot out from under him; his head went under again. Now at last he knew how the fish must feel when the line tightens and drags him toward the alien element that is his doom. Now he knew.

Desperately he dug the fingers of his free hand into the ooze, felt them dredge a futile channel through broken shells and the ribbon-like sea grasses. He tried to raise his head, but could not get it clear. Torrents of spray choked him as the ray plunged toward deep water.

His eyes were of no use to him in the foam-streaked blackness. He closed them tight, and at once an insane sequence of pictures flashed through his mind. He saw his wife sitting in their living room, reading, waiting calmly for his return. He saw the mullet he had just caught, gasping its life away on the floor boards of the skiff. He saw the cigarette he had flung from the sea wall touch the water and expire with a tiny hiss. He saw all these things and many others simultaneously in his mind as his body fought silently and tenaciously for its existence. His hand touched something hard and closed on it in a death grip, but it was only the sharp-edged helmet of a horseshoe crab, and after an instant he let it go.

He had been under the water perhaps fifteen seconds now, and something in his brain told him quite calmly that he could last another forty or fifty and then the red flashes behind his eyes would merge into darkness, and the water would pour into his lungs in one sharp painful shock, and he would be finished.

This thought spurred him to a desperate effort. He reached up and caught his pinioned wrist with his free hand. He doubled up his knees to create more drag. He thrashed his body madly, like a fighting fish, from side to side. This did not disturb the ray, but now one of the great wings tore through the mesh, and the net slipped lower over the fins projecting like horns from below the nightmare head, and the sea devil jumped again.

And once more the man was able to get his feet on the bottom and his head above water, and he saw ahead of him the pair of ancient stakes that marked the approach to the channel. He knew that if he was dragged much beyond those stakes he would be in eight feet of water, and the ray would go down to hug the bottom as rays always do, and then no power on earth could save him. So in the moment of respite that was granted him, he flung himself toward them. For a moment he thought his captor yielded a bit. Then the ray moved off again, but more slowly now, and for a few yards the man was able to keep his feet on the bottom. Twice he hurled himself back against the rope with all his strength, hoping that something would break. But nothing broke. The mesh of the net was ripped and torn, but the draw lines were strong, and the stout perimeter cord threaded through the sinkers was even stronger.

The man could feel nothing now in his trapped hand, it was numb; but the ray could feel the powerful lunges of the unknown thing that was trying to restrain it. It drove its great wings against the unyielding water and forged ahead, dragging the man and pushing a sullen wave in front of it.

The man had swung as far as he could toward the stakes. He plunged toward one and missed it by inches. His feet slipped and he went down on his knees. Then the ray swerved sharply and the second stake came right at him. He reached out with his free hand and caught it.

He caught it just above the surface, six or eight inches below high-water mark. He felt the razor-sharp barnacles bite into his hand, collapse under the pressure, drive their tiny slime-covered shell splinters deep into his flesh. He felt the pain, and he welcomed it, and he made his fingers into an iron claw that would hold until the tendons were severed or the skin was shredded from the bone. The ray felt the pressure increase with a jerk that stopped it dead in the water. For a moment all was still as the tremendous forces came into equilibrium.

Then the net slipped again, and the perimeter cord came down over the sea devil's eyes, blinding it momentarily. The great ray settled to the bottom and braced its wings against the mud and hurled itself forward and upward.

The stake was only a four-by-four creosoted pine, and it was old. Ten thousand tides had swirled around it. Worms had bored; parasites had clung. Under the crust of barnacles it still had some heart left, but not enough. The man's grip was five feet above the floor of the bay; the leverage was too great. The stake snapped off at its base.

The ray lunged forward, dragging the man and the useless timber. The man had his lungs full of air, but when the stake snapped he thought of expelling the air and inhaling the water so as to have it finished quickly. He thought of this, but he did not do it. And then, just at the channel's edge, the ray met the porpoise coming in.

The porpoise had fed well this night and was in no hurry, but it was a methodical creature and it intended to make a sweep around the old dock before the tide dropped too low. It had no quarrel with any ray, but it feared no fish in the sea, and when the great black shadow came rushing blindly and unavoidably, it rolled fast and struck once with its massive horizontal tail.

The blow descended on the ray's flat body with a sound like a pistol shot. It would have broken a buffalo's back, and even the sea devil was half stunned. It veered wildly and turned back toward shallow water. It passed within ten feet of the man, face down in the water. It slowed and almost stopped, wing tips moving faintly, gathering strength for another rush.

The man had heard the tremendous slap of the great mammal's tail and the snorting gasp as it plunged away. He felt the line go slack again, and he raised his dripping face, and he reached for the bottom with his feet. He found it, but now the water was up to his neck. He plucked at the noose once more with his lacerated hand, but there was no strength in his fingers. He felt the tension come back into the line as the ray began to move again, and for half a second he was tempted to throw himself backward and fight as he had been doing, pitting his strength against the vastly superior strength of the brute.

But the acceptance of imminent death had done something to his brain. It had driven out the fear, and with the fear had gone the panic. He could think now, and he knew with absolute certainty that if he was to make any use of this last chance that had been given him, it would have to be based on the one faculty that had carried man to his pre-eminence above all beasts, the faculty of reason. Only by using his brain could he possibly survive, and he called on his brain for a solution, and his brain responded. It offered him one.

He did not know whether his body still had the strength to carry out the brain's commands, but he began to swim forward, toward the ray that was still moving hesitantly away from the channel. He swam forward, feeling the rope go slack as he gained on the creature.

Ahead of him he saw the one remaining stake, and he made himself swim faster until he was parallel with the ray and the rope trailed behind both of them in a deep U. He swam with a surge of desperate energy that came from nowhere so that he was slightly in the lead as they came to the stake. He passed on one side of it; the ray was on the other.

Then the man took one last deep breath, and he went down under the black water until he was sitting on the bottom of the bay. He put one foot over the line so that it passed under his bent knee. He drove both his heels into the mud, and he clutched the slimy grass with his bleeding hand, and he waited for the tension to come again.

The ray passed on the other side of the stake, moving faster now. The rope grew taut again, and it began to drag the man back toward the stake. He held his prisoned wrist close to the bottom, under his knee, and he prayed that the stake would not break. He felt the rope vibrate as the barnacles bit into it. He did not know whether the rope would crush the barnacles or whether the barnacles would cut the rope. All he knew was that in five seconds or less he would be dragged into the stake and cut to ribbons if he tried to hold on; or drowned if he didn't.

He felt himself sliding slowly, and then faster, and suddenly the ray made a great leap forward, and the rope burned around the base of the stake, and the man's foot hit it hard. He kicked himself backward with his remaining strength, and the rope parted and he was free.

He came slowly to the surface.

Thirty feet away the sea devil made one tremendous leap

and disappeared into the darkness. The man raised his wrist and looked at the frayed length of rope dangling from it. Twenty inches, perhaps. He lifted his other hand and felt the hot blood start instantly, but he didn't care. He put his hand on the stake above the barnacles and held on to the good, rough, honest wood. He heard a strange noise, and realized that it was himself, sobbing.

High above, there was a droning sound, and looking up he saw the nightly plane from New Orleans inbound for Tampa. Calm and serene, it sailed, symbol of man's proud mastery over nature. Its lights winked red and green for a moment; then it was gone.

Slowly, painfully, the man began to move through the placid water. He came to the skiff at last and climbed into it. The mullet, still alive, slapped convulsively with its tail. The man reached down with his torn hand, picked up the mullet, let it go.

He began to work on the slip-knot doggedly with his teeth. His mind was almost a blank, but not quite. He knew one thing. He knew he would do no more casting alone at night. Not in the dark of the moon. No, not he.

ARTHUR GORDON, who hails from Savannah, Georgia, served as a combat correspondent with the Eighth Air Force during World War II and attained the rank of major. After the war he continued as a writer and became editor-in-chief of *Cosmopolitan* magazine, a job he held until 1948, when he turned to writing full time. Since then he has written a novel, *Reprisal,* and many short stories and magazine articles.

Jim Kjelgaard

*What kind of courage does it take to face one of
nature's most ferocious jungle animals?*

*Would you go out alone and track a South
American jaguar and then try to kill it with only a
machete and an old muzzle-loading rifle?*

*Pepe's great courage must remain unknown
in*

THE TIGER'S HEART

The approaching jungle night was, in itself, a threat. As it
deepened, an eerie silence enveloped the thatched village. People
were silent. Tethered cattle stood quietly. Roosting chickens did
not stir and wise goats made no noise. Thus it had been for
countless centuries and thus it would continue to be. The brown-
skinned inhabitants of the village knew the jungle. They had trod-
den its dim paths, forded its sulky rivers, borne its streaming heat
and were intimately acquainted with its deer, tapir, crocodiles,
screaming green parrots and countless other creatures.

That was the daytime jungle they could see, feel and hear,
but at night everything became different. When darkness came,
the jungle was alive with strange and horrible things which no man
had ever seen and no man could describe. They were shadows
that had no substance and one was unaware of them until they
struck and killed. Then, with morning, they changed themselves

back into the shape of familiar things. Because it was a time of the unknown, night had to be a time of fear.

Except, Pepe Garcia reflected, to the man who owned a rifle. As the night closed in, Pepe reached out to fondle his rifle and make sure that it was close beside him. As long as it was, he was king.

That was only just, for the rifle had cost him dearly. With eleven others from his village, Pepe had gone to help chop a right of way for the new road. They used machetes, the indispensable long knife of all jungle dwellers, and they had worked hard. Unlike the rest, Pepe had saved every peso he didn't have to spend for immediate living expenses. With his savings, and after some haggling, he had bought his muzzle-loading rifle, a supply of powder, lead, and a mold in which he could fashion bullets for his rifle.

Eighty pesos the rifle had cost him. But it was worth the price. Though the jungle at night was fear itself, no man with a rifle had to fear. The others, who had only machetes with which to guard themselves from terrors that came in the darkness, were willing to pay well for protection. Pepe went peacefully to sleep.

He did not know what awakened him, only that something was about. He listened intently, but there was no change in the jungle's monotonous night sounds. Still, something was not as it should be.

Then he heard it. At the far end of the village, near Juan Aria's hut, a goat bleated uneasily. Silence followed. The goat bleated again, louder and more fearful. There was a pattering rush of small hoofs, a frightened bleat cut short, again silence.

Pepe, who did not need to people the night with fantastic creatures because he owned a rifle, interpreted correctly what he had heard. A tiger, a jaguar, had come in the night, leaped the thorn fence with which the village was surrounded, and made off with one of Juan Aria's goats.

Pepe went peacefully back to sleep. With morning, certainly, Juan Aria would come to him.

He did not awaken until the sun was up. Then he emerged from his hut, breakfasted on a papaya he had gathered the day before, and awaited his expected visitor. They must always come to him; it ill befitted a man with a rifle to seek out anyone at all.

Presently Pepe saw two men, Juan Aria and his brother, coming up one of the paths that wound through the village. Others stared curiously, but nobody else came because their flocks had not been raided. They had no wish to pay, or to help pay, a hunter.

Pepe waited until the two were near, then said, *"Buenos dias."*

"Buenos dias," they replied.

They sat down in the sun, looking at nothing in particular, not afraid any more, because the day was never a time of fear. By daylight, only now and again did a tiger come to raid a flock of goats, or kill a burro or a cow.

After a suitable lapse of time, Juan Aria said, "I brought my goats into the village last night, thinking they would be safe."

"And were they not?"

"They were not. Something came and killed one, a fine white and black nanny, my favorite. When the thing left, the goat went too. Never again shall I see her alive."

"What killed your goat?" Pepe inquired.

"A devil, but this morning I saw only the tracks of a tiger."

"Did you hear it come?"

"I heard it."

"Then why did you not defend your flock?"

Juan Aria gestured with eloquent hands. "To attack a devil, or a tiger, with nothing but a machete would be madness."

"That is true," Pepe agreed. "Let us hope that the next time it is hungry, this devil, or tiger, will not come back for another goat."

"But it will!"

Pepe relaxed, for Juan Aria's admission greatly improved Pepe's bargaining position. And it was true that, having had a taste of easy game, the tiger would come again. Only death would end his forays, and since he knew where to find Juan Aria's goats, he would continue to attack them.

Pepe said, "That is bad, for a man may lose many goats to a tiger."

"Unless a hunter kills him," Juan Aria said.

"Unless a hunter kills him," Pepe agreed.

"That is why I have come to you, Pepe," Juan Aria said. A

troubled frown overspread his face. "I hope you will follow and kill this tiger, for you are the only man who can do so."

"It would give me pleasure to kill him, but I cannot work for nothing."

"Nor do I expect you to. Even a tiger will not eat an entire goat, and you are sure to find what is left of my favorite nanny. Whatever the tiger has not eaten, you may have for your pay."

Pepe bristled. "You are saying that I should put myself and my rifle to work for carrion left by a tiger?"

"No, no!" Juan Aria protested. "In addition I will give you one live goat!"

"Three goats."

"I am a poor man!" the other wailed. "You would bankrupt me!"

"No man with twenty-nine goats is poor, though he may be if a tiger raids his flock a sufficient number of times," Pepe said.

"I will give you one goat and two kids."

"Two goats and one kid."

"You drive a hard bargain," Juan Aria said, "but I cannot deny you now. Kill the tiger."

Affecting an air of nonchalance, as befitted the owner of a firearm, Pepe took his rifle from the fine blanket upon which it lay when he was not carrying it. He looked to his powder horn and bullet pouch, strapped his machete on, and sauntered toward Juan Aria's hut. A half-dozen worshipful children followed.

"Begone!" Pepe ordered.

They fell behind, but continued to follow until Pepe came to that place where Juan Aria's flock had passed the night. He glanced at the dust, and saw the tiger's great paw marks imprinted there. It was a huge cat, lame in the right front paw, or it might have been injured in battle with another tiger.

Expertly, Pepe located the place where it had gone back over the thorn fence. Though the tiger had carried the sixty-pound goat in its jaws, only a couple of thorns were disturbed at the place where it had leaped.

Though he did not look around, Pepe was aware of the villagers watching him and he knew that their glances would be very respectful. Most of the men went into the jungle from time to time to work with their machetes, but none would work where tigers were known to be. Not one would dare to take a tiger's trail. Only Pepe dared and, because he did, he must be revered.

Still affecting nonchalance, Pepe sauntered through the gate. Behind him, he heard the village's collective sigh of mingled relief and admiration. A raiding tiger was a very real and terrible threat, and goats and cattle were not easily come by. The man with a rifle, the man able to protect them, must necessarily be a hero.

Once in the jungle, and out of the villagers' sight, Pepe underwent a transformation.

He shed his air of indifference and became as alert as the little doe that showed him only her white tail. A rifle might be a symbol of power, but unless a man was also a hunter, a rifle did him no good. Impressing the villagers was one thing: hunting a tiger was quite another.

Pepe knew the great cats were dappled death incarnate. They could move with incredible swiftness and were strong enough to kill an ox. They feared nothing.

Jungle-born, Pepe slipped along as softly as a jungle shadow. His machete slipped a little, and he shifted it to a place where his legs would not be bumped. From time to time he glanced at the ground before him.

To trained eyes, there was a distinct trail. It consisted of an occasional drop of blood from the dead goat, a bent or broken plant, a few hairs where the tiger had squeezed between trees, paw prints in soft places. Within the first quarter mile Pepe knew many things about this tiger.

He was not an ordinary beast, or he would have gone only far enough from the village so his nostrils could not be assailed by its unwelcome scents and eaten what he wanted there, then covered the remainder of the goat with sticks and leaves. He was not old, for his was not the lagging gait of an old cat, and the ease with which he had leaped the thorn fence with a goat in his jaws was evidence of his strength.

Pepe stopped to look to the loading and priming of his rifle. There seemed to be nothing amiss, and there had better not be. When he saw the tiger, he must shoot straight and true. Warned by some super jungle sense, Pepe slowed his pace. A moment later he found his game.

He came upon it suddenly in a grove of scattered palms. Because he had not expected it there, Pepe did not see it until it was nearer than safety allowed.

The tiger crouched at the base of a palm whose fronds waved at least fifty feet above the roots. Both the beast's front paws were on what remained of the dead goat. It did not snarl or grimace, or even twitch its tail. But there was a lethal quality about the great cat and an extreme tension. The tiger was bursting with raw anger that seemed to swell and grow.

Pepe stopped in his tracks and cold fear crept up his spine. But he did not give way to fear. With deliberate, studied slowness he brought the rifle to his shoulder and took aim. He had only one bullet and there would be no time to reload, but even a tiger could not withstand the smash of that enormous leaden ball right between the eyes. Pepe steadied the rifle.

His finger tightened slowly on the trigger, for he must not let nervousness spoil his aim. When the hammer fell Pepe's brain and body became momentarily numb.

There was no satisfying roar and no puff of black powder smoke wafting away from the muzzle. Instead there was only a sudden hiss, as though cold water had spilled on a hot stone, and the metallic click of the falling hammer. Pepe himself had loaded the rifle, but he could not have done so correctly. Only the powder in the priming pan flashed.

It was the spark needed to explode the anger in the tiger's lithe and deadly body. He emitted a coughing snarl and launched his charge. Lord of the jungle, he would crush this puny man who dared interfere with him.

Pepe jerked back to reality, but he took time to think of his rifle, leaning it lovingly against a tree and in the same motion jerking his machete from its sheath.

It was now a hopeless fight, to be decided in the tiger's favor, because not within the memory of the village's oldest inhabitant had any man ever killed a tiger with a machete. But it was as well to fight hopelessly, as to turn and run, for if he did that he would surely be killed. No tiger that attacked anything was ever known to turn aside.

Machete in hand, Pepe studied the onrushing cat. He had

read the tracks correctly, for from pad to joint the tiger's right front foot was swollen to almost twice the size of the other. It must have stepped on a poisonous thorn or been bitten by a snake.

Even with such a handicap, a tiger was more than a match for a man armed only with a machete—but Pepe watched the right front paw carefully. If he had any advantage, it lay there. Then the tiger, a terrible, pitiless engine of destruction, flung himself at Pepe. Pepe had known from the first that the tiger's initial strike would be exactly this one, and he was ready for it. He swerved, bending his body outward as the great cat brushed past him. With all the strength in his powerful right arm, he swung the machete. He stopped his downward stroke just short of the tiger's silken back, for he knew suddenly that there was just one way to end this fight.

The tiger whirled, and hot spittle from his mouth splashed on the back of Pepe's left hand. Holding the machete before him, like a sword, he took a swift backward step. The tiger sprang, launching himself from the ground as though his rear legs were made of powerful steel springs, and coming straight up. His flailing left paw flashed at Pepe. It hooked in his shirt, ripping it away from the arm as though it were paper, and burning talons sank into the flesh. Red blood welled out.

Pepe did not try again to slash with the machete, but thrust, as he would have thrust with a knife or sword. The machete's point met the tiger's throat, and Pepe put all his strength and weight behind it. The blade explored its way into living flesh, and the tiger gasped. Blood bubbled over the machete.

With a convulsive effort, the tiger pulled himself away. But blood was rushing from his throat now and he shook his head, then stumbled and fell. He pulled himself erect, looked with glazing' eyes at Pepe and dragged himself toward him. There was a throttled snarl. The tiger slumped to the ground. The tip of his tail twitched and was still.

Pepe stared, scarcely seeing the blood that flowed from his lacerated arm. He had done the impossible, he had killed a tiger with a machete. Pepe brushed a hand across his eyes and took a trembling forward step.

He picked up his rifle and looked again to the priming.

There seemed to be nothing wrong. Repriming, Pepe clasped the rifle with his elbow and seized the machete's hilt. Bracing one foot against the tiger's head, he drew the machete out.

Then he held his rifle so close to the machete wound that the muzzle caressed silken fur. He pulled the trigger. The wound gaped wider and smoke-blackened fur fringed it. All traces of the machete wound were obliterated. Pepe knew a second's anguished regret, then steeled himself, for this was the way it must be.

Everybody had a machete. In his village, the man who owned a rifle must remain supreme.

JIM KJELGAARD was born in 1910 and grew up on a farm in Tioga County, Pennsylvania. There he acquired a great love of the outdoors—hunting, fishing, trapping, and forest lore. Before he became a writer, he worked as a laborer, factory worker, Teamster, plumber's apprentice, and surveyor's assistant. He died in 1959. His books include *Big Red, Red Siege,* and *Forest Patrol.*

Ted Hughes

Do animals sometimes react strangely and unpredictably in stormy weather?

If a domestic animal, such as a dog or horse, attacked and tried to kill you, how would you try to protect yourself?

A man alone in a field one rainy night tries to escape from

THE RAIN HORSE

As the young man came over the hill the first thin blowing of rain met him. He turned his coat collar up and stood on top of the long rabbit-riddled hedge bank, looking down into the valley.

He had come too far. What had set out as a walk along pleasantly remembered Tarmac lanes had somehow, almost dreamily, turned into a cross-plowland trek, his shoes ruined, and the mud working up the trouser legs of his suit where they rubbed against each other. There was a raw flapping wetness in the air that would be downpour again at any moment.

Still, this was the view he had been thinking of. Looking down from this point, he had felt, he would get the whole thing. The valley lay open in front of him, its shallow bare fields black and sodden as the bed of an old drained lake after the weeks of rain, utterly deserted.

Nothing happened.

Not that he had expected any very overpowering experience, but he had looked forward to something, some pleasant feeling, he wasn't quite sure what.

So he waited, trying to nudge the right feelings alive by the remembered details of the scene—the surprisingly familiar curve of the hedges, the great stone gate-pillar and the iron hook let into it that he had so often used as a target, the long bank of the rabbit warren on which he stood and which had been the first thing he had ever noticed about the hill when twenty years ago, from the distance of the village, he had said: "That looks like rabbits."

But twelve years had transformed him. This land no longer recognized him. He looked back at it coldly, remotely, as at a finally visited home country known only through the stories of a grandfather; felt nothing but the dullness of feeling nothing. Boredom. Then, suddenly, impatience, with a whole swarm of little anxieties about his shoes and this spitting rain and his new suit and that sky and the two-mile trudge through the mud back to the road.

A quicker way out of it would be to go straight forward to the farm, a mile away, behind which the road looped. But the thought of meeting the farmer—whether to be embarrassingly remembered or shouted at as a trespasser—deterred him. Now the rain was pulling up out of the distance, dragging its gray broken columns, smudging the trees and farms.

A wave of anger went over him, against himself for blundering into this mud-trap and against the land for making him feel so hardened, so old and stiff and stupid. He turned to get away out of it as quickly as he could and at that moment caught a movement in his eye-corner. All his senses startled alert. He stopped.

Over to his right a thin black horse was running across the plowland toward the hill, its head down, its neck stretched out. It seemed to be running on its toes like a cat, a long low sidling run like a dog up to no good. Something unnatural about the way it ran hypnotized him.

From the high point on which he stood the hill dipped slightly in a ridge that rose to another high point three hundred yards to his right. The horse ran up to this crest that was fringed with the tops of trees, showed against the sky, for a moment like a nightmarish leopard, then disappeared over the other side.

For several seconds he stood, stunned by the unpleasantly strange impression the sight of the horse made on him. Then the plastering beat of the cold rain on his bare skull brought him back to himself. The distance had vanished in a wall of gray and all around him the fields were jumping and streaming.

Holding his collar close about his chin, he lowered his head and ran back over toward the town side of the hill, the lee side, his feet sucking and splashing, occasionally skidding.

This hill was shaped like a wave, a gently rounded back lifting up out of the valley with a sharply crested, almost concave front hanging over the river meadows toward the town. Down this front, from the crest, hung two small woods separated by a fallow field. The nearer wood was nothing more than a quarry, circular, full of stones and bracken, with a few thorns and non-descript saplings, foxholes, and rabbit holes. The other was rectangular, mainly a planting of scrub oak trees. Beyond the river smoldered the town like a great heap of blue cinders.

He ran along the top of the first wood and, finding no shelter but the thin leafless thorns of the hedge, dipped below the crest, so that he was at least out of the wind, and jogged along through thick grass toward the wood of oaks. The rain still driving blindly, he plunged into the tangle of bramble stems at the wood's edge. The little crippled trees were small choice in the way of shelter and under a sudden fierce thickening of the rain he took one at random, crouching down beneath the leaning trunk.

Still panting from his run, drawing up his knees, he watched the bleak lines of rain, gray as hail, slanting into the bracken and clumps of bramble. He felt hidden and safe: the sound of the rain as it rushed and lulled sealed him from the world. The chilly sheet lead of his suit became a tight warm mold, and gradually he sank into a state of comfort that was all but trance, though the drops still beat uninterruptedly on his shoulders and knees and trickled down the oak trunk and onto his neck.

All around him the boughs angled down, glistening like black iron. From their tips and elbows the drops hurried steadily, and the channels of the bark pulsed and gleamed. For a time he amused himself calculating the variation in the rainfall by the variations in a dribble of water from a trembling twig-end two feet in front of his nose. He studied the twig itself, bringing dwarfs and continents and animals out of its scurfy bark. Beyond the boughs the blue shoal of the town was rising and falling, and darkening and fading again, in the white backdrop of rain.

He wanted this rain to go on forever. Whenever it seemed to be drawing off he listened anxiously until it closed in again. Sitting there, he felt suspended from life and from time in a delicious freedom and peace. He didn't want to return to his sodden shoes and his possibly ruined suit and the walk back over that land of mud.

All at once he began to feel uneasy. At the same moment he thought of the horse, and the hair on the nape of his neck prickled slightly as he remembered how it had run up to the crest and showed against the sky.

He tried to dismiss the thought. Horses wandered about the countryside often enough. But the vision of the horse as it had appeared against the sky stuck in his mind. It must have come over the crest just above the wood in which he was now sitting. As if to clear his mind he twisted round and looked up the wood between the tree stems, to his left.

At the wood top, with the silvered gray light coming in behind it, the black horse was standing under the oaks, its head high and alert, its ears pricked, watching him.

A horse sheltering from the rain usually goes into a sort of stupor, tilts a hind hoof and hangs its head low and lets its eyelids droop, and so it remains as long as the rain lasts. This horse was nothing like that. It was watching him intently, standing perfectly still, its soaked neck and flank shining in the hard light.

As he turned back he felt the same crawling dismay as when he first saw it coming across the land. The hair on his head went icy suddenly and he shivered. There was surely something queer about this horse. But what was he to do? It seemed ridiculous to try driving it away; and to leave the wood, with the rain still coming down so heavily, was out of the question. The idea of being watched became more and more disturbing until at last he had to twist around again, to see if the horse had moved. It stood exactly as before.

This was absurd. He took control of himself and deliberately turned back, determined not to give the horse one more thought. If it wanted to share the wood with him, let it. If it

wanted to stare at him, let it. He was settling firmly into these
resolutions when the ground shook and he heard the crash of
a heavy body coming down the wood. Like lightning his legs
bounded him upright and about face. The horse was almost on
top of him, its head stretching forward, ears flattened and lips
lifted back from the long yellow teeth. He got one photograph
glimpse of the red-veined eyeball as he flung himself backwards
round the tree; then he was away up the slope, whipped by oak
twigs as he leapt the brambles and brushwood, twisting between
the close trees till he tripped and sprawled. As he fell the thought
flashed through his head that he must at all costs keep his suit
out of the leaf-mold, but a more urgent instinct was already rolling
him sideways. He spun round, sat up, and looked back, ready to
scramble off in a flash to one side. He was panting from the sudden excitement and effort. The horse had disappeared. The wood
was empty except for the slant gray rain, dancing the bracken and
glittering from the branches.

He got up, furious. Knocking the dirt and leaves from his
suit as well as he could he looked round for a weapon. The horse
was evidently mad, had an abcess on its brain or something of the
sort. Or maybe it was just spiteful—rain sometimes puts creatures
into funny states. Whatever it was, he decided to get away from
the wood just as quickly as possible, rain or no rain.

Since the horse seemed to have gone on down the wood,
his way to the farm over the hill was clear. As he went he broke
a yard length of wrist-thick dead branch from one of the oaks,
but immediately threw it aside and wiped the slough of rotten wet
bark from his hands with his soaked handkerchief. Already he
was thinking it incredible that the horse should have meant to
attack him. Most likely it was just going down the wood for
better shelter and had made a feint at him in passing—as much
out of curiosity or playfulness as anything. He thought of the way
horses menace each other when they are playing and galloping
round in a paddock.

The wood rose to a steep bank topped by the hawthorn
hedge that ran along the whole ridge of the hill. He scrambled
up this bank toward a thin place in the hedge, and was pulling
himself up by the bare stem of one of the hawthorns when he
checked and shrank down again. The swelling gradient of fields

lay in front of him, smoking in the slowly crossing rain. Out in the middle of the first field, tall as a statue, and a ghostly silver in the undercloud light, stood the horse, watching the wood.

He lowered his head slowly, and as he slithered back down the bank an awful feeling of helplessness came over him. He felt certain the horse had been looking straight at him, waiting for him. Was it clairvoyant? Maybe a mad animal can be clairvoyant. At the same time he was ashamed to find himself acting so fool-ishly, ducking and creeping about in this way just to keep out of sight of a horse as if it were an enemy with a rifle. He tried to imagine how anybody in their senses would just walk off home. This cooled him a little, and he retreated further down the wood, determined to go straight back the way he had come, along under the ridge.

The rain was still falling, a cold steady weight, but he observed this rather than felt it. The water was running down inside his clothes and squelching in his shoes as he eased his way carefully over the bedded leaves. At every moment he expected to see the prick-eared black head looking down at him from the hedge above.

At the woodside he paused. The success of this last ma-neuver had restored his confidence, but he didn't want to venture out into the open field without making sure that the horse was just where he had left it. Then he could withdraw quietly and leave the horse standing out there in the rain. He crept up again among the trees to the crest and peeped through the hedge.

The gray field and the whole slope were empty. He searched the distance since the horse was quite likely to have forgotten him altogether and wandered off. Then he raised him-self and leaned out to see if it had come in close to the hedge. Before he was aware of anything the ground shook. He twisted round wildly to see how he had been outwitted. The black shape was above him, its whinnying snort and the spattering whack of its hooves seemed to be actually inside his head as he fell backwards down the bank, and leaped again like a madman, dodging among the oaks, imagining how the buffet would come and how he would be knocked headlong. Halfway down the wood the oaks gave way to bracken and old roots and stony rabbit diggings. He was well out into the middle of this before he realized that he was running alone.

He was gasping for breath now and cursing mechanically. Without a thought for his suit he sat down where he was, to rest his shaken legs, letting the rain plaster the hair down over his forehead and watching the dense flashing lines disappear abruptly into the earth all round him as if he were watching from safe shelter and through thick plate glass. His lungs trembled as he took deep breaths in an effort to steady his heart and regain control of himself. His right trouser turn-up was ripped at the seam and his suit jacket was splashed with the yellow mud of the top field.

Obviously the horse had been further along the hedge above the steep field, waiting for him to come out at the wood-side just as he had intended, and he must have peeped through the hedge—peeping the wrong way—within yards of it.

However, this last attack had cleared up one thing. He need no longer act like a fool out of simple uncertainty as to whether the horse was his antagonist or merely crazy. It was definitely after him. He picked up two stones about the size of goose eggs and set off towards the bottom of the wood, striding carelessly.

The whole hill was skirted by a loop of the river. His plan was to cross the little meadow at the bottom of the wood and follow the river, a three-mile circuit, back to the road. There were deep hollows in the river bank, full of stones as he remembered, excellent places to defend himself from if the horse should come after him out there.

The bottom of the wood was choked with hawthorns, some of them good-sized trees, and they knitted into an almost impassable barrier. He walked along, looking for a way through. Then he stopped. Through the bluish veil of their bare twigs he could see the familiar shape out in the field below, waiting for him.

The horse was facing away from the wood, looking toward the river. It seemed not to have noticed him. Quietly he turned back and climbed across the clearing toward the one side of the wood he had not yet tried. If the horse would only stay down there he could follow his first and easiest plan, up the woodside and over the hilltop to the farm. As he made for the straggling line of oaks hedging the wood on that side, the rain suddenly pressed down as if the whole sky were to be emptied in a few minutes.

The oaks ahead blurred and the ground drummed. As he broke into a run, he heard a deeper sound running with him. He whirled round, a stone ready in his hand. The horse was charging straight at him across the middle of the clearing, scattering the clay and stones in an immensely supple and powerful motion. He let out a tearing roar and threw the stone in his right hand. The result was instantaneous. Whether at the roar or the stone the horse reared as if against a wall and shied to the left. As it dropped back onto its forefeet his second stone, at ten yards' range, landed with a thwack and he saw the bright mud blotch suddenly appear on the glistening black flank. The horse surged down the wood, splashing the earth like water, tossing its long tail as it plunged out of sight among the hawthorns.

He looked around for stones. The sharp encounter had set the blood beating in his head and given him a savage energy. He could have killed the horse at that moment. That this brute should play with him in such a spiteful, deliberate way was more than he could bear. Whoever owned that horse, he thought, deserved to have its neck broken for letting the dangerous thing loose.

He came out at the woodside, still searching for the right stones. There were plenty here, piled and scattered where they had been plowed out of the field over the years. He selected two. As he looked up, the horse was within twenty yards of him, in the middle of the field, watching him calmly. They looked at each other.

"Out of it!" he shouted, brandishing his arm. "Out of it! Go on!" The horse ignored him, only twitching its pricked ears. With all his force he threw a stone that soared and landed beyond with a soft thud. He rearmed and threw again. For several minutes he kept up his bombardment, without a single hit, working himself into a fury and throwing more and more wildly, till his arm began to ache with the unaccustomed exercise. All the time the horse watched him fixedly. Finally he had to stop and ease his shoulder muscles, and as if the horse had been waiting for just this, it dipped its head twice and came at him.

He spun round, snatched up two stones and roaring with all his strength flung the one in his right hand. He was astonished at the crack of the impact—sharp as if he had struck a tile—and the horse actually stumbled. With another roar he ran forward and hurled the second stone. His aim seemed to be under superior guidance. The stone struck and rebounded straight up into the air, spinning fiercely, as the horse swirled away and went careering down toward the far bottom corner of the field, at first with great swinging leaps, then at a canter, leaving deep churned holes in the soil.

It turned up the far side of the field, climbing till it was level with him. He felt a little surprise of pity to see it shaking its head, and once it paused to lower its head and paw over its ear with its forehoof as a cat does.

"You stay there!" he shouted. "Keep your distance and you'll not get hurt."

And indeed the horse did stop at that moment, almost obediently. It stood watching him as he climbed to the crest.

The rain swept into his face and he realized that he was freezing, as if his very flesh were sodden. The farm seemed miles away over the dreary fields. Keeping an eye on the horse now, that still watched him alertly, he loaded the crook of his left arm with stones and plunged out onto the waste of gray mud.

The horse was lost to sight immediately below the ridge, but he kept twisting around every few strides to see if it was following him. Before he was halfway over the first field it appeared, silhouetted against the sky at the corner of the wood, head high and attentive, watching his laborious retreat over the three fields.

The ankle-deep clay dragged at him as he stumbled on, burdened by his sogged clothes and the armful of stones, his limbs weighing like great clods of mud. He had to fight to keep his breathing even, two strides in, two strides out, the air ripping his lungs. Upwards and out of the sucking earth he forced himself till in the middle of the last field he stopped, dropped all the stones from the cramp of his left arm, keeping just one in his hand, and continued at a walk. The horse, tiny on the skyline, had not moved.

He slumped over the top bar of the gate that led out of the field into the lane behind the farm. He became conscious of the rain again and suddenly longed to collapse full length under it, to take the cooling, healing drops all over his body, forgetting himself in the last wretchedness of the mud. Instead he made an effort, pulled himself exhaustedly over the gate-top into the lane, and leaned again, looking up at the hill.

The rain was dissolving land into sky like a wet water color as the afternoon darkened. He concentrated, raising his head, searching the skyline from end to end. The horse had vanished. The hill looked lifeless and desolate as some island lifting out of the sea, awash with every tide.

Under the long shed where the tractors, plow, binders, and the rest were drawn up, waiting for their seasons, he sat on a sack thrown over a petrol drum, trembling, his lungs heaving. He began to look around. The ragged swallows' nests were still there in the angles of the beams; the mingled smell of paraffin, creosote, fertilizer, dust—all exactly as he had left it twelve years ago. He remembered three dead foxes hanging in a row from one of the beams, their teeth bloody.

The nightmare he had just been through had already sunk from reality. It hung under the surface of his mind, an obscure confusion of fright and shame, as after a narrowly escaped street accident. There was a solid pain in his chest, like a spike of bone stabbing, that made him wonder if he had strained his heart on that last stupid burdened run. Piece by piece he began to take off his clothes, wringing the gray water out of them, but soon he stopped that and just sat staring at the ground, as if some important part had been cut out of his brain.

TED HUGHES was born in 1930 in Mytholmroyd, Yorkshire, England, where he grew up. After World War II he enlisted in the Royal Air Force and served as a ground wireless mechanic (radio technician). Later he studied at Cambridge, where he received his B.A. Although primarily noted for his poetry, he has also written short stories and children's books. Much of his writing deals with animals, both symbolically and realistically. His books include *The Hawk in the Rain, Lupercal,* and *Wodwo.*

Charles Einstein

Is it true that a man makes his own luck when he gambles?

Do you believe that gambling casinos, such as those in Las Vegas, are completely honest?

In this story Mr. Rafferty faces professional gamblers and wins not only the new deck but

THE NEW DEAL

Rafferty was not the only one losing at the blackjack table, but he had been there the longest. He had been sitting there since ten in the morning; now it was after three, and the waitress of the Wanderlust, Las Vegas' fanciest and newest hotel, had offered him drinks on the house half-a-dozen times at least. The hotel could well afford buying him a drink to keep him where he was.

But he was not drinking; he was only losing. Losers are, by profession, doubters. This was Las Vegas and the Wanderlust was a brand-new hotel and the dealers' faces were not familiar.

The dealer gave Rafferty two fives. He himself had a six showing. Rafferty had bet $40. He put eight more five-dollar chips on the line to double his bet and took one card face down. He sneaked a look under the corner: a queen. Rafferty had 20 going for him.

The dealer turned up his down card: a seven. Now he had

13. Then, an ace. Fourteen. He hit himself again: a two. Sixteen. He hit himself for the last time. A five. Twenty-one. His practiced side-hand motion swept away all of Rafferty's chips.

"I want a new deck," Rafferty said.

"What's that?"

"I said I want a new deck."

"We just broke this one ten minutes ago."

"And it's breaking me. I want a new deck." Rafferty moistened his lips. "And a new dealer."

The two other men who were playing at the table shifted uneasily. They were losing, too, and perhaps secretly they shared Rafferty's spoken sentiments, but they did not want to be drawn in on this.

They were drawn in on it. The dealer drew them in: "Either of you gentlemen want to complain?"

The two men looked down at the green of the table, studying the pattern and the arc inscription: DEALER MUST HIT 16 & STAND ON ALL 17s.

"Don't drag anybody else into it," Rafferty said coldly to the dealer. "It only takes one man to make a complaint. I'm making it."

Out of nowhere, the pit boss appeared. That is not a definitive statement; all pit bosses appear from nowhere. This one was small, cushion-footed, leathery-faced, black-haired. He said to the dealer: "And?"

The dealer nodded toward Rafferty.

"Yes, Mr. Rafferty?" the pit boss said. They knew his name. He had cashed three checks so far today.

"I don't like the cards."

The dealer said, "New deck ten minutes ago."

"Spread 'em," the pit boss said to him.

The dealer spread the deck face up.

"No," Rafferty said. "You're wasting your time. If I knew what to look for I'd be on your side of the table."

"All right," the pit boss said. "New deck."

"Ah, what for?" Rafferty said. He sighed. "They all come out of the same box, don't they?"

"Well, then," the pit boss said, "what can we do?"

Rafferty sighed again. "You know," he said, "it'd be terrible for a new place like this to get into trouble. Take away your gambling license, you're dead. You know that, don't you?"

"He asked for a new deck," the dealer said defensively to the pit boss. "You offer him one and now he says 'no.' Maybe he's got a little case of loser's fatigue."

"Oh, I want a new deck," Rafferty said. "But not out of the box backstage. Suppose I told you I had a deck upstairs in my room. Would you play with my cards?"

The pit boss laughed. Then he looked at Rafferty's face and stopped laughing. He said, "You know better than that, Mr. Rafferty. The house supplies the cards."

"I bought them at the cigar counter over there," Rafferty said. "They're the same brand the house uses, aren't they?"

"We didn't see you buy them," the dealer said. "We don't know what you did upstairs."

"Shut up," the pit boss said to him.

"And I don't know what you do downstairs," Rafferty said to the dealer. "All I know is, there's a lot of fives in your deck."

"Nobody's making you play," the dealer said to him. "You don't like the game, nobody's making you sit there."

"I told you, shut up," the pit boss said to him. Four or five people had gathered behind Rafferty and the other players to listen. "Mr. Rafferty, can I talk to you for a minute?"

"We can talk here," Rafferty said. But there was something in the way the pit boss looked at him. He shrugged and stood up. "All right." He moved away from the playing area and the pit boss ducked under the rope and joined him.

"How much are you out?" the pit boss said in a low voice.

"I don't know exactly," Rafferty said. "Couple of thousand, maybe. Does it make any difference?"

"Look," the pit boss said, "on the one hand, we run an honest game. On the other hand, we don't want any trouble. We'll do anything reasonable to prove we're on the level."

"You won't play with my cards, will you?"

"I said anything reasonable," the pit boss said.

"But they're the same cards you use. I bought them right over there."

The pit boss shook his head patiently. "Nobody would call that reasonable, Mr. Rafferty. The dealer had it right. Nobody knows you bought them here. And nobody knows how long ago it was. If you were to buy a deck right now and we played them fresh, that would be another thing."

"All right," Rafferty said.

"I beg your pardon?"

"I said all right. They're your terms. I accept."

"I don't understand."

"I will walk with you this minute to the cigar counter," Rafferty said, "and I will buy a deck of cards, and then we will walk back to the table and play blackjack with those cards."

"Ah, Mr. Rafferty," the pit boss said. "Don't be ridiculous."

"Ridiculous?" Rafferty's voice went up and the other man looked uncertainly around. "All I've just done is agree to something you yourself proposed."

"But it isn't worked that way," the pit boss said. "Suppose everybody came in wanting to play with his own cards or his own dice. We'd have to make a career out of checking up on people."

"I'm not everybody," Rafferty said. "You proposed something and the minute I agree, you change your mind. You say the cards over here are the same as the cards over there. So I'm not playing with my cards. I'm playing with your cards."

"Then what difference does it make?"

"The difference is that you said they were the same cards; I didn't. I'd like to see if the cards you sell over the counter to the public are the same as the ones you play with. Call it an experiment."

Rafferty grinned coldly, then suddenly turned and walked the few steps to the cigar counter. The pit boss followed him. He said, "What are you going to do?"

"Just buy a deck of cards," Rafferty said. He nodded at the girl behind the counter. "Cards?"

"A dollar, sir," the girl said and slid a deck across the glass top of the counter.

Rafferty set a silver dollar on the counter. He turned and held out the deck to the pit boss. "Here," he said. "You hold them. Just to make sure I'm not cheating."

The pit boss took the deck and stared at him. "You figure we're sensitive, so you're trying to make trouble, aren't you?"

"No," Rafferty said. "You're the one who's looking for trouble. All I'm looking for is an even shake. To repeat, all I'm doing is taking up your offer."

The pit boss swallowed. "Suppose you have a run of luck."

"Then I have a run of luck."

"Then you can go around saying this proves we're crooked."

"If you're not, you don't have anything to worry about."

"And if you keep on losing? What then? Do you hang it on the dealer?"

"There'll be people watching," Rafferty said. "I'm not worried about card tricks. Not this time around."

"You could still sit there and complain and cause us more trouble."

"Not really," Rafferty said. "A deck lasts about an hour in play, doesn't it? And if I went back to the counter for another deck, that *would* be unreasonable, wouldn't it? No, I've made my play. I'm truly interested in whether you think it's asking too much."

The pit boss looked down at his shoes. "This doesn't prove a thing, you know. If we were dishonest, the easiest thing in the world now would be to rig it so you win."

"I'd be delighted," Rafferty said. "Except that doing that would make you look really bad."

"Then what do you want?"

"A fresh start with a new deck of cards."

"Mr. Rafferty," the pit boss said, "I . . ." He paused. "All right. You've got an hour."

"Thank you," Rafferty said, and they went back to the table. A new dealer was called over. The pit boss himself broke the seal and spread the cards.

Rafferty played for an hour, while the pit boss and an ever-growing crowd of onlookers watched.

At the end of the hour, Rafferty stood up. He had won $18,000.

"Are you satisfied?" the pit boss said to him.

"Not quite," Rafferty said smoothly. "I'm out a dollar."

"You're out a . . . ?"

"For the cards."

"I see," the pit boss said. His voice struggled for control. "But that's not a dollar, Mr. Rafferty, because the cards at this point aren't worth a dollar anymore. They're used. So here are the cards, Mr. Rafferty, and you sell them for what you can get for them. And I'm not supposed to say this, but I'm going to say it anyway—don't come back here, Mr. Rafferty. It costs us too much to prove to you we're honest, and I'm not talking just about money. We like people who take our word for it, because we *are* honest, and we have their good will and the only way we can stay in business is to stay honest and settle for the house edge. You understand, Mr. Rafferty?"

"Perfectly," Rafferty said. "You don't have to worry about me coming back. It's unlikely I'd ever have another run like this one."

He nodded, fended his way through the group of onlookers and went to the elevators and up to his room. When he got there, he found there was a young woman seated at the writing table. She had an extremely thin artist's pen in her hand and she was marking the backs of a new deck of cards. The package the cards came in had been opened so that the seal was left unbroken.

"Hi," she said to Rafferty. "How'd you do?" She was the girl who had been behind the cigar counter downstairs.

"Fifteen net," Rafferty said, "and I told you not to be seen up here. And lay off the cards for now. Wait till we get to Reno."

CHARLES EINSTEIN became Midwest Sports Editor for the International News Service (INS) while he was still in college, and he continued with INS until 1958. Since then he has worked as a freelance writer and has edited the Simon and Schuster *Fireside Books of Baseball*. Although he has written numerous short stories, he specializes in the short-short story form and contributes to many magazines.

John Steinbeck

Have you ever thought you'd like to rob a bank?

Do you think a mild-mannered grocery clerk could rob a bank in broad daylight and get away with it?

In this story we learn

HOW MR. HOGAN ROBBED A BANK

I

On the Saturday before Labor Day, 1955, at 9:04½ A.M., Mr. Hogan robbed a bank. He was forty-two years old, married, and the father of a boy and a girl, named John and Joan, twelve and thirteen respectively. Mrs. Hogan's name was Joan and Mr. Hogan's was John, but since they called themselves Papa and Mama that left their names free for the children, who were considered very smart for their ages, each having jumped a grade in school. The Hogans lived at 215 East Maple Street, in a brown-shingle house with white trim—there are two. 215 is the one across from the street light and it is the one with the big tree in the yard, either oak or elm—the biggest tree in the whole street, maybe in the whole town.

John and Joan were in bed at the time of the robbery, for it was Saturday. At 9:10 A.M., Mrs. Hogan was making the cup of tea she always had. Mr. Hogan went to work early. Mrs. Hogan drank her tea slowly, scalding hot, and read her fortune in the tea leaves. There was a cloud and a five-pointed star with two short points in the bottom of the cup, but that was at 9:12 and the robbery was all over by then.

The way Mr. Hogan went about robbing the bank was very interesting. He gave it a great deal of thought and had for a long time, but he did not discuss it with anyone. He just read his newspaper and kept his own counsel. But he worked it out to his own satisfaction that people went to too much trouble robbing banks and that got them in a mess. The simpler the better, he always thought. People went in for too much hullabaloo and hankypanky. If you didn't do that, if you left hanky-panky out, robbing a bank would be a relatively sound venture—barring accidents, of course, of an improbable kind, but then they could happen to a man crossing the street or anything. Since Mr. Hogan's method worked fine, it proved that his thinking was sound. He often considered writing a little booklet on his technique when the how-to rage was running so high. He figured out the first sentence, which went: "To successfully rob a bank, forget all about hanky-panky."

Mr. Hogan was not just a clerk at Fettucci's grocery store. He was more like the manager. Mr. Hogan was in charge, even hired and fired the boy who delivered groceries after school. He even put in orders with the salesmen, sometimes when Mr. Fettucci was right in the store too, maybe talking to a customer. "You do it, John," he would say and he would nod at the customer, "John knows the ropes. Been with me—how long you been with me, John?"

"Sixteen years."

"Sixteen years. Knows the business as good as me. John, why he even banks the money."

And so he did. Whenever he had a moment, Mr. Hogan went into the storeroom on the alley, took off his apron, put on his necktie and coat, and went back through the store to the cash register. The checks and bills would be ready for him inside the bankbook with a rubber band around it. Then he went next door and stood at the teller's window and handed the checks and bankbook through to Mr. Cup and passed the time of day with him too. Then, when the bankbook was handed back, he checked the entry, put the rubber band around it, and walked next door to Fettucci's grocery and put the bankbook in the cash register, continued on to the storeroom, removed his coat and tie, put on his apron, and went back into the store ready for business. If there was no line at the teller's window, the whole thing didn't take more than five minutes, even passing the time of day.

Mr. Hogan was a man who noticed things, and when it came to robbing the bank, this trait stood him in good stead. He had noticed, for instance, where the big bills were kept right in the drawer under the counter and he had noticed also what days there were likely to be more than other days. Thursday was payday at the American Can Company's local plant, for instance, so there would be more then. Some Fridays people drew more money to tide them over the weekend. But it was even Steven, maybe not a thousand dollars difference, between Thursdays and Fridays and Saturday mornings. Saturdays were not terribly good because people didn't come to get money that early in the morning, and the bank closed at noon. But he thought it over and came to the conclusion that the Saturday before a long weekend in the summer would be the best of all. People going on trips, vacations, people with relatives visiting, and.the bank closed Monday. He thought it out and looked, and sure enough the Saturday morning before Labor Day the cash drawer had twice as much money in it—he saw it when Mr. Cup pulled out the drawer.

Mr. Hogan thought about it during all that year, not all the time, of course, but when he had some moments. It was a busy year too. That was the year John and Joan had the mumps and Mrs. Hogan got her teeth pulled and was fitted for a denture. That was the year when Mr. Hogan was Master of the Lodge, with all the time that takes. Larry Shield died that year—he was Mrs. Hogan's brother and was buried from the Hogan house at 215 East Maple. Larry was a bachelor and had a room in the Pine Tree House and he played pool nearly every night. He worked at the Silver Diner but that closed at nine and so Larry would go to Louie's and play pool for an hour. Therefore, it was a surprise when he left enough so that after funeral expenses there were twelve hundred dollars left. And even more surprising that he left a will in Mrs. Hogan's favor, but his double-barreled twelve-gauge shotgun he left to John Hogan, Jr. Mr. Hogan was pleased, although he never hunted. He put the shotgun away in the back of the closet in the bathroom, where he kept his things, to keep it for young John. He didn't want children handling guns and he never bought any shells. It was some of that twelve hundred that got Mrs. Hogan her dentures. Also, she bought a bicycle for John and a doll buggy and walking-talking doll for Joan—a doll with three changes of dresses and a little suitcase, complete with play make-up. Mr. Hogan thought it might spoil the children, but it didn't seem to. They made just as good marks in school and John even got a job delivering papers. It was a very busy year. Both John and Joan wanted to enter the W. R. Hearst National "I Love America" Contest and Mr. Hogan thought it was almost too much, but they promised to do the work during their summer vacation, so he finally agreed.

II

During that year, no one noticed any difference in Mr. Hogan. It was true, he was thinking about robbing the bank, but he only thought about it in the evening when there was neither a Lodge meeting nor a movie they wanted to go to, so it did not become an obsession and people noticed no change in him.

He had studied everything so carefully that the approach of Labor Day did not catch him unprepared or nervous. It was hot that summer and the hot spells were longer than usual. Saturday was the end of two weeks heat without a break and people were irritated with it and anxious to get out of town, although the country was just as hot. They didn't think of that. The children were excited because the "I Love America" Essay Contest was due to be concluded and the winners announced, and the first prize was an all-expense-paid two days trip to Washington, D.C., with every fixing—hotel room, three meals a day, and side trips in a limousine —not only for the winner, but for an accompanying chaperone; visit to the White House—shake hands with the President—everything. Mr. Hogan thought they were getting their hopes too high and he said so.

"You've got to be prepared to lose," he told his children. "There're probably thousands and thousands entered. You get your hopes up and it might spoil the whole autumn. Now I don't want any long faces in this house after the contest is over."

"I was against it from the start," he told Mrs. Hogan. That was the morning she saw the Washington Monument in her tea-cup, but she didn't tell anybody about that except Ruth Tyler, Bob Tyler's wife. Ruthie brought over her cards and read them in the Hogan kitchen, but she didn't find a journey. She did tell Mr. Hogan that the cards were often wrong. The cards had said Mrs. Winkle was going on a trip to Europe and the next week Mrs. Winkle got a fishbone in her throat and choked to death. Ruthie, just thinking out loud, wondered if there was any connection between the fishbone and the ocean voyage to Europe. "You've got to interpret them right." Ruthie did say she saw money coming to the Hogans.

"Oh, I got that already from poor Larry," Mrs. Hogan explained.

"I must have got the past and future cards mixed," said Ruthie. "You've got to interpret them right."

Saturday dawned a blaster. The early morning weather report on the radio said "Continued hot and humid, light scattered rain Sunday night and Monday." Mrs. Hogan said, "Wouldn't you know? Labor Day." And Mr. Hogan said, "I'm sure glad we didn't plan anything." He finished his egg and mopped the plate with his toast. Mrs. Hogan said, "Did I put coffee on the list?" He took the paper from his handkerchief pocket and consulted it. "Yes, coffee, it's here."

"I had a crazy idea I forgot to write it down," said Mrs. Hogan. "Ruth and I are going to Altar Guild this afternoon. It's at Mrs. Alfred Drake's. You know, they just came to town. I can't wait to see their furniture."

"They trade with us," said Mr. Hogan. "Opened an account last week. Are the milk bottles ready?"

"On the porch."

Mr. Hogan looked at his watch just before he picked up the bottles and it was five minutes to eight. He was about to go down the stairs, when he turned and looked back through the opened door at Mrs. Hogan. She said, "Want something, Papa?"

"No," he said. "No," and he walked down the steps.

He went down to the corner and turned right on Spooner, and Spooner runs into Main Street in two blocks, and right across from where it runs in, there is Fettucci's and the bank around the corner and the alley beside the bank. Mr. Hogan picked up a handbill in front of Fettucci's and unlocked the door. He went through to the storeroom, opened the door to the alley, and looked out. A cat tried to force its way in, but Mr. Hogan blocked it with his foot and leg and closed the door. He took off his coat and put on his long apron, tied the strings in a bowknot behind his back. Then he got the broom from behind the counter and swept out behind the counters and scooped the sweepings into a dustpan; and, going through the storeroom, he opened the door to the alley. The cat had gone away. He emptied the dustpan into the garbage can and tapped it smartly to dislodge a piece of lettuce leaf. Then he went back to the store and worked for a while on the order sheet. Mrs. Clooney came in for a half a pound of bacon. She said it was hot and Mr. Hogan agreed. "Summers are getting hotter," he said.

"I think so myself," said Mrs. Clooney. "How's Mrs. standing up?"

"Just fine," said Mr. Hogan. "She's going to Altar Guild."

"So am I. I just can't wait to see their furniture," said Mrs. Clooney, and she went out.

III

Mr. Hogan put a five-pound hunk of bacon on the slicer and stripped off the pieces and laid them on wax paper and then he put the wax-paper-covered squares in the cooler cabinet. At ten minutes to nine, Mr. Hogan went to a shelf. He pushed a spaghetti box aside and took down a cereal box, which he emptied in the little closet toilet. Then, with a banana knife, he cut out the Mickey Mouse mask that was on the back. The rest of the box he took to the toilet and tore up the cardboard and flushed it down. He went into the store then and yanked a piece of string loose and tied the ends through the side holes of the mask and then he looked at his watch—a large silver Hamilton with black hands. It was two minutes to nine.

Perhaps the next four minutes were his only time of nervousness at all. At one minute to nine, he took the broom and went out to sweep the sidewalk and he swept it very rapidly—was sweeping it, in fact, when Mr. Warner unlocked the bank door. He said good morning to Mr. Warner and a few seconds later the bank staff of four emerged from the coffee shop. Mr. Hogan saw them across the street and he waved at them and they waved back. He finished the sidewalk and went back in the store. He laid his watch on the little step of the cash register. He sighed very deeply, more like a deep breath than a sigh. He knew that Mr. Warner would have the safe open now and he would be carrying the cash trays to the teller's window. Mr. Hogan looked at the watch on the cash register step. Mr. Kenworthy paused in the store entrance, then shook his head vaguely and walked on and Mr. Hogan let out his breath gradually. His left hand went behind his back and pulled the bowknot on his apron, and then the black hand on his watch crept up on the four-minute mark and covered it.

Mr. Hogan opened the charge account drawer and took out the store pistol, a silver-colored Iver Johnson .38. He moved quickly to the storeroom, slipped off his apron, put on his coat, and stuck the revolver in his side pocket. The Mickey Mouse mask he shoved up under his coat where it didn't show. He opened the alley door and looked up and down and stepped quickly out, leaving the door slightly ajar. It is sixty feet to where the alley enters Main Street, and there he paused and looked up and down and then he turned his head toward the center of the street as he passed the bank window. At the bank's swinging door, he took out the mask from under his coat and put it on. Mr. Warner was just entering his office and his back was to the door. The top of Will Cup's head was visible through the teller's grill.

Mr. Hogan moved quickly and quietly around the end of the counter and into the teller's cage. He had the revolver in his right hand now. When Will Cup turned his head and saw the revolver, he froze. Mr. Hogan slipped his toe under the trigger of the floor alarm and he motioned Will Cup to the floor with the revolver and Will went down quick. Then Mr. Hogan opened the cash drawer and with two quick movements he piled the large bills from the tray together. He made a whipping motion to Will on the floor, to indicate that he should turn over and face the wall, and Will did. Then Mr. Hogan stepped back around the counter. At the door of the bank, he took off the mask, and as he passed the window he turned his head toward the middle of the street. He moved into the alley, walked quickly to the storeroom, and entered. The cat had got in. It watched him from a pile of canned goods cartons. Mr. Hogan went to the toilet closet and tore up the mask and flushed it. He took off his coat and put on his apron. He looked out into the store and then moved to the cash register. The revolver went back into the charge account drawer. He punched No Sale and, lifting the top drawer, distributed the stolen money underneath the top tray and then pulled the tray forward and closed the register, and only then did he look at his watch and it was 9:07½.

He was trying to get the cat out of the storeroom when the commotion boiled out of the bank. He took his broom and went out on the sidewalk. He heard all about it and offered his opinion when it was asked for. He said he didn't think the fellow could get away—where could he get to? Still, with the holiday coming up—

It was an exciting day. Mr. Fettucci was as proud as though it were his bank. The sirens sounded around town for hours. Hundreds of holiday travelers had to stop at the roadblocks set up all around the edge of town and several sneaky-looking men had their cars searched.

Mrs. Hogan heard about it over the phone and she dressed earlier than she would have ordinarily and came to the store on her way to Altar Guild. She hoped Mr. Hogan would have seen or heard something new, but he hadn't. "I don't see how the fellow can get away," he said.

Mrs. Hogan was so excited, she forgot her own news. She only remembered when she got to Mrs. Drake's house, but she asked permission and phoned the store the first moment she could. "I forgot to tell you. John's won honorable mention."

"What?"

"In the 'I Love America' Contest."

"What did he win?"

"Honorable mention."

"Fine. Fine—Anything come with it?"

"Why, he'll get his picture and his name all over the country. Radio too. Maybe even television. They've already asked for a photograph of him."

"Fine," said Mr. Hogan. "I hope it don't spoil him." He put up the receiver and said to Mr. Fettucci, "I guess we've got a celebrity in the family."

Fettucci stayed open until nine on Saturdays. Mr. Hogan ate a few snacks from cold cuts, but not much, because Mrs. Hogan always kept his supper warming.

It was 9:05, or :06, or :07, when he got back to the brown-shingle house at 215 East Maple. He went in through the front door and out to the kitchen where the family was waiting for him.

"Got to wash up," he said, and went up to the bathroom. He turned the key in the bathroom door and then he flushed the toilet and turned on the water in the basin and tub while he counted the money. Eight thousand three hundred and twenty dollars. From the top shelf of the storage closet in the bathroom, he took down the big leather case that held his Knight Templar's uniform. The plumed hat lay there on its form. The white ostrich feather was a little yellow and needed changing. Mr. Hogan lifted out the hat and pried the form up from the bottom of the case. He put the money in the form and then he thought again and removed two bills and shoved them in his side pocket. Then he put the form back over the money and laid the hat on top and closed the case and shoved it back on the top shelf. Finally he washed his hands and turned off the water in the tub and the basin.

In the kitchen, Mrs. Hogan and the children faced him, beaming. "Guess what some young man's going on?"

"What?" asked Mr. Hogan.

"Radio," said John. "Monday night. Eight o'clock."

"I guess we got a celebrity in the family," said Mr. Hogan.

Mrs. Hogan said, "I just hope some young lady hasn't got her nose out of joint."

Mr. Hogan pulled up to the table and stretched his legs. "Mama, I guess I got a fine family," he said. He reached in his pocket and took out two five-dollar bills. He handed one to John. "That's for winning," he said. He poked the other bill at Joan. "And that's for being a good sport. One celebrity and one good sport. What a fine family!" He rubbed his hands together and lifted the lid of the covered dish. "Kidneys," he said. "Fine."

And that's how Mr. Hogan did it.

JOHN STEINBECK was born in Salinas, California, in 1902 and died in New York in 1968. He attended Stanford University but left without a degree in 1925. Before he became a successful writer he worked at a variety of jobs—ranch hand, hod carrier, laboratory assistant, reporter, and fruit picker. He won the Pulitzer Prize for his novel *Grapes of Wrath* in 1940 and the Nobel Prize in literature in 1962. Some of his other famous novels include *Cannery Row, Tortilla Flat, Of Mice and Men,* and *Travels with Charley.*

James Thurber

*Have you ever seen a female bully hard at work
frightening the men around her?*

   *What would be the perfect "put-down" for
a loud-mouthed office bully?*

   Mr. Martin thinks of one in

THE CATBIRD SEAT

Mr. Martin bought the pack of Camels on Monday night
in the most crowded cigar store on Broadway. It was theatre time
and seven or eight men were buying cigarettes. The clerk didn't
even glance at Mr. Martin, who put the pack in his overcoat
pocket and went out. If any of the staff at F & S had seen him
buy the cigarettes, they would have been astonished, for it was
generally known that Mr. Martin did not smoke, and never had.
No one saw him.

It was just a week to the day since Mr. Martin had decided
to rub out Mrs. Ulgine Barrows. The term "rub out" pleased him
because it suggested nothing more than the correction of an error
—in this case an error of Mr. Fitweiler. Mr. Martin had spent each
night of the past week working out his plan and examining it. As
he walked home now he went over it again. For the hundredth
time he resented the element of imprecision, the margin of guess-

work that entered into the business. The project as he had worked it out was casual and bold, the risks were considerable. Something might go wrong anywhere along the line. And therein lay the cunning of his scheme. No one would ever see in it the cautious, painstaking hand of Erwin Martin, head of the filing department at F & S, of whom Mr. Fitweiler had once said, "Man is fallible but Martin isn't." No one would see his hand, that is, unless it were caught in the act.

Sitting in his apartment, drinking a glass of milk, Mr. Martin reviewed his case against Mrs. Ulgine Barrows, as he had every night for seven nights. He began at the beginning. Her quacking voice and braying laugh had first profaned the halls of F & S on March 7, 1941 (Mr. Martin had a head for dates). Old Roberts, the personnel chief, had introduced her as the newly appointed special adviser to the president of the firm, Mr. Fitweiler. The woman had appalled Mr. Martin instantly, but he hadn't shown it. He had given her his dry hand, a look of studious concentration, and a faint smile. "Well," she had said, looking at the paper on his desk, "are you lifting the oxcart out of the ditch?" As Mr. Martin recalled that moment, over his milk, he squirmed slightly. He must keep his mind on her crimes as a special adviser, not on her peccadillos as a personality. This he found difficult to do, in spite of entering an objection and sustaining it. The faults of the woman as a woman kept chattering on in his mind like an unruly witness. She had, for almost two years now, baited him. In the halls, in the elevator, even in his own office, into which she romped now and then like a circus horse, she was constantly shouting these silly questions at him. "Are you lifting the oxcart out of the ditch? Are you tearing up the pea patch? Are you hollering down the rain barrel? Are you scaping around the bottom of the pickle barrel? Are you sitting in the catbird seat?"

It was Joey Hart, one of Mr. Martin's two assistants, who had explained what the gibberish meant. "She must be a Dodger fan," he had said. "Red Barber announces the Dodger games over the radio and he uses those expressions—picked 'em up down South." Joey had gone on to explain one or two. "Tearing up the pea patch" meant going on a rampage; "sitting in the catbird seat" meant sitting pretty, like a batter with three balls and no strikes on him. Mr. Martin dismissed all this with an effort. It had been annoying, it had driven him near to distraction, but he was too solid a man to be moved to murder by anything so childish. It was fortunate, he reflected as he passed on to the important charges against Mrs. Barrows, that he had stood up under it so well. He had maintained always an outward appearance of polite tolerance. "Why, I even believe you like the woman," Miss Paird, his other assistant, had once said to him. He had simply smiled.

A gavel rapped in Mr. Martin's mind and the case proper was resumed. Mrs. Ulgine Barrows stood charged with willful, blatant, and persistent attempts to destroy the efficiency and system of F & S. It was competent, material, and relevant to review her advent and rise to power. Mr. Martin had got the story from Miss Paird, who seemed always able to find things out. According to her, Mrs. Barrows had met Mr. Fitweiler at a party, where she had rescued him from the embraces of a powerfully built drunken man who had mistaken the president of F & S for a famous retired Middle Western football coach. She had led him to a sofa and somehow worked upon him a monstrous magic. The aging gentleman had jumped to the conclusion there and then that this was a woman of singular attainments, equipped to bring out the best in him and in the firm. A week later he had introduced her into F & S as his special adviser. On that day confusion got its foot in the door. After Miss Tyson, Mr. Brundage, and Mr. Bartlett had been fired and Mr. Munson had taken his hat and stalked out, mailing in his resignation later, old Roberts had been emboldened to speak to Mr. Fitweiler. He mentioned that Mr. Munson's department had been "a little disrupted" and hadn't they perhaps better resume the old system there? Mr. Fitweiler had said certainly not. He had the greatest faith in Mrs. Barrows' ideas. "They require a little seasoning, a little seasoning, is all," he had added. Mr. Roberts had given it up. Mr. Martin reviewed in detail all the changes wrought by Mrs. Barrows. She had begun chipping at the cornices of the firm's edifice and now she was swinging at the foundation stones with a pickaxe.

Mr. Martin came now, in his summing up, to the afternoon of Monday, November 2, 1942—just one week ago. On that day, at 3 P.M., Mrs. Barrows had bounced into his office. "Boo!" she had yelled. "Are you scraping around the bottom of the pickle barrel?" Mr. Martin had looked at her from under his green eyeshade,

saying nothing. She had begun to wander about the office, taking
it in with her great, popping eyes. "Do you really need *all* these
filing cabinets?" she had demanded suddenly. Mr. Martin's heart
had jumped. "Each of these files," he had said, keeping his voice
even, "play an indispensable part in the system of F & S." She
had brayed at him, "Well, don't tear up the pea patch!" and gone
to the door. From there she had bawled, "But you sure have got
a lot of fine scrap in here!" Mr. Martin could no longer doubt that
the finger was on his beloved department. Her pickaxe was on
the upswing, poised for the first blow. It had not come yet; he had
received no blue memo from the enchanted Mr. Fitweiler bearing
nonsensical instructions deriving from the obscene woman. But
there was no doubt in Mr. Martin's mind that one would be forth-
coming. He must act quickly. Already a precious week had gone
by. Mr. Martin stood up in his living room, still holding his milk
glass. "Gentlemen of the jury," he said to himself, "I demand the
death penalty for this horrible person."

The next day Mr. Martin followed his routine, as usual. He
polished his glasses more often and once sharpened an already
sharp pencil, but not even Miss Paird noticed. Only once did he
catch sight of his victim; she swept past him in the hall with a
patronizing "Hi!" At five-thirty he walked home, as usual, and
had a glass of milk, as usual. He had never drunk anything stronger
in his life—unless you could count ginger ale. The late Sam
Schlosser, the S of F & S, had praised Mr. Martin at a staff meeting
several years before for his temperate habits. "Our most efficient
worker neither drinks nor smokes," he had said. "The results
speak for themselves." Mr. Fitweiler had sat by, nodding approval.

Mr. Martin was still thinking about that red-letter day as
he walked over to Schrafft's on Fifth Avenue near Forty-sixth Street.
He got there, as he always did, at eight o'clock. He finished his
dinner and the financial page of the *Sun* at a quarter to nine, as
he always did. It was his custom after dinner to take a walk.
This time he walked down Fifth Avenue at a casual pace. His
gloved hands felt moist and warm, his forehead cold. He transferred the Camels from his overcoat to a jacket pocket. He wondered, as he did so, if they did not represent an unnecessary
strain. Mrs. Barrows smoked only Luckies. It was his idea to puff

a few puffs on a Camel (after the rubbing-out), stub it out in the ashtray holding her lipstick-stained Luckies, and thus drag a small red herring across the trail. Perhaps it was not a good idea. It would take time. He might even choke, too loudly.

Mr. Martin had never seen the house on West Twelfth Street where Mrs. Barrows lived, but he had a clear enough picture of it. Fortunately, she had bragged to everybody about her ducky first-floor apartment in the perfectly darling three-story red-brick. There would be no doorman or other attendants; just the tenants of the second and third floors. As he walked along, Mr. Martin realized that he would get there before nine-thirty. He had considered walking north on Fifth Avenue from Schrafft's to a point from which it would take him until ten o'clock to reach the house. At that hour people were less likely to be coming in or going out. But the procedure would have made an awkward loop in the straight thread of his casualness, and he had abandoned it. It was impossible to figure when people would be entering or leaving the house, anyway. There was a great risk at any hour. If he ran into anybody, he would simply have to place the rubbing-out of Ulgine Barrows in the inactive file forever. The same thing would hold true if there were someone in her apartment. In that case he would just say that he had been passing by, recognized her charming house and thought to drop in.

It was eighteen minutes after nine when Mr. Martin turned into Twelfth Street. A man passed him, and a man and a woman talking. There was no one within fifty paces when he came to the house, halfway down the block. He was up the steps and in the small vestibule in no time, pressing the bell under the card that said "Mrs. Ulgine Barrows." When the clicking in the lock started, he jumped forward against the door. He got inside fast, closing the door behind him. A bulb in a lantern hung from the hall ceiling on a chain seemed to give a monstrously bright light. There was nobody on the stair, which went up ahead of him along the left wall. A door opened down the hall in the wall on the right. He went toward it swiftly, on tiptoe.

"Well, for God's sake, look who's here!" bawled Mrs. Barrows, and her braying laugh rang out like the report of a shotgun. He rushed past her like a football tackle, bumping her. "Hey,

quit shoving!" she said, closing the door behind them. They were
in her living room, which seemed to Mr. Martin to be lighted by
a hundred lamps. "What's after you?" she said. "You're as jumpy
as a goat." He found he was unable to speak. His heart was
wheezing in his throat. "I—yes," he finally brought out. She was
jabbering and laughing as she started to help him off with his
coat. "No, no," he said. "I'll put it here." He took it off and put
it on a chair near the door. "Your hat and gloves, too," she said.
"You're in a lady's house." He put his hat on top of the coat. Mrs.
Barrows seemed larger than he had thought. He kept his gloves
on. "I was passing by," he said. "I recognized—is there anyone
here?" She laughed louder than ever. "No," she said, "we're all
alone. You're as white as a sheet, you funny man. Whatever *has*
come over you? I'll mix you a toddy." She started toward a door
across the room. "Scotch-and-soda be all right? But say, you
don't drink, do you?" She turned and gave him her amused look.
Mr. Martin pulled himself together. "Scotch-and-soda will be all
right," he heard himself say. He could hear her laughing in the
kitchen.

Mr. Martin looked quickly around the living room for the
weapon. He had counted on finding one there. There were and-
irons and a poker and something in a corner that looked like an
Indian club. None of them would do. It couldn't be that way.
He began to pace around. He came to a desk. On it lay a metal
paper knife with an ornate handle. Would it be sharp enough?
He reached for it and knocked over a small brass jar. Stamps
spilled out of it and it fell to the floor with a clatter. "Hey," Mrs.
Barrows yelled from the kitchen, "are you tearing up the pea
patch?" Mr. Martin gave a strange laugh. Picking up the knife, he
tried its point against his left wrist. It was blunt. It wouldn't do.

When Mrs. Barrows reappeared, carrying two highballs,
Mr. Martin, standing there with his gloves on, became acutely
conscious of the fantasy he had wrought. Cigarettes in his pocket,
a drink prepared for him—it was all too grossly improbable. It was
more than that; it was impossible. Somewhere in the back of his
mind a vague idea stirred, sprouted. "For heaven's sake, take off
those gloves," said Mrs. Barrows. "I always wear them in the
house," said Mr. Martin. The idea began to bloom, strange and

wonderful. She put the glasses on a coffee table in front of a sofa and sat on the sofa. "Come over here, you odd little man," she said. Mr. Martin went over and sat beside her. It was difficult getting a cigarette out of the pack of Camels, but he managed it. She held a match for him, laughing. "Well," she said, handing him his drink, "this is perfectly marvelous. You with a drink and a cigarette."

Mr. Martin puffed, not too awkwardly, and took a gulp of the highball. "I drink and smoke all the time," he said. He clinked his glass against hers. "Here's nuts to that old windbag, Fitweiler," he said, and gulped again. The stuff tasted awful, but he made no grimace. "Really, Mr. Martin," she said, her voice and posture changing, "you are insulting our employer." Mrs. Barrows was now all special adviser to the president. "I am preparing a bomb," said Mr. Martin, "which will blow the old goat higher than hell." He had only had a little of the drink, which was not strong. It couldn't be that. "Do you take dope or something?" Mrs. Barrows asked coldly. "Heroin," said Mr. Martin. "I'll be coked to the gills when I bump that old buzzard off." "Mr. Martin!" she shouted, getting to her feet. "That will be all of that. You must go at once." Mr. Martin took another swallow of his drink. He tapped his cigarette out in the ashtray and put the pack of Camels on the coffee table. Then he got up. She stood glaring at him. He walked over and put on his hat and coat. "Not a word about this," he said, and laid an index finger against his lips. All Mrs. Barrows could bring out was "Really!" Mr. Martin put his hand on the doorknob. "I'm sitting in the catbird seat," he said. He stuck his tongue out at her and left. Nobody saw him go.

Mr. Martin got to his apartment, walking, well before eleven. No one saw him go in. He had two glasses of milk after brushing his teeth, and he felt elated. It wasn't tipsiness, because he hadn't been tipsy. Anyway, the walk had worn off all effects of the whiskey. He got in bed and read a magazine for a while. He was asleep before midnight.

Mr. Martin got to the office at eight-thirty the next morning, as usual. At a quarter to nine, Ulgine Barrows, who had never arrived at work before ten, swept into his office. "I'm reporting to Mr. Fitweiler now!" she shouted. "If he turns you over to the

police, it's no more than you deserve!" Mr. Martin gave her a look
of shocked surprise. "I beg your pardon?" he said. Mrs. Barrows
snorted and bounced out of the room, leaving Miss Paird and Joey
Hart staring after her. "What's the matter with that old devil
now?" asked Miss Paird. "I have no idea," said Mr. Martin, resuming his work. The other two looked at him and then at each other.
Miss Paird got up and went out. She walked slowly past the
closed door of Mr. Fitweiler's office. Mrs. Barrows was yelling
inside, but she was not braying. Miss Paird could not hear what
the woman was saying. She went back to her desk.

Forty-five minutes later, Mrs. Barrows left the president's
office and went into her own, shutting the door. It wasn't until
half an hour later that Mr. Fitweiler sent for Mr. Martin. The head
of the filing department, neat, quiet, attentive, stood in front of
the old man's desk. Mr. Fitweiler was pale and nervous. He took
his glasses off and twiddled them. He made a small, bruffing
sound in his throat. "Martin," he said, "you have been with us
more than twenty years." "Twenty-two, sir," said Mr. Martin. "In
that time," pursued the president, "your work and your—uh—
manner have been exemplary." "I trust so, sir," said Mr. Martin.
"I have understood, Martin," said Mr. Fitweiler, "that you have
never taken a drink or smoked." "That is correct, sir," said Mr.
Martin. "Ah, yes." Mr. Fitweiler polished his glasses. "You may
describe what you did after leaving the office yesterday, Mr.
Martin," he said. Mr. Martin allowed less than a second for his
bewildered pause. "Certainly, sir," he said. "I walked home.
Then I went to Schrafft's for dinner. Afterward I walked home
again. I went to bed early, sir, and read a magazine for a while.
I was asleep before eleven." "Ah, yes," said Mr. Fitweiler again.
He was silent for a moment, searching for the proper words to say
to the head of the filing department. "Mrs. Barrows," he said finally, "Mrs. Barrows has worked hard, Martin, very hard. It grieves
me to report that she has suffered a severe breakdown. It has
taken the form of a persecution complex accompanied by distress-
ing hallucinations." "I am very sorry, sir," said Mr. Martin. "Mrs.
Barrows is under the delusion," continued Mr. Fitweiler, "that you
visited her last evening and behaved yourself in an—uh—unseemly
manner." He raised his hand to silence Mr. Martin's little pained
outcry. "It is the nature of these psychological diseases," Mr.

Fitweiler said, "to fix upon the least likely and most innocent party as the—uh—source of persecution. These matters are not for the lay mind to grasp, Martin. I've just had my psychiatrist, Dr. Fitch, on the phone. He would not, of course, commit himself, but he made enough generalizations to substantiate my suspicions. I suggested to Mrs. Barrows when she had completed her—uh— story to me this morning, that she visit Dr. Fitch, for I suspected a condition at once. She flew, I regret to say, into a rage, and demanded—uh—requested that I call you on the carpet. You may not know, Martin, but Mrs. Barrows had planned a reorganization of your department—subject to my approval, of course, subject to my approval. This brought you, rather than anyone else, to her mind—but again that is a phenomenon for Dr. Fitch and not for us. So, Martin, I am afraid Mrs. Barrows' usefulness here is at an end."
"I am dreadfully sorry, sir," said Mr. Martin.

It was at this point that the door to the office blew open with the suddenness of a gas-main explosion and Mrs. Barrows catapulted through it. "Is the little rat denying it?" she screamed. "He can't get away with that!" Mr. Martin got up and moved discreetly to a point beside Mr. Fitweiler's chair. "You drank and smoked at my apartment," she bawled at Mr. Martin, "and you know it! You called Mr. Fitweiler an old windbag and said you were going to blow him up when you got coked to the gills on your heroin!" She stopped yelling to catch her breath and a new glint came into her popping eyes. "If you weren't such a drab, ordinary little man," she said, "I'd think you'd planned it all. Sticking your tongue out, saying you were sitting in the catbird seat, because you thought no one would believe me when I told it! My God, it's really too perfect!" She brayed loudly and hysterically, and the fury was on her again. She glared at Mr. Fitweiler. "Can't you see how he has tricked us, you old fool? Can't you see his little game?" But Mr. Fitweiler had been surreptitiously pressing all the buttons under the top of his desk and employees of F & S began pouring into the room. "Stockton," said Mr. Fitweiler, "you and Fishbein will take Mrs. Barrows to her home. Mrs. Powell, you will go with them." Stockton, who had played a little football in high school, blocked Mrs. Barrows as she made for Mr. Martin. It took him and Fishbein together to force her out of the door into the hall, crowded with stenographers and office boys. She was still screaming imprecations at Mr. Martin, tangled and contradictory imprecations. The hubbub finally died out down the corridor.

"I regret that this has happened," said Mr. Fitweiler. "I shall ask you to dismiss it from your mind, Martin." "Yes, sir," said Mr. Martin, anticipating his chief's "That will be all" by moving to the door. "I will dismiss it." He went out and shut the door, and his step was light and quick in the hall. When he entered his department he had slowed down to his customary gait, and he walked quietly across the room to the W20 file, wearing a look of studious concentration.

JAMES THURBER, one of America's funniest writers, was born in Columbus, Ohio, in 1894 and died in 1961. He attended Ohio State University and began his journalistic career as a newspaper reporter in Columbus. He later traveled to France, worked in the American Embassy, and was a reporter for the Paris edition of the *Herald Tribune*. In 1926 he began a long and distinguished career as a writer and humorist for the *New Yorker* magazine, to which he contributed stories, sketches, articles, and cartoons. One of the best-known collections of his writings is *The Thurber Carnival*.

A. B. Guthrie, Jr.

Do you think there might have been times when the white man's efforts to impress and frighten the American Indian backfired miserably?

Are the ingredients of a mule, a cannon, and showmanship a mixture for explosive laughter?

See what Chief Two Plumes thinks of the white man's medicine in

THE BIG IT

Two Plumes was that Injun chief's name. It just hit my mind. Two Plumes, a Piegan, and the place was Fort Benton, Montana Territory, and the time somewheres between 1870 and 1875. I had showed up in the town from over in the Deer Lodge country, lookin' for fun but not for what come.

The place was lively as a hot carcass, for the nabobs from the fur companies had come up from St. Louis, like they did every year, to see how much they'd been cheated out of their legal and honorable earnin's. Steamboats on the levee. Other visitors aplenty in town—bullwhackers, muleskinners, prospectors, traders, tinhorn gamblers, crews from the boats, new crop of girls, all bein' merry.

And to boot, there was a big bunch of Injuns, mostly Piegans, but Bloods, too, and other kinds I didn't savvy. A passel, I tell you. Their tepees was pitched out a ways, God knows why, for mornin', noon and night they hung around town.

People was a little ticklish, seein' them Injuns was so many. Give them savages some little excuse, they said between hiccups and rumpuses, and they might forget their manners, which wasn't high-toned at the best.

Then, from some tradin' post, a pack train showed up. Tied on one of the mules, with the muzzle pointin' the same way as the mule's, was a little brass cannon, or what they call a mountain howitzer.

It took a little time to see that here was the big IT. The trouble with opportunity is that its name's wrote on its butt. But this time somebody seen it before it went over the hill. Fire that cannon, the smart somebody said. Make boom. Make goddam big hole in far bluff of river. Show Injuns real medicine. Scare devil out of red devils.

There wasn't no argument on that motion. It had just to be put to get a unanimous vote. So the boys went out to round up the Injuns, tellin' 'em by tongue and by sign to come see the big show. Meantime some others said they'd cut the mule from the string and plant him close to the river. Them with no special duties kept circulatin', makin' sure that all hands was informed.

Everyone was, Injun and white. The Injuns came in a herd, in blankets and buckskins and bare skins, and so did the whites, all of 'em, includin' some ladies not so damn ladylike they couldn't enjoy theirselves. You never seen such a crowd.

Like now, of course, Front Street was half-faced, buildin's on one side, river on t'other. The mule men had led the mule to the shore. On yon side was a cut bank they figured would make a good target. The rest of us pushed around close, makin' a kind of a half circle, the heathens composin' one horn of it and us redeemers the other, though there was some mixin' up, it bein' hard to remember it was them that needed to see and get educated.

Now in the front row of the Injuns I spotted this old chief, Two Plumes, that I had smoked with a time or two. He had his arms folded and the look on his face that a redskin can wear which says nothin' will ever surprise him, in particular white men and their doin's. The other bucks was wearin' it, too. You can't beat an Injun for lookin' like he wouldn't let on that you stink.

The men with the mule got the cannon loaded, one standin' on a box so's to get at the muzzle and feed it a whole hatful of powder and then poke the ball home.

So then all was ready save for the sightin'. Aimin' the piece meant aimin' the mule first and then seein' to the refinements. Wasn't no trouble. That sleepy old mule was agreeable. He led around and whoaed with his tail dead on the target and went back to sleep. With one man at his head, another climbed up and squinted over the barrel and fiddled with doodads and got down, claimin' the piece was trained finer than frog hair.

The ramrod of this frolic, whoever he was, made a little speech then, tellin' the Injuns to look-see across the far water where the white man's terrible medicine iron would blow the dust tall. With that, he turned to his terrible crew. "Ready?" he said.

They sighted again and nodded for yes, and he told 'em, "Fire away, men!"

One of 'em touched a match to the fuse.

The fuse fizzed and fizzed, and Mister Mule opened one eye and then both, and he flapped his ears back and let out a snort while the crew hollered whoa and hung hard to his head. Huh-uh! The mule hunched a hump in his back and began buck-jumpin' around in a wheel, the cannon bobbin' its big eye at one and another and all of us innocent bystanders while the fuse et down toward the charge.

For a shake no one could move, but just for a shake. Me, I found myself lyin' behind a scatter of driftwood, and some feller was tryin' to scratch under me like a mole, prayin', "No! Don't shoot! No!" to the mule.

That feller tunneled me up over my fort. The mule was wheelin' and the fuse fusin' and the cannon pickin' up targets, and them innocent targets, I tell you, was wild on the wing or dead flat on the ground or neck-deep in the river, duckin' like hell-divers when the muzzle swung around. But the Injuns stood still, waitin' for the tall dust to blow.

Then, like a close clap of thunder, the cannon went off!

It didn't hurt anything. What with the mule's jumpin', it had slid back, down on the slope of his hump, so's the ball skimmed his tail and went into the ground.

Men began comin' from cover and trailin' up in the dust and the powder smoke, smilin' pale and damn silly.

I walked over to Two Plumes, who was standin' with his arms folded like before, with nothin' in his face that showed anything.

"How?" I said. "How chief like 'im?"

He answered, "How?" and let the rest of it wait, but in that Injun eye was a gleam. Then he said, "Paleface jackass poop."

A. B. GUTHRIE, JR., was born in Bedford, Indiana, on January 13, 1901, and was raised in Choteau, Montana. While working as a printer's devil on the Choteau *Ocantha* during high school, he became interested in journalism and Western history. He graduated from Montana State University. During the summers of his college years he worked in the Lewis and Clark National Forest in Montana and on ranches. After his graduation he and a friend went to Mexico in a Model T Ford and worked in the Yaqui Valley on an irrigation project. Guthrie then held many jobs, from grocery clerking to taking the federal census on horseback. Two of his best novels are *The Big Sky* (1947) and *The Way West* (1949).

Herman Melville

How many superstitions about lightning do you know? Can lightning strike twice in the same place? Where is the safest place to be in an electrical storm?

Are certain people "doom sayers" who predict terrible things for the future?

Listen to one man who is called

THE LIGHTNING-ROD
MAN

What grand irregular thunder, thought I, standing on my hearthstone among the Acroceraunian hills, as the scattered bolts boomed overhead, and crashed down among the valleys, every bolt followed by zigzag irradiations, and swift slants of sharp rain, which audibly rang, like a charge of spearpoints, on my low shingled roof. I suppose, though, that the mountains hereabouts break and churn up the thunder, so that it is far more glorious here than on the plain. Hark!—some one at the door. Who is this that chooses a time of thunder for making calls? And why don't he, man-fashion, use the knocker, instead of making that doleful undertaker's clatter with his fist against the hollow panel? But let him in. Ah, here he comes. "Good day, sir": an entire stranger. "Pray be seated." What is that strange-looking walking-stick he carries: "A fine thunder-storm sir."

"Fine?—Awful!"

"You are wet. Stand here on the hearth before the fire."

"Not for worlds!"

The stranger still stood in the exact middle of the cottage, where he had first planted himself. His singularity impelled a closer scrutiny. A lean, gloomy figure. Hair dark and lank, mattedly streaked over his brow. His sunken pitfalls of eyes were ringed by indigo halos, and played with an innocuous sort of lightning: the gleam without the bolt. The whole man was dripping. He stood in a puddle on the bare oak floor: his strange walking-stick vertically resting at his side.

It was a polished copper rod, four feet long, lengthwise attached to a neat wooden staff, by insertion into two balls of greenish glass, ringed with copper bands. The metal rod terminated at the top tripodwise, in three keen tines, brightly gilt. He held the thing by the wooden part alone.

"Sir," said I, bowing politely, "have I the honor of a vision from that illustrious god, Jupiter Tonans? So stood he in the Greek statue of old, grasping the lightning-bolt. If you be he, or his viceroy, I have to thank you for this noble storm you have brewed among our mountains. Listen: That was a glorious peal. Ah, to a lover of the majestic, it is a good thing to have the Thunderer himself in one's cottage. The thunder grows finer for that. But pray be seated. This old rush-bottomed arm-chair, I grant, is a poor substitute for your evergreen throne on Olympus; but, condescend to be seated."

While I thus pleasantly spoke, the stranger eyed me, half in wonder, and half in a strange sort of horror; but did not move a foot.

"Do, sir, be seated; you need to be dried ere going forth again."

I planted the chair invitingly on the broad hearth, where a little fire had been kindled that afternoon to dissipate the dampness, not the cold; for it was early in the month of September.

But without heeding my solicitation, and still standing in the middle of the floor, the stranger gazed at me portentously and spoke.

"Sir," said he, "excuse me; but instead of my accepting your invitation to be seated on the hearth there, I solemnly warn *you*, that you had best accept *mine*, and stand with me in the middle of the room. Good heavens!" he cried, starting—"there is another of those awful crashes. I warn you, sir, quit the hearth."

"Mr. Jupiter Tonans," said I, quietly rolling my body on the stone, "I stand very well here."

"Are you so horridly ignorant, then," he cried, "as not to know, that by far the most dangerous part of a house, during such a terrific tempest as this, is the fire-place?"

"Nay, I did not know that," involuntarily stepping upon the first board next to the stone.

The stranger now assumed such an unpleasant air of successful admonition, that—quite involuntarily again—I stepped back upon the hearth, and threw myself into the erectest, proudest posture I could command. But I said nothing.

"For Heaven's sake," he cried, with a strange mixture of alarm and intimidation—"for Heaven's sake, get off the hearth! Know you not, that the heated air and soot are conductors;—to say nothing of those immense iron fire-dogs? Quit the spot—I conjure—I command you."

"Mr. Jupiter Tonans, I am not accustomed to be commanded in my own house."

"Call me not by that pagan name. You are profane in this time of terror."

"Sir, will you be good as to tell me your business? If you seek shelter from the storm, you are welcome, so long as you be civil; but if you come on business, open it forthwith. Who are you?"

"I am a dealer in lightning-rods," said the stranger, softening his tone; "my special business is—Merciful heaven! what a crash!—Have you ever been struck—your premises, I mean? No? It's best to be provided";—significantly rattling his metallic staff on the floor;—"by nature, there are no castles in thunder-storms; yet, say but the word, and of this cottage I can make a Gibraltar by a few waves of this wand. Hark, what Himalayas of concussions!"

"You interrupted yourself; your special business you were to speak of."

"My special business is to travel the country for orders for lightning-rods. This is my specimen-rod"; tapping his staff; "I have the best of references"—fumbling in his pockets. "In

Criggan last month, I put up three-and-twenty rods on only five buildings."

"Let me see. Was it not at Criggan last week, about midnight on Saturday, that the steeple, the big elm, and the assembly-room cupola were struck? Any of your rods there?"

"Not on the tree and cupola, but the steeple."

"Of what use is your rod, then?"

"Of life-and-death use. But my workman was heedless. In fitting the rod at top to the steeple, he allowed a part of the metal to graze the tin sheeting. Hence the accident. Not my fault, but his. Hark!"

"Never mind. That clap burst quite loud enough to be heard without finger-pointing. Did you hear of the event at Montreal last year? A servant girl struck at her bed-side with a rosary in her hand; the beads being metal. Does your beat extend into the Canadas?"

"No. And I hear that there, iron rods only are in use. They should have *mine,* which are copper. Iron is easily fused. Then they draw out the rod so slender, that it has not body enough to conduct the full electric current. The metal melts; the building is destroyed. My copper rods never act so. Those Canadians are fools. Some of them knob the rod at the top, which risks a deadly explosion, instead of imperceptibly carrying down the current into the earth, as this sort of rod does. *Mine* is the only true rod. Look at it. Only one dollar a foot."

"This abuse of your own calling in another might make one distrustful with respect to yourself."

"Hark! The thunder becomes less muttering. It is nearing us, and nearing the earth, too. Hark! One crammed crash! All the vibrations made one by nearness. Another flash. Hold!"

"What do you?" I said, seeing him now, instantaneously relinquishing his staff, lean intently forward towards the window, with his right fore and middle fingers on his left wrist.

But ere the words had well escaped me, another exclamation escaped him.

"Crash! only three pulses—less than a third of a mile off—yonder, somewhere in that wood. I passed three stricken oaks there, ripped out new and glittering. The oak draws lightning more than other timber, having iron in solution in its sap. Your floor here seems oak."

"Heart-of-oak. From the peculiar time of your call upon me, I suppose you purposely select stormy weather for your journeys. When the thunder is roaring, you deem it an hour peculiarly favorable for producing impressions favorable to your trade."

"Hark!—Awful!"

"For one who would arm others with fearlessness, you seem unbeseemingly timorous yourself. Common men choose fair weather for their travels: you choose thunder-storms; and yet—"

"That I travel in thunder-storms, I grant; but not without particular precautions, such as only a lightning-rod man may know. Hark! Quick—look at my specimen rod. Only one dollar a foot."

"A very fine rod, I dare say. But what are these particular precautions of yours? Yet first let me close yonder shutters; the slanting rain is beating through the sash. I will bar up."

"Are you mad? Know you not that yon iron bar is a swift conductor? Desist."

"I will simply close the shutters, then, and call my boy to bring me a wooden bar. Pray, touch the bell-pull there."

"Are you frantic? That bell-wire might blast you. Never touch bell-wire in a thunder-storm, nor ring a bell of any sort."

"Nor those in belfries? Pray, will you tell me where and how one may be safe in a time like this? Is there any part of my house I may touch with hopes of my life?"

"There is; but not where you now stand. Come away from the wall. The current will sometimes run down a wall, and—a man being a better conductor than a wall—it would leave the wall and run into him. Swoop! *That* must have fallen very nigh. That must have been globular lightning."

"Very probably. Tell me at once, which is, in your opinion, the safest part of this house?"

"This room, and this one spot in it where I stand. Come hither."

"The reasons first."

"Hark!—after the flash the gust—the sashes shiver—the house, the house!—Come hither to me!"

"The reasons, if you please."

"Come hither to me!"

"Thank you again, I think I will try my old stand—the hearth. And now, Mr. Lightning-rod man, in the pauses of the thunder, be so good as to tell me your reasons for esteeming this one room of the house the safest, and your own one stand-point there the safest spot in it."

There was now a little cessation of the storm for a while. The Lightning-rod man seemed relieved and replied:—

"Your house is a one-storied house, with an attic and a cellar; this room is between. Hence its comparative safety. Because lightning sometimes passes from the clouds to the earth, and sometimes from the earth to the clouds. Do you comprehend?—and I choose the middle of the room, because, if the lightning should strike the house at all, it would come down the chimney or walls; so, obviously, the further you are from them, the better. Come hither to me, now."

"Presently. Something you just said, instead of alarming me, has strangely inspired confidence."

"What have I said?"

"You said that sometimes lightning flashes from the earth to the clouds."

"Aye, the returning-stroke, as it is called; when the earth, being overcharged with the fluid, flashes its surplus upward."

"The returning-stroke; that is, from earth to sky. Better and better. But come here on the hearth and dry yourself."

"I am better here, and better wet."

"How?"

"It is the safest thing you can do—Hark, again!—to get yourself thoroughly drenched in a thunder-storm. Wet clothes are better conductors than the body; and so, if the lightning strikes, it might pass down the wet clothes without touching the body. The storm deepens again. Have you a rug in the house? Rugs are non-conductors. Get one, that I may stand on it here, and you, too. The skies blacken—it is dusk at noon. Hark!—the rug, the rug!"

I gave him one; while the hooded mountains seemed closing and tumbling into the cottage.

"And now, since our being dumb will not help us," said I, resuming my place, "let me hear your precautions in traveling during thunder-storms."

"Wait till this one is passed."

"Nay, proceed with the precautions. You stand in the safest possible place according to your own account. Go on."

"Briefly, then. I avoid pine-trees, high houses, lonely barns, upland pastures, running water, flocks of cattle and sheep, a crowd of men. If I travel on foot—as to-day—I do not walk fast; if in my buggy, I touch not its back or sides; if on horseback, I dismount and lead the horse. But of all things, I avoid tall men."

"Do I dream? Man avoid man? and in danger-time, too."

"Tall men in a thunder-storm I avoid. Are you so grossly ignorant as not to know, that the height of a six-footer is sufficient to discharge an electric cloud upon him? Are not lonely Kentuckians, ploughing, smit in the unfinished furrow? Nay, if the six-footer stand by running water, the cloud will sometimes *select* him as its conductor to that running water. Hark! Sure, yon black pinnacle is split. Yes, a man is a good conductor. The lightning goes through and through a man, but only peels a tree. But sir, you have kept me so long answering your questions, that I have not yet come to business. Will you order one of my rods? Look at this specimen one? See: it is of the best of copper. Copper's the best conductor. Your house is low; but being upon the mountains, that lowness does not one whit depress it. You mountaineers are most exposed. In mountainous countries the lightning-rod man should have most business. Look at the specimen, sir. One rod will answer for a house so small as this. Look over these recommendations. Only one rod, sir; cost, only twenty dollars. Hark! There go all the granite Taconics and Hoosics dashed together like pebbles. By the sound, that must have struck something. An elevation of five feet above the house, will protect twenty feet radius all about the rod. Only twenty dollars, sir—a dollar a foot. Hark!—Dreadful!—Will you order? Will you buy? Shall I put down your name? Think of being a heap of charred offal, like a haltered horse burnt in his stall; and all in one flash!"

"You pretended envoy extraordinary and minister plenipotentiary to and from Jupiter Tonans," laughed I; "you mere man who come here to put you and your pipestem between clay and sky, do you think that because you can strike a bit of green light from the Leyden jar, that you can thoroughly avert the supernal bolt? Your rod rusts, or breaks, and where are you? Who has empowered you, you Tetzel, to peddle round your indulgences from divine ordinations? The hairs of our heads are numbered, and the days of our lives. In thunder as in sunshine, I stand at ease in the hands of my God. False negotiator, away! see, the scroll of the storm is rolled back; the house is unharmed; and in the blue heavens I read in the rainbow, that the Deity will not, of purpose, make war on man's earth."

"Impious wretch!" foamed the stranger, blackening in the face as the rainbow beamed, "I will publish your infidel notions."

The scowl grew blacker on his face; the indigo-circles enlarged round his eyes as the storm-rings round the midnight moon. He sprang upon me; his tri-forked thing at my heart.

I seized it; I snapped it; I dashed it; I trod it; and dragging the dark lightning-king out of my door, flung his elbowed, copper sceptre after him.

But spite of my treatment, and spite of my dissuasive talk of him to my neighbors, the Lightning-rod man still dwells in the land; still travels in storm time, and drives a brave trade with the fears of man.

HERMAN MELVILLE was born in New York City in 1819 and died there in 1891. As a young man he became fascinated by the sea and made several voyages. On one voyage to the South Seas in a whaling ship he deserted ship and, together with a friend, lived among the natives of the Marquesas Islands for some weeks. Later he turned these events into the novels *Typee*, *Omoo*, and *Moby Dick*. He spent his last years as an Inspector of Customs in New York City, remaining close to the sea that he loved.

John Collier

Do you think "a woman scorned" would resort to violent murder?

     Is it possible to commit the perfect murder?

     See how one father protects his daughter

on a

WET SATURDAY

It was July. In the large, dull house they were imprisoned by the swish and the gurgle and all the hundred sounds of rain. They were in the drawing-room, behind four tall and weeping windows, in a lake of damp and faded chintz.

This house, ill-kept and unprepossessing, was necessary to Mr. Princey, who detested his wife, his daughter, and his hulking son. His life was to walk through the village, touching his hat, not smiling. His cold pleasure was to recapture snap-shot memories of the infinitely remote summers of his childhood —coming into the orangery and finding his lost wooden horse, the tunnel in the box hedge, and the little square of light at the end of it. But now all this was threatened—his austere pride of position in the village, his passionate attachment to the house— and all because Millicent, his cloddish daughter Millicent, had

103

done this shocking and incredibly stupid thing. Mr. Princey turned from her in revulsion and spoke to his wife.

"They'd send her to a lunatic asylum," he said. "A criminal-lunatic asylum. We should have to move away. It would be impossible."

His daughter began to shake again. "I'll kill myself," she said.

"Be quiet," said Mr. Princey. "We have very little time. No time for nonsense. I intend to deal with this." He called to his son, who stood looking out of the window. "George, come here. Listen. How far did you get with your medicine before they threw you out as hopeless?"

"You know as well as I do," said George.

"Do you know enough—did they drive enough into your head for you to be able to guess what a competent doctor could tell about such a wound?"

"Well, it's a—it's a knock or blow."

"If a tile fell from the roof? Or a piece of the coping?"

"Well, guv'nor, you see, it's like this—"

"Is it possible?"

"No."

"Why not?"

"Oh, because she hit him several times."

"I can't stand it," said Mrs. Princey.

"You have got to stand it, my dear," said her husband. "And keep that hysterical note out of your voice. It might be overheard. We are talking about the weather. If he fell down the well, George, striking his head several times?"

"I really don't know, guv'nor."

"He'd have had to hit the sides several times in thirty or forty feet, and at the correct angles. No, I'm afraid not. We must go over it all again. Millicent."

"No! No!"

"Millicent, we must go over it all again. Perhaps you have forgotten something. One tiny irrelevant detail may save or ruin us. Particularly you, Millicent. You don't *want* to be put in an asylum, do you? Or be hanged? They might hang you, Millicent. You must stop that shaking. You must keep your voice quiet. We are talking of the weather. Now."

"I can't. I . . . I . . ."

"Be quiet, child. Be quiet." He put his long, cold face very near to his daughter's. He found himself horribly revolted by her. Her features were thick, her jaw heavy, her whole figure repellently powerful. "Answer me," he said. "You were in the stable?"

"Yes."

"One moment, though. Who knew you were in love with this wretched curate?"

"No one. I've never said a—"

"Don't worry," said George. "The whole god-damned village knows. They've been sniggering about it in the Plough for three years past."

"Likely enough," said Mr. Princey. "Likely enough. What filth!" He made as if to wipe something off the backs of his hands. "Well, now, we continue. You were in the stable?"

"Yes."

"You were putting the croquet set into its box?"

"Yes."

"You heard someone crossing the yard?"

"Yes."

"It was Withers?"

"Yes."

"So you called him?"

"Yes."

"Loudly? Did you call him loudly? Could anyone have heard?"

"No, Father. I'm sure not. I didn't call him. He saw me as I went to the door. He just waved his hand and came over."

"How *can* I find out from you whether there was anyone about? Whether he *could* have been seen?"

"I'm sure not, Father. I'm quite sure."

"So you both went into the stable?"

"Yes. It was raining hard."

"What did he say?"

"He said 'Hullo, Milly.' And to excuse him coming in the back way, but he'd set out to walk over to Bass Hill."

"Yes."

"And he said, passing the park, he'd seen the house

and suddenly thought of me, and he thought he'd just look in for a minute, just to tell me something. He said he was so happy, he wanted me to share it. He'd heard from the Bishop he was to have the vicarage. And it wasn't only that. It meant he could marry. And he began to stutter. And I thought he meant me."

"Don't tell me what you thought. Exactly what he said. Nothing else."

"Well . . . Oh dear!"

"Don't cry. It is a luxury you cannot afford. Tell me."

"He said no. He said it wasn't me. It's Ella Brangwyn-Davies. And he was sorry. And all that. Then he went to go."

"And then?"

"I went mad. He turned his back. I had the winning post of the croquet set in my hand—"

"Did you shout or scream? I mean, as you hit him?"

"No. I'm sure I didn't."

"Did he? Come on. Tell me."

"No, Father."

"And then?"

"I threw it down. I came straight into the house. That's all. I wish I were dead!"

"And you met none of the servants. No one will go into the stable. You see, George, he probably told people he was going to Bass Hill. Certainly no one knows he came here. He might have been attacked in the woods. We must consider every detail . . . A curate, with his head battered in—"

"Don't, Father!" cried Millicent.

"Do you want to be hanged? A curate, with his head battered in, found in the woods. Who'd want to kill Withers?"

There was a tap on the door, which opened immediately. It was little Captain Smollett, who never stood on ceremony. "Who'd kill Withers?" he said. "I would, with pleasure. How d'you do, Mrs. Princey. I walked right in."

"He heard you, Father," moaned Millicent.

"My dear, we can all have our little joke," said her father. "Don't pretend to be shocked. A little theoretical curate-killing, Smollett. In these days we talk nothing but thrillers."

"Parsonicide," said Captain Smollett. "Justifiable parson-icide. Have you heard about Ella Brangwyn-Davies? I shall be laughed at."

"Why?" said Mr. Princey. "Why should you be laughed at?"

"Had a shot in that direction myself," said Smollett, with careful sang-froid. "She half said yes, too. Hadn't you heard? She told most people. Now it'll look as if I got turned down for a white rat in a dog collar."

"Too bad!" said Mr. Princey.

"Fortune of war," said the little captain.

"Sit down," said Mr. Princey. "Mother, Millicent, console Captain Smollett with your best light conversation. George and I have something to look to. We shall be back in a minute or two, Smollett. Come, George."

It was actually five minutes before Mr. Princey and his son returned.

"Excuse me, my dear," said Mr. Princey to his wife. "Smollett, would you care to see something rather interesting? Come out to the stables for a moment."

They went into the stable yard. The buildings were now unused except as odd sheds. No one ever went there. Captain Smollett entered, George followed him, Mr. Princey came last. As he closed the door he took up a gun which stood behind it. "Smollett," said he, "we have come out to shoot a rat which George heard squeaking under that tub. Now, you must listen to me very carefully or you will be shot by accident. I mean that."

Smollett looked at him. "Very well," said he. "Go on."

"A very tragic happening has taken place this afternoon," said Mr. Princey. "It will be even more tragic unless it is smoothed over."

"Oh?" said Smollett.

"You heard me ask," said Mr. Princey, "who would kill Withers. You heard Millicent make a comment, an unguarded comment."

"Well?" said Smollett. "What of it?"

"Very little," said Mr. Princey. "Unless you heard that Withers had met a violent end this very afternoon. And that, my dear Smollett, is what you are going to hear."

"Have you killed him?" cried Smollett.

"Millicent has," said Mr. Princey.

"Hell!" said Smollett.

"It *is* hell," said Mr. Princey. "You would have remembered—and guessed."

"Maybe," said Smollett. "Yes. I suppose I should."

"Therefore," said Mr. Princey, "you constitute a problem."

"Why did she kill him?" said Smollett.

"It is one of these disgusting things," said Mr. Princey. "Pitiable, too. She deluded herself that he was in love with her."

"Oh, of course," said Smollett.

"And he told her about the Brangwyn-Davies girl."

"I see," said Smollett.

"I have no wish," said Mr. Princey, "that she should be proved either a lunatic or a murderess. I could hardly live here after that."

"I suppose not," said Smollett.

"On the other hand," said Mr. Princey, "*you* know about it."

"Yes," said Smollett. "I am wondering if I could keep my mouth shut. If I promised you—"

"I am wondering if I could believe you," said Mr. Princey.

"If I promised," said Smollett.

"If things went smoothly," said Mr. Princey. "But not if there was any sort of suspicion, any questioning. You would be afraid of being an accessory."

"I don't know," said Smollett.

"I do," said Mr. Princey. "What are we going to do?"

"I can't see anything else," said Smollett. "You'd never be fool enough to do me in. You can't get rid of two corpses."

"I regard it," said Mr. Princey, "as a better risk than the other. It could be an accident. Or you and Withers could both disappear. There are possibilities in that."

"Listen," said Smollett. "You can't—"

"Listen," said Mr. Princey. "There may be a way out. There *is* a way out, Smollett. You gave me the idea yourself."

"Did I?" said Smollett. "What?"

"You said you would kill Withers," said Mr. Princey. "You have a motive."

"I was joking," said Smollett.

"You are always joking," said Mr. Princey. "People think there must be something behind it. Listen, Smollett, I can't trust you, therefore you must trust me. Or I will kill you now, in the next minute. I mean that. You can choose between dying and living."

"Go on," said Smollett.

"There is a sewer here," said Mr. Princey, speaking fast and forcefully. "That is where I am going to put Withers. No outsider knows he has come up here this afternoon. No one will ever look there for him unless you tell them. You must give me evidence that you have murdered Withers."

"Why?" said Smollett.

"So that I shall be dead sure that you will never open your lips on the matter," said Mr. Princey.

"What evidence?" said Smollett.

"George," said Mr. Princey, "hit him in the face, hard."

"Good God!" said Smollett.

"Again," said Mr. Princey. "Don't bruise your knuckles."

"Oh!" said Smollett.

"I'm sorry," said Mr. Princey. "There must be traces of a struggle between you and Withers. Then it will not be altogether safe for you to go to the police."

"Why won't you take my word?" said Smollett.

"I will when we've finished," said Mr. Princey. "George, get that croquet post. Take your handkerchief to it. As I told you. Smollett, you'll just grasp the end of this croquet post. I shall shoot you if you don't."

"Oh, hell," said Smollett. "All right."

"Pull two hairs out of his head, George," said Mr. Princey, "and remember what I told you to do with them. Now, Smollett, you take that bar and raise the big flagstone with the ring in it. Withers is in the next stall. You've got to drag him through and dump him in."

"I won't touch him," said Smollett.

"Stand back, George," said Mr. Princey, raising his gun.

"Wait a minute," cried Smollett. "Wait a minute." He did as he was told.

Mr. Princey wiped his brow. "Look here," said he. "Everything is perfectly safe. Remember, no one knows that

Withers came here. Everyone thinks he walked over to Bass Hill. That's five miles of country to search. They'll never look in our sewer. Do you see how safe it is?"

"I suppose it is," said Smollett.

"Now come into the house," said Mr. Princey. "We shall never get that rat."

They went into the house. The maid was bringing tea into the drawing-room. "See, my dear," said Mr. Princey to his wife, "we went to the stable to shoot a rat and we found Captain Smollett. Don't be offended, my dear fellow."

"You must have walked up the back drive," said Mrs. Princey.

"Yes. Yes. That was it," said Smollett in some confusion.

"You've cut your lip," said George, handing him a cup of tea.

"I . . . I just knocked it."

"Shall I tell Bridget to bring some iodine?" said Mrs. Princey. The maid looked up, waiting.

"Don't trouble, please," said Smollett. "It's nothing."

"Very well, Bridget," said Mrs. Princey. "That's all."

"Smollett is very kind," said Mr. Princey. "He knows all our trouble. We can rely on him. We have his word."

"Oh, have we, Captain Smollett?" cried Mrs. Princey. "You *are* good."

"Don't worry, old fellow," Mr. Princey said. "They'll never find anything."

Pretty soon Smollett took his leave. Mrs. Princey pressed his hand very hard. Tears came into her eyes. All three of them watched him go down the drive. Then Mr. Princey spoke very earnestly to his wife for a few minutes and the two of them went upstairs and spoke still more earnestly to Millicent. Soon after, the rain having ceased, Mr. Princey took a stroll round the stable yard.

He came back and went to the telephone. "Put me through to Bass Hill police station," said he. "Quickly . . . Hullo, is that the police station? This is Mr. Princey, of Abbott's Laxton. I'm afraid something rather terrible has happened up here. Can you send someone at once?"

JOHN COLLIER was born in London, England, in 1901. He was educated in English private schools and began writing verse at age nineteen, publishing his first poems at twenty. Although he has been a poetry editor for the magazine *Time and Tide*, he is best known for his wry, ironic, or satiric short stories.

Ervin D. Krause

Why would it be wrong to kill an animal just for the fun of it?

   Should an adult frighten a child with the body of a dead animal?

   Observe a man and boy in

THE SNAKE

   I was thinking of the heat and of water that morning when I was plowing the stubble field far across the hill from the farm buildings. It had grown hot early that day, and I hoped that the boy, my brother's son, would soon come across the broad black area of plowed ground, carrying the jar of cool water. The boy usually was sent out at about that time with the water, and he always dragged an old snow-fence lath or a stick along, to play with. He pretended that the lath was a tractor and he would drag it through the dirt and make buzzing, tractor sounds with his lips.

   I almost ran over the snake before I could stop the tractor in time. I had turned at the corner of the field and I had to look back to raise the plow and then to drop it again into the earth, and I was thinking of the boy and the water anyway, and when I looked again down the furrow, the snake was there. It lay half in the furrow and half out, and the front wheels had rolled nearly up to it when I put in the clutch. The tractor was heavily loaded with the weight of the plow turning the earth, and the tractor stopped instantly.

The snake slid slowly and with great care from the new ridge the plow had made, into the furrow and did not go any further. I had never liked snakes much, I still had that kind of quick panic that I'd had as a child whenever I saw one, but this snake was clean and bright and very beautiful. He was multi-colored and graceful and he lay in the furrow and moved his arched and tapered head only so slightly. Go out of the furrow, snake, I said, but he did not move at all. I pulled the throttle of the tractor in and out, hoping to frighten him with the noise, but the snake only flicked its black, forked tongue and faced the huge tractor wheel, without fright or concern.

I let the engine idle then, and I got down and went around the wheel and stood beside it. My movement did frighten the snake and it raised its head and trailed delicately a couple of feet and stopped again, and its tongue was working very rapidly. I followed it, looking at the brilliant colors on its tubular back, the colors clear and sharp and perfect, in orange and green and brown diamonds the size of a baby's fist down its back, and the diamonds were set one within the other and interlaced with glistening jet-black. The colors were astonishing, clear and bright, and it was as if the body held a fire of its own, and the colors came through that transparent flesh and skin, vivid and alive and warm. The eyes were clear and black and the slender body was arched slightly. His flat and gracefully tapered head lifted as I looked at him and the black tongue slipped in and out of that solemn mouth.

You beauty, I said, I couldn't kill you. You are much too beautiful. I had killed snakes before, when I was younger, but there had been no animal like this one, and I knew it was unthinkable that an animal such as that should die. I picked him up, and the length of him arched very carefully and grace-fully and only a little wildly, and I could feel the coolness of that radiant, fire-colored body, like splendid ice, and I knew that he had eaten only recently because there were two whole and solid little lumps in the forepart of him, like fieldmice swallowed whole might make.

The body caressed through my hands like cool satin, and my hands, usually tanned and dark, were pale beside it, and I asked it where the fire colors could come from the coolness of that body. I lowered him so he would not fall and his body slid out onto the cool, newly-plowed earth, from between my pale hands. The snake worked away very slowly and delicately and with a gorgeous kind of dignity and beauty, and he carried his head a little above the rolled clods. The sharp, burning colors of his body stood brilliant and plain against the black soil, like a target.

I felt good and satisfied, looking at the snake. It shone in its bright diamond color against the sun-burned stubble and the crumbled black clods of soil and against the paleness of myself. The color and beauty of it were strange and wonderful and somehow alien, too, in that dry and dusty and uncolored field.

I got on the tractor again and I had to watch the plow closely because the field was drawn across the long hillside and even in that good soil there was a danger of rocks. I had my back to the corner of the triangular field that pointed towards the house. The earth was a little heavy and I had to stop once and clean the plowshares because they were not scouring properly, and I did not look back towards the place until I had turned the corner and was plowing across the upper line of the large field, a long way from where I had stopped because of the snake.

I saw it all at a glance. The boy was there at the lower corner of the field, and he was in the plowed earth, stamping with ferocity and a kind of frenzied impatience. Even at that distance, with no sound but the sound of the tractor, I could tell the fierce mark of brutality on the boy. I could see the hunched-up shoulders, the savage determination, the dance of his feet as he ground the snake with his heels, and the pirouette of his arms as he whipped at it with the stick.

Stop it, I shouted, but the lumbering and mighty tractor

roared on, above anything I could say. I stopped the tractor and I shouted down to the boy, and I knew he could hear me, for the morning was clear and still, but he did not even hesitate in that brutal, murdering dance. It was no use. I felt myself tremble, thinking of the diamond light of that beauty I had held a few moments before, and I wanted to run down there and halt, if I could, that frenetic pirouette, catch the boy in the moment of his savagery, and save a glimmer, a remnant, of that which I remembered, but I knew it was already too late. I drove the tractor on, not looking down there; I was afraid to look for fear the evil might still be going on. My head began to ache, and the fumes of the tractor began to bother my eyes, and I hated the job suddenly, and I thought, there are only moments when one sees beautiful things, and these are soon crushed, or they vanish. I felt the anger mount within me.

The boy waited at the corner, with the jar of water held up to me in his hands, and the water had grown bubbly in the heat of the morning. I knew the boy well. He was eleven and we had done many things together. He was a beautiful boy, really, with finely-spun blonde hair and a smooth and still effeminate face, and his eyelashes were long and dark and brushlike, and his eyes were blue. He waited there and he smiled as the tractor came up, as he would smile on any other day. He was my nephew, my brother's son, handsome and warm and newly-scrubbed, with happiness upon his face and his face resembled my brother's and mine as well.

I saw then, too, the stake driven straight and hard into the plowed soil, through something there where I had been not long before.

I stopped the tractor and climbed down and the boy came eagerly up to me. "Can I ride around with you?" he asked, as he often did, and I had as often let him be on the tractor beside me. I looked closely at his eyes, and he was already innocent; the killing was already forgotten in that clear mind of his.

"No, you cannot," I said, pushing aside the water jar he offered to me. I pointed to the splintered, upright snake. "Did you do that?" I asked.

"Yes," he said, eagerly, beginning a kind of dance of excitement. "I killed a snake; it was a big one." He tried to take my hand to show me.

"Why did you kill it?"

"Snakes are ugly and bad."

"This snake was very beautiful. Didn't you see how beautiful it was?"

"Snakes are ugly," he said again.

"You saw the colors of it, didn't you? Have you ever seen anything like it around here?"

"Snakes are ugly and bad, and it might have bitten somebody, and they would have died."

"You know there are no poisonous snakes in this area. This snake could not harm anything."

"They eat chickens sometimes," the boy said. "They are ugly and they eat chickens and I hate snakes."

"You are talking foolishly," I said. "You killed it because you wanted to kill it, for no other reason."

"They're ugly and I hate them," the boy insisted. "Nobody likes snakes."

"It was beautiful," I said, half to myself.

The boy skipped along beside me, and he was contented with what he had done.

The fire of the colors was gone; there was a contorted ugliness now; the colors of its back were dull and gray-looking, torn and smashed in, and dirty from the boy's shoes. The beautifully-tapered head, so delicate and so cool, had been flattened as if in a vise, and the forked tongue splayed out of the twisted, torn mouth. The snake was hideous, and I remembered, even then, the cool, bright fire of it only a little while before, and I thought perhaps the boy had always seen it dead and hideous like that, and had not even stopped to see the beauty of it in its life.

I wrenched the stake out, that the boy had driven through it in the thickest part of its body, between the colored diamond crystals. I touched it and the coolness, the ice-feeling, was gone, and even then it moved a little, perhaps a tiny spasm of the dead muscles, and I hoped that it was truly dead, so that I would not have to kill it. And then it moved a little more, and I knew the snake was dying, and I would have to kill it there. The boy stood off a few feet and he had the stake again and he was racing innocently in circles, making the buzzing tractor sound with his lips.

I'm sorry, I thought to the snake, for you were beautiful. I took the broken length of it around the tractor and I took one of the wrenches from the tool-kit and I struck its head, not looking at it, to kill it at last, for it could never live.

The boy came around behind me, dragging the stake. "It's a big snake, isn't it?" he said. "I'm going to tell everybody how big a snake I killed."

"Don't you see what you have done?" I said. "Don't you see the difference now?"

"It's an ugly, terrible snake," he said. He came up and was going to push at it with his heavy shoes. I could see the happiness in the boy's eyes, the gleeful brutality.

"Don't," I said. I could have slapped the boy. He looked up at me, puzzled, and he swayed his head from side to side. I thought, you little brute, you nasty, selfish, little beast, with brutality already developed within that brain and in those eyes. I wanted to slap his face, to wipe forever the insolence and brutal glee from his mouth, and I decided then, very suddenly, what I would do.

I drew the snake up and I saw the blue eyes of the boy open wide and change and fright, and I stepped towards him as he cringed back, and I shouted, "It's alive, it's alive!" and I looped the tube of the snake's body around the boy's neck.

The boy shrieked and turned in his terror and ran, and I followed a few steps, shouting after him, "It's alive, it's alive, alive!"

The boy gasped and cried out in his terror and he fled towards the distant house, stumbling and falling and rising to run again, and the dead snake hung on him, looped around his neck, and the boy tore at it, but it would not fall off.

The little brute, I thought, the little cruel brute, to hurt and seek to kill something so beautiful and clean, and I couldn't help smiling and feeling satisfied because the boy, too, had suffered a little for his savageness, and I felt my mouth trying to smile about it. And I stopped suddenly and I said, oh God, with the fierce smile of brutality frightening my face, and I thought, oh God, oh God. I climbed quickly onto the tractor and I started it and pulled the throttle open to drown the echoes of the boy shrieking down there in the long valley. I was trembling and I could not steer the tractor well, and I saw that my hands were suffused and flushed, red with a hot blood color.

ERVIN D. KRAUSE grew up on farms in Nebraska and Iowa and attended Iowa State College. He has worked for an aircraft company and has taught English at the Universities of Nebraska, Wyoming, and Honolulu. His stories have appeared in the *Prairie Schooner* and in *O'Henry Awards: Prize Stories,* 1963.

John Collier

Can the perfect crime be committed by an ordinary person, or is the amateur criminal always caught eventually?

What kind of nasty gossip could cause a loving husband to want to kill his wife?

In this story the doctor's prescription is

DE MORTUIS

Dr. Rankin was a large and rawboned man on whom the newest suit at once appeared outdated, like a suit in a photograph of twenty years ago. This was due to the squareness and flatness of his torso, which might have been put together by a manufacturer of packing cases. His face also had a wooden and a roughly constructed look; his hair was wiglike and resentful of the comb. He had those huge and clumsy hands which can be an asset to a doctor in a small upstate town where people still retain a rural relish for paradox, thinking that the more apelike the paw, the more precise it can be in the delicate business of a tonsillectomy.

This conclusion was perfectly justified in the case of Dr. Rankin. For example, on this particular fine morning, though his task was nothing more ticklish than the cementing over of a large patch on his cellar floor, he managed those large and clumsy hands with all the unflurried certainty of one who would never leave a sponge within or create an unsightly scar without.

The doctor surveyed his handiwork from all angles. He added a touch here and a touch there till he had achieved a smoothness altogether professional. He swept up a few last crumbs of soil and dropped them into the furnace. He paused before putting away the pick and shovel he had been using, and found occasion for yet another artistic sweep of his trowel, which made the new surface precisely flush with the surrounding floor. At this moment of supreme concentration the porch door upstairs slammed with the report of a minor piece of artillery, which, appropriately enough, caused Dr. Rankin to jump as if he had been shot.

The Doctor lifted a frowning face and an attentive ear. He heard two pairs of heavy feet clump across the resonant floor of the porch. He heard the house door opened and the visitors enter the hall, with which his cellar communicated by a short flight of steps. He heard whistling and then voices of Buck and Bud crying, "Doc! Hi, Doc! They're biting!"

Whether the Doctor was not inclined for fishing that day, or whether, like others of his large and heavy type, he experienced an especially sharp, unsociable reaction on being suddenly startled, or whether he was merely anxious to finish undisturbed the job in hand and proceed to more important duties, he did not respond immediately to the inviting outcry of his friends. Instead, he listened while it ran its natural course, dying down at last into a puzzled and fretful dialogue.

"I guess he's out."

"I'll write a note—say we're at the creek to come on down."

"We could tell Irene."

"But she's not here, either. You'd think *she'd* be around."

"Ought to be, by the look of the place."

"You said it, Bud. Just look at this table. You could write your name—"

"Sh-h-h! Look!"

Evidently the last speaker had noticed that the cellar door was ajar and that a light was shining below. Next moment the door was pushed wide open and Bud and Buck looked down.

"Why, Doc! There you are!"

"Didn't you hear us yelling?"

The Doctor, not too pleased at what he had overheard, nevertheless smiled his rather wooden smile as his two friends made their way down the steps. "I thought I heard someone," he said.

"We were bawling our heads off," Buck said. "Thought nobody was home. Where's Irene?"

"Visiting," said the Doctor. "She's gone visiting."

"Hey, what goes on?" said Bud. "What are you doing? Burying one of your patients, or what?"

"Oh, there's been water seeping up through the floor," said the Doctor. "I figured it might be some spring opened up or something."

"You don't say!" said Bud, assuming instantly the high ethical standpoint of the realtor. "Gee, Doc, I sold you this property. Don't say I fixed you up with a dump where there's an underground spring."

"There was water," said the Doctor.

"Yes, but, Doc, you can look on that geological map the Kiwanis Club got up. There's not a better section of subsoil in the town."

"Looks like he sold you a pup," said Buck, grinning.

"No," said Bud. "Look. When the Doc came here he was green. You'll admit he was green. The things he didn't know!"

"He bought Ted Webber's jalopy," said Buck.

"He'd have bought the Jessop place if I'd let him," said Bud. "But I wouldn't give him a bum steer."

"Not the poor, simple city slicker from Poughkeepsie," said Buck.

"Some people would have taken him," said Bud. "Maybe some people did. Not me. I recommended this property. He and Irene moved straight in as soon as they were married. I wouldn't have put the Doc on to a dump where there'd be a spring under the foundations."

"Oh, forget it," said the Doctor, embarrassed by this conscientiousness. "I guess it was just the heavy rains."

"By gosh!" Buck said, glancing at the besmeared point of the pickaxe. "You certainly went deep enough. Right down into the clay, huh?"

"That's four feet down, the clay," Bud said.

"Eighteen inches," said the Doctor.

"Four feet," said Bud. "I can show you on the map."

"Come on. No arguments," said Buck. "How's about it, Doc? An hour or two at the creek, eh? They're biting."

"Can't do it, boys," said the Doctor. "I've got to see a patient or two."

"Aw, live and let live, Doc," Bud said. "Give 'em a chance to get better. Are you going to depopulate the whole darn town?"

The Doctor looked down, smiled, and muttered, as he always did when this particular jest was trotted out. "Sorry, boys," he said. "I can't make it."

"Well," said Bud, disappointed, "I suppose we'd better get along. How's Irene?"

"Irene?" asked the Doctor. "Never better. She's gone visiting. Albany. Got the eleven o'clock train."

"Eleven o'clock?" said Buck. "For Albany?"

"Did I say Albany?" said the Doctor. "Watertown, I meant."

"Friends in Watertown?" Buck asked.

"Mrs. Slater," said the Doctor. "Mr. and Mrs. Slater. Lived next door to 'em when she was a kid, Irene said, over on Sycamore Street."

"Slater?" said Bud. "Next door to Irene. Not in *this* town."

"Oh, yes," said the Doctor. "She was telling me all about them last night. She got a letter. Seems this Mrs. Slater looked after her when her mother was in the hospital one time."

"No," said Bud.

"That's what she told me," said the Doctor. "Of course, it was a good many years ago."

"Look, Doc," said Buck. "Bud and I were raised in this town. We've known Irene's folks all our lives. We were in and out of their house all the time. There was never anybody next door called Slater."

"Perhaps," said the Doctor, "she married again, this woman. Perhaps it was a different name."

Bud shook his head.

"What time did Irene go to the station?" Buck asked.

"Oh, about a quarter of an hour ago," said the Doctor.

"You didn't drive her?" said Buck.

"She walked," said the Doctor.

"We came down Main Street," Buck said. "We didn't meet her."

"Maybe she walked across the pasture," said the Doctor.

"That's a tough walk with a suitcase," said Buck.

"She just had a couple of things in a little bag," said the Doctor.

Bud was still shaking his head.

Buck looked at Bud, and then at the pick, at the new, damp cement on the floor. "Jesus Christ!" he said.

"Oh, God, Doc!" Bud said. "A guy like you!"

"What in the name of heaven are you two bloody fools thinking?" asked the Doctor. "What are you trying to say?"

"A spring!" said Bud. "I ought to have known right away it wasn't any spring."

The Doctor looked at his cement-work, at the pick, at the large worried faces of his two friends. His own face turned livid. "Am I crazy?" he said. "Or are you? You suggest that I've—that Irene—my wife—oh, go on! Get out! Yes, go and get the sheriff. Tell him to come here and start digging. You—get out!"

Bud and Buck looked at each other, shifted their feet, and stood still again.

"Go on," said the Doctor.

"I don't know," said Bud.

"It's not as if he didn't have the provocation," Buck said.

"God knows," Bud said.

"God knows," Buck said. "You know. I know. The whole town knows. But try telling it to a jury."

The Doctor put his hand to his head. "What's that?" he said. "What is it? Now what are you saying? What do you mean?"

"If this ain't being on the spot!" said Buck. "Doc, you

can see how it is. It takes some thinking. We've been friends right from the start. Damn good friends."

"But we've got to think," said Bud. "It's serious. Provocation or not, there's a law in the land. There's such a thing as being an accomplice."

"You were talking about provocation," said the Doctor.

"You're right," said Buck. "And you're our friend. And if ever it could be called justified—"

"We've got to fix this somehow," said Bud.

"Justified?" said the Doctor.

"You were bound to get wised up sooner or later," said Buck.

"We could have told you," said Bud. "Only—what the hell?"

"We could," said Buck. "And we nearly did. Five years ago. Before ever you married her. You hadn't been here six months, but we sort of cottoned to you. Thought of giving you a hint. Spoke about it. Remember, Bud?"

Bud nodded. "Funny," he said. "I came right out in the open about that Jessop property. I wouldn't let you buy that, Doc. But getting married, that's something else again. We could have told you."

"We're that much responsible," Buck said.

"I'm fifty," said the Doctor. "I suppose it's pretty old for Irene."

"If you was Johnny Weissmuller at the age of twenty-one, it wouldn't make any difference," said Buck.

"I know a lot of people think she's not exactly a perfect wife," said the Doctor. "Maybe she's not. She's young. She's full of life."

"Oh, skip it!" said Buck sharply, looking at the raw cement. "Skip it, Doc, for God's sake."

The Doctor brushed his hand across his face. "Not everybody wants the same thing," he said. "I'm a sort of dry fellow. I don't open up very easily. Irene—you'd call her gay."

"You said it," said Buck.

"She's no housekeeper," said the Doctor. "I know it. But that's not the only thing a man wants. She's enjoyed herself."

"Yeah," said Buck. "She did."

"That's what I love," said the Doctor. "Because I'm not that way myself. She's not very deep, mentally. All right. Say she's stupid. I don't care. Lazy. No system. Well, I've got plenty of system. She's enjoyed herself. It's beautiful. It's innocent. Like a child."

"Yes. If that was all," Buck said.

"But," said the Doctor, turning his eyes full on him, "You seem to know there was more."

"Everybody knows it," said Buck.

"A decent, straightforward guy comes to a place like this and marries the town floozy," Bud said bitterly. "And nobody'll tell him. Everybody just watches."

"And laughs," said Buck. "You and me, Bud, as well as the rest."

"We told her to watch her step," said Bud. "We warned her."

"Everybody warned her," said Buck. "But people get fed up. When it got to truck-drivers—"

"It was never us, Doc," said Bud, earnestly. "Not after you came along, anyway."

"The town'll be on your side," said Buck.

"That won't mean much when the case comes to trial in the county seat," said Bud.

"Oh!" cried the Doctor, suddenly. "What shall I do? What shall I do?"

"It's up to you, Bud," said Buck. "I can't turn him in."

"Take it easy, Doc," said Bud. "Calm down. Look, Buck. When we came in here the street was empty, wasn't it?"

"I guess so," said Buck. "Anyway, nobody saw us come down cellar."

"And we haven't been down," Bud said, addressing himself forcefully to the Doctor. "Get that, Doc? We shouted upstairs, hung around a minute or two, and cleared out. But we never came down into this cellar."

"I wish you hadn't," the Doctor said heavily.

"All you have to do is say Irene went out for a walk and never came back," said Buck. "Bud and I can swear we saw her headed out of town with a fellow in a—well, say in a Buick sedan. Everybody'll believe that, all right. We'll fix it. But later. Now we'd better scram."

"And remember, now. Stick to it. We never came down here and we haven't seen you today," said Bud. "So long!"

Buck and Bud ascended the steps, moving with a rather absurd degree of caution. "You'd better get that . . . that thing covered up," Buck said over his shoulder.

Left alone, the Doctor sat down on an empty box, holding his head with both hands. He was still sitting like this when the porch door slammed again. This time he did not start. He listened. The house door opened and closed. A voice cried, "Yoo-hoo! Yoo-hoo! I'm back."

The Doctor rose slowly to his feet. "I'm down here, Irene!" he called.

The cellar door opened. A young woman stood at the head of the steps. "Can you beat it?" she said. "I missed the damn train."

"Oh!" said the Doctor. "Did you come back across the field?"

"Yes, like a fool," she said. "I could have hitched a ride and caught the train up the line. Only I didn't think. If you'd run me over to the junction, I could still make it."

"Maybe," said the Doctor. "Did you meet anyone coming back?"

"Not a soul," she said. "Aren't you finished with that old job yet?"

"I'm afraid I'll have to take it all up again," said the Doctor. "Come down here, my dear, and I'll show you."

JOHN COLLIER (For biography, see p. 111.)

A. B. Guthrie, Jr.

For the badmen of the Old West, would the ability to read and write be as necessary for survival as the ability to fight and shoot?

What kinds of tactics could a peace-loving store owner use to handle a mean, ornery, and drunken cowboy?

In this story Mr. Baumer waits patiently and then finally drives a hard

BARGAIN

Mr. Baumer and I had closed the Moon Dance Mercantile Company and were walking to the post office, and he had a bunch of bills in his hand ready to mail. There wasn't anyone or anything much on the street because it was suppertime. A buckboard and a saddle horse were tied at Hirsch's rack, and a rancher in a wagon rattled for home ahead of us, the sound of his going fading out as he prodded his team. Freighter Slade stood alone in front of the Moon Dance Saloon, maybe wondering whether to have one more before going to supper. People said he could hold a lot without showing it except in being ornerier even than usual.

Mr. Baumer didn't see him until he was almost on him, and then he stopped and fingered through the bills until he found the right one. He stepped up to Slade and held it out.

Slade said, "What's this, Dutchie?"

Mr. Baumer had to tilt his head up to talk to him. "You know vat it is."

Slade just said, "Yeah?" You never could tell from his face what went on inside his skull. He had dark skin and shallow cheeks and a thick-growing mustache that fell over the corners of his mouth.

"It is a bill," Mr. Baumer said. "I tell you before it is a bill. For twenty-vun dollars and fifty cents."

"'You know what I do with bills, don't you, Dutchie?" Slade asked.

Mr. Baumer didn't answer the question. He said, "For merchandise."

Slade took the envelope from Mr. Baumer's hand and squeezed it up in his fist and let it drop on the plank sidewalk. Not saying anything, he reached down and took Mr. Baumer's nose between the knuckles of his fingers and twisted it up into his eyes. That was all. That was all at the time. Slade half turned and slouched to the door of the bar and let himself in. Some men were laughing in there.

Mr. Baumer stooped and picked up the bill and put it on top of the rest and smoothed it out for mailing. When he straightened up I could see tears in his eyes from having his nose screwed around.

He didn't say anything to me, and I didn't say anything to him, being so much younger and feeling embarrassed for him. He went into the post office and slipped the bills in the slot, and we walked on home together. At the last, at the crossing where I had to leave him, he remembered to say, "Better study, Al. Is good to know to read and write and figure." I guess he felt he had to push me a little, my father being dead.

I said, "Sure. See you after school tomorrow"— Which he knew I would anyway. I had been working in the store for him during the summer and after classes ever since pneumonia took my dad off.

Three of us worked there regularly, Mr. Baumer, of course, and me and Colly Coleman, who knew enough to drive the delivery wagon but wasn't much help around the store except for carrying orders out to the rigs at the hitchpost and handling heavy things like the whisky barrel at the back of the store which Mr. Baumer sold quarts and gallons out of.

The store carried quite a bit of stuff—sugar and flour and dried fruits and canned goods and such on one side and yard goods and coats and caps and aprons and the like of that on the other, besides kerosene and bran and buckets and linoleum and pitchforks in the storehouse at the rear—but it wasn't a big store like Hirsch Brothers up the street. Never would be, people guessed, going on to say, with a sort of slow respect, that it would have gone under long ago if Mr. Baumer hadn't been half mule and half beaver. He had started the store just two years before and, the way things were, worked himself close to death.

He was at the high desk at the end of the grocery counter when I came in the next afternoon. He had an eyeshade on and black sateen protectors on his forearms, and his pencil was in his hand instead of behind his ear and his glasses were roosted on the nose that Slade had twisted. He didn't hear me open and close the door or hear my feet as I walked back to him, and I saw he wasn't doing anything with the pencil but holding it over a paper. I stood and studied him for a minute, seeing a small, stooped man with a little paunch bulging through his unbuttoned vest. He was a man you wouldn't remember from meeting once. There was nothing in his looks to set itself in your mind unless maybe it was his chin, which was a small, pink hill in the gentle plain of his face.

While I watched him, he lifted his hand and felt carefully of his nose. Then he saw me. His eyes had that kind of mistiness that seems to go with age or illness, though he wasn't really old or sick, either. He brought his hand down quickly and picked up the pencil, but he saw I was still looking at the nose, and finally he sighed and said, "That Slade."

Just the sound of the name brought Slade to my eye. I saw him slouched in front of the bar, and I saw him and his string coming down the grade from the buttes, the wheel horses held snug and the rest lined out pretty, and then the string leveling off and Slade's whip lifting hair from a horse that wasn't up in the collar. I had heard it said that Slade could make a horse scream with that whip. Slade's name wasn't Freighter, of course. Our town nicknamed him that because that was what he was.

"I don't think it's any good to send him a bill, Mr. Baumer," I said. "He can't even read."

"He could pay yet."

"He don't pay anybody," I said.

"I think he hate me," Mr. Baumer went on. "That is the thing. He hate me for coming not from this country. I come here, sixteen years old, and learn to read and write, and I make a business, and so I think he hate me."

"He hates everybody."

Mr. Baumer shook his head. "But not to pinch the nose. Not to call Dutchie."

The side door squeaked open, but it was only Colly Coleman coming in from a trip so I said, "Excuse me, Mr. Baumer, but you shouldn't have trusted him in the first place."

"I know," he answered, looking at me with his misty eyes. "A man make mistakes. I think some do not trust him, so he will pay me because I do. And I do not know him well then. He only came back to town three-four months ago, from being away since before I go into business."

"People who knew him before could have told you," I said.

"A man makes mistakes," he explained again.

"It's not my business, Mr. Baumer, but I would forget the bill."

His eyes rested on my face for a long minute, as if they didn't see me but the problem itself. He said, "It is not twenty-vun dollars and fifty cents now, Al. It is not that any more."

"What is it?"

He took a little time to answer. Then he brought his two hands up as if to help him shape the words. "It is the thing. You see, it is the thing."

I wasn't quite sure what he meant.

He took his pencil from behind his ear where he had put it and studied the point of it. "That Slade. He steal whisky and call it evaporation. He sneak things from his load. A thief, he is. And too big for me."

I said, "I got no time for him, Mr. Baumer, but I guess there never was a freighter didn't steal whiskey. That's what I hear."

It was true, too. From the railroad to Moon Dance was fifty miles and a little better—a two day haul in good weather, heck knew how long in bad. Any freight string bound home with a load had to lie out at least one night. When a freighter had his stock tended to and maybe a little fire going against the dark, he'd tackle a barrel of whiskey or of grain alcohol if he had one aboard, consigned to Hirsch Brothers or Mr. Baumer's or the Moon Dance Saloon or the Gold Leaf Bar. He'd drive a hoop out of place, bore a little hole with a nail or bit and draw off what he wanted. Then he'd plug the hole with a whittled peg and pound the hoop back. That was evaporation. Nobody complained much. With freighters you generally took what they gave you, within reason.

"Moore steals it, too," I told Mr. Baumer. Moore was Mr. Baumer's freighter.

"Yah," he said, and that was all, but I stood there for a minute, thinking there might be something more. I could see thought swimming in his eyes, above that little hill of chin. Then a customer came in, and I had to go wait on him.

Nothing happened for a month, nothing between Mr. Baumer and Slade, that is, but fall drew on toward winter and the first flight of ducks headed south and Mr. Baumer hired Miss Lizzie Webb to help with the just-beginning Christmas trade, and here it was, the first week in October, and he and I walked up the street again with the monthly bills. He always sent them out. I guess he had to. A bigger store, like Hirsch's would wait on the ranchers until their beef or wool went to market.

Up to a point things looked and happened almost the same as they had before, so much the same that I had the crazy feeling I was going through that time again. There was a wagon and a rig tied up at Hirsch's rack and a saddle horse standing hipshot in front of the harness shop. A few more people were on the street now, not many, and lamps had been lit against the shortened day.

It was dark enough that I didn't make out Slade right away. He was just a figure that came out of the yellow wash of light from the Moon Dance Saloon and stood on the board walk and with his head made the little motion of spitting. Then I recognized the lean, raw shape of him and the muscles flowing down into the sloped shoulders, and in the settling darkness I filled the picture in—the dark skin and the flat cheeks and the peevish eyes and the mustache growing rank.

There was Slade and here was Mr. Baumer with his bills
and here I was, just as before, just like in the second go-round
of a bad dream. I felt like turning back, being embarrassed and
half scared by trouble even when it wasn't mine. Please, I said
to myself, don't stop, Mr. Baumer! Don't bite off anything!
Please, shortsighted the way you are, don't catch sight of him
at all! I held up and stepped around behind Mr. Baumer and
came up on the outside so as to be between him and Slade
where maybe I'd cut off his view.

But it wasn't any use. All along I think I knew it was no
use, not the praying or the walking between or anything. The
act had to play itself out.

Mr. Baumer looked across the front of me and saw Slade
and hesitated in his step and came to a stop. Then in his slow,
business way, his chin held firm against his mouth, he began
fingering through the bills, squinting to make out the names.
Slade had turned and was watching him, munching on a cud of
tobacco like a bull waiting.

"You look, Al," Mr. Baumer said without lifting his face
from the bills. "I cannot see so good."

So I looked, and while I was looking Slade must have
moved. The next I knew Mr. Baumer was staggering ahead, the
envelopes spilling out of his hands. There had been a thump,
the clap of a heavy hand swung hard on his back.

Slade said, "Haryu, Dutchie?"

Mr. Baumer caught his balance and turned around, the
bills he had trampled shining white between them and, at Slade's
feet, the hat that Mr. Baumer had stumbled out from under.

Slade picked up the hat and scuffed through the bills
and held it out. "Cold to be goin' without a sky-piece," he said.

Mr. Baumer hadn't spoken a word. The lampshine from
inside the bar caught his eyes, and in them it seemed to me a
light came and went as anger and the uselessness of it took turns
in his head.

Two men had come up on us and stood watching. One
of them was Angus McDonald, who owned the Ranchers' Bank,
and the other was Dr. King. He had his bag in his hand.

Two others were drifting up, but I didn't have time to tell
who. The light came in Mr. Baumer's eyes, and he took a step

ahead and swung. I could have hit harder myself. The first landed on Slades's cheek without hardly so much as jogging his head, but it let hell loose in the man. I didn't know he could move so fast. He slid in like a practiced fighter and let Mr. Baumer have it full in the face.

Mr. Baumer slammed over on his back, but he wasn't out. He started lifting himself. Slade leaped ahead and brought a boot heel down on the hand he was lifting himself by. I heard meat and bone under that heel and saw Mr. Baumer fall back and try to roll away.

Things had happened so fast that not until then did anyone have a chance to get between them. Now Mr. McDonald pushed at Slade's chest, saying, "That's enough, Freighter. That's enough now," and Dr. King lined up, too, and another man I didn't know, and I took a place, and we formed a kind of screen between them. Dr. King turned and bent to look at Mr. Baumer.

"Damn fool hit me first," Slade said.

"That's enough," Mr. McDonald told him again while Slade looked at all of us as if he'd spit on us for a nickel. Mr. McDonald went on, using a half-friendly tone, and I knew it was because he didn't want to take Slade on any more than the rest of us did. "You go on home and sleep it off, Freighter. That's the ticket."

Slade just snorted.

From behind us Dr. King said, "I think you've broken this man's hand."

"Lucky for him I didn't kill him," Slade answered. "Damn Dutch penny-pincher!" He fingered the chew out of his mouth. "Maybe he'll know enough to leave me alone now."

Dr. King had Mr. Baumer on his feet. "I'll take him to the office," he said.

Blood was draining from Mr. Baumer's nose and rounding the curve of his lip and dripping from the sides of his chin. He held his hurt right hand in the other. But a thing was that he didn't look beaten even then, not the way a man who has given up looks beaten. Maybe that was why Slade said, with a show of that fierce anger, "You stay away from me! Hear? Stay clear away, or you'll get more of the same!"

Dr. King led Mr. Baumer away, Slade went back into the

bar, and the other men walked off, talking about the fight. I got down and picked up the bills, because I knew Mr. Baumer would want me to, and mailed them at the post office, dirty as they were. It made me sorer, someway, that Slade's bill was one of the few that wasn't marked up. The cleanness of it seemed to say that there was no getting the best of him.

Mr. Baumer had his hand in a sling the next day and wasn't much good at waiting on the trade. I had to hustle all afternoon and so didn't have a chance to talk to him even if he had wanted to talk. Mostly he stood at his desk, and once, passing it, I saw he was practicing writing with his left hand. His nose and the edges of the cheeks around it were swollen some.

At closing time I said, "Look, Mr. Baumer, I can lay out of school a few days until you kind of get straightened out here."

"No," he answered as if to wave the subject away. "I get somebody else. You go to school. Is good to learn."

I had a half notion to say that learning hadn't helped him with Slade. Instead, I blurted out that I would have the law on Slade.

"The law?" he asked.

"The sheriff or somebody."

"No, Al," he said. "You would not."

I asked why.

"The law, it is not for plain fights," he said. "Shooting? Robbing? Yes, the law come quick. The plain fights, they are too many. They not count enough."

He was right. I said, "Well, I'd do something anyhow."

"Yes," he answered with a slow nod of his head. "Something you vould do, Al." He didn't tell me what.

Within a couple of days he got another man to clerk for him—it was Ed Hempel, who was always finding and losing jobs—and we made out. Mr. Baumer took his hand from the sling in a couple or three weeks, but with the tape on it it still wasn't any use to him. From what you could see of the fingers below the tape it looked as if it never would be.

He spent most of his time at the high desk, sending me or Ed out on the errands he used to run, like posting and getting the mail. Sometimes I wondered if that was because he was afraid of meeting Slade. He could just as well have gone himself. He wasted a lot of hours just looking at nothing, though I will have to say he worked hard at learning to write left-handed.

Then, a month and a half before Christmas, he hired Slade to haul his freight for him.

Ed Hempel told me about the deal when I showed up for work. "Yessir," he said, resting his foot on a crate in the storeroom where we were supposed to be working. "I tell you he's throwed in with Slade. Told me this morning to go out and locate him if I could and bring him in. Slade was at the saloon, o' course, and says to hell with Dutchie, but I told him this was honest-to-God business, like Baumer had told me to, and there was a quart of whisky right there in the store for him if he'd come and get it. He was out of money, I reckon, because the quart fetched him."

"What'd they say?" I asked him.

"Search me. There was two or three people in the store and Baumer told me to wait on 'em, and he and Slade palavered back by the desk."

"How do you know they made a deal?"

Ed spread his hands out. " 'Bout noon, Moore came in with his string, and I heard Baumer say he was makin' a change. Moore didn't like it too good, either."

It was a hard thing to believe, but there one day was Slade with a pile of stuff for the Moon Dance Mercantile Company, and that was proof enough with something left for boot.

Mr. Baumer never opened the subject up with me, though I gave him plenty of chances. And I didn't feel like asking. He didn't talk much these days but went around absent-minded, feeling now and then of the fingers that curled yellow and stiff out of the bandage like the toes on the leg of a dead chicken. Even on our walks home he kept his thoughts to himself.

I felt different about him now, and was sore inside. Not that I blamed him exactly. A hundred and thirty-five pounds wasn't much to throw against two hundred. And who could tell what Slade would do on a bellyful of whisky? He had promised Mr. Baumer more of the same, hadn't he?, But I didn't feel good. I couldn't look up to Mr. Baumer like I used to and still wanted to. I didn't have the beginning of an answer when men cracked jokes or shook their heads in sympathy with Mr. Baumer, saying Slade had made him come to time.

Slade hauled in a load for the store, and another, and Christmas time was drawing on and trade heavy, and the winter that had started early and then pulled back came on again. There was a blizzard and then a still cold and another blizzard and afterwards a sunshine that was ice-shine on the drifted snow. I was glad to be busy, selling overshoes and sheep-lined coats and mitts and socks as thick as saddle blankets and Christmas candy out of buckets and hickory nuts and the fresh oranges that the people in our town never saw except when Santa Claus was coming.

One afternoon when I lit out from class the thermometer on the school porch read 42° below. But you didn't have to look at it to know how cold the weather was. Your nose and fingers and toes and ears and the bones inside you told you. The snow cried when you stepped on it.

I got to the store and took my things off and scuffed my hands at the stove for a minute so's to get life enough in them to tie a parcel. Mr. Baumer—he was always polite to me—said, "Hello, Al. Not so much to do today. Too cold for customers." He shuddered a little, as if he hadn't got the chill off even yet, and rubbed his broken hand with the good one. "Ve need Christmas goods," he said, looking out the window to the furrows that wheels had make in the snow-banked street, and I knew he was thinking of Slade's string, inbound from the railroad, and the time it might take even Slade to travel those hard miles.

Slade never made it at all.

Less than an hour later our old freighter, Moore, came in, his beard white and stiff with frost. He didn't speak at first but looked around and clumped to the stove and took off his heavy mitts, holding his news inside him.

Then he said, not pleasantly, "Your new man's dead, Baumer."

"My new man?" Mr. Baumer said.

"Who the hell do you think? Slade. He's dead."

All Mr. Baumer could say was, "Dead!"

"Froze to death, I figger," Moore told him while Colly

Coleman and Ed Hempel and Miss Lizzie and I and a couple of customers stepped closer.

"Not Slade," Mr. Baumer said. "He know too much to freeze."

"Maybe so, but he sure's God's froze now. I got him in the wagon."

We stood looking at one another and at Moore. Moore was enjoying his news, enjoying feeding it out bit by bit so's to hold the stage. "Heart might've give out for all I know."

The side door swung open, letting in a cloud of cold and three men who stood, like us, waiting on Moore. I moved a little and looked through the window and saw Slade's freight outfit tied outside with more men around it. Two of them on a wheel of one of the wagons, looking inside.

"Had a extra man, so I brought your stuff in," Moore went on. "Figgered you'd be glad to pay for it."

"Not Slade," Mr. Baumer said again.

"You can take a look at him."

Mr. Baumer answered no.

"Someone's takin' word to Connor to bring his hearse. Anyhow I told 'em to. I carted old Slade this far. Connor can have him now."

Moore pulled on his mitts. "Found him there by the Deep Creek crossin', doubled up in the snow an' his fire out." He moved toward the door. "I'll see to the horses, but your stuff'll have to set there. I got more'n enough work to do at Hirsch's."

Mr. Baumer just nodded.

I put on my coat and went out and waited my turn and climbed on a wagon wheel and looked inside, and there was Slade piled on some bags of bran. Maybe because of being frozen, his face was whiter than I ever saw it, whiter and deader, too, though it never had been lively. Only the mustache seemed still alive, sprouting thick like greasewood from alkali. Slade was doubled up all right, as if he had died and stiffened leaning forward in a chair.

I got down from the wheel, and Colly and then Ed climbed up. Moore was unhitching, tossing off his pieces of information while he did so. Pretty soon Mr. Connor came up with his old hearse, and he and Moore tumbled Slade into it, and the team that was as old as the hearse made off, the tires squeaking in the snow. The people trailed on away with it, their breaths leaving little ribbons of mist in the air. It was beginning to get dark.

Mr. Baumer came out of the side door of the store, bundled up, and called to Colly and Ed and me. "We unload," he said. "Already is late. Al, better you get a couple lanterns now."

We did a fast job, setting the stuff out of the wagons on to the platform and then carrying it or rolling it on the one truck that the store owned and stowing it inside according to where Mr. Baumer's good hand pointed.

A barrel was one of the last things to go in. I edged it up and Colly nosed the truck under it, and then I let it fall back. "Mr. Baumer," I said, "we'll never sell all this, will we?"

"Yah," he answered. "Sure we sell it. I get it cheap. A bargain, Al, so I buy it."

I looked at the barrel head again. There in big letters I saw *Wood Alcohol—Deadly Poison.*

"Hurry now," Mr. Baumer said. "Is late." For a flash and no longer I saw through the mist in his eyes, saw, you might say, that hilly chin repeated there. "Then ve go home, Al. Is good to know to read."

A. B. GUTHRIE, JR. (For biography, see p. 94.)

John Updike

Is there an appropriate code of dress for public places, such as stores, or should a person be allowed to wear or not wear anything he or she wants?

Have you ever acted impulsively without fear of consequences when you got "fed up"?

In this story there is a clash between a clerk and the great

A & P

In walks these three girls in nothing but bathing suits. I'm in the third checkout slot, with my back to the door, so I don't see them until they're over by the bread. The one that caught my eye first was the one in the plaid green two-piece. She was a chunky kid, with a good tan and a sweet broad soft-looking can with those two crescents of white just under it, where the sun never seems to hit, at the top of the backs of her legs. I stood there with my hand on a box HiHo crackers trying to remember if I rang it up or not. I ring it up again and the customer starts giving me hell. She's one of these cash-register-watchers, a witch about fifty with rouge on her cheekbones and no eyebrows, and I know it made her day to trip me up. She'd been watching cash registers for fifty years and probably never seen a mistake before.

By the time I got her feathers smoothed and her goodies

into a bag—she gives me a little snort in passing, if she'd been born at the right time they would have burned her over in Salem —by the time I get her on her way the girls had circled around the bread and were coming back, without a pushcart, back my way along the counters, in the aisle between the checkouts and the Special bins. They didn't even have shoes on. There was this chunky one, with the two-piece—it was bright green and the seams on the bra were still sharp and her belly was still pretty pale so I guessed she just got it (the suit)—there was this one, with one of those chubby berry-faces, the lips all bunched together under her nose, this one, and a tall one, with black hair that hadn't quite frizzed right, and one of these sunburns right across under the eyes, and a chin that was too long—you know, the kind of girl other girls think is very "striking" and "attractive" but never quite makes it, as they very well know, which is why they like her so much—and then the third one, that wasn't quite so tall. She was the queen. She kind of led them, the other two peeking around and making their shoulders round. She didn't look around, not this queen, she just walked straight on slowly, on these long white prima-donna legs. She came down a little hard on her heels, as if she didn't walk in her bare feet that much, putting down her heels and then letting the weight move along to her toes as if she was testing the floor with every step, putting a little deliberate extra action into it. You never know for sure how girls' minds work (do you really think it's a mind in there or just a little buzz like a bee in a glass jar?) but you got the idea she had talked the other two into coming in here with her, and now she was showing them how to do it, walk slow and hold yourself straight.

She had on a kind of dirty-pink—beige maybe, I don't know—bathing suit with a little nubble all over it and, what got me, the straps were down. They were off her shoulders looped loose around the cool tops of her arms, and I guess as a result the suit had slipped a little on her, so all around the top of the cloth there was this shining rim. If it hadn't been there you wouldn't have known there could have been anything whiter than those shoulders. With the straps pushed off, there was nothing between the top of the suit and the top of her head except just *her,* this clean bare plane of the top of her chest down from the

shoulder bones like a dented sheet of metal tilted in the light. I
mean, it was more than pretty.

She had sort of oaky hair that the sun and salt had
bleached, done up in a bun that was unravelling, and a kind of
prim face. Walking into the A & P with your straps down, I suppose it's the only kind of face you *can* have. She held her head
so high her neck, coming up out of those white shoulders,
looked kind of stretched, but I didn't mind. The longer her neck
was, the more of her there was.

She must have felt in the corner of her eye me and over
my shoulder Stokesie in the second slot watching, but she didn't
tip. Not this queen. She kept her eyes moving across the racks,
and stopped, and turned so slow it made my stomach rub the inside of my apron, and buzzed to the other two, who kind of
huddled against her for relief, and then they all three of them
went up the cat-and-dog-food-breakfast-cereal-macaroni-rice-
raisins-seasonings-spreads-spaghetti-soft-drinks-crackers-and-
cookies aisle. From the third slot I look straight up this aisle to
the meat counter, and I watched them all the way. The fat one
with the tan sort of fumbled with the cookies, but on second
thought she put the package back. The sheep pushing their carts
down the aisle—the girls were walking against the usual traffic
(not that we have one-way signs or anything)—were pretty hilari-
ous. You could see them, when Queenie's white shoulders
dawned on them, kind of jerk, or hop, or hiccup, but their eyes
snapped back to their own baskets and on they pushed. I bet
you could set off dynamite in an A & P and the people would by
and large keep reaching and checking oatmeal off their lists and
muttering "Let me see, there was a third thing, began with A,
asparagus, no ah, yes, applesauce!" or whatever it is they do
mutter. But there was no doubt, this jiggled them. A few house-
slaves in pin curlers even looked around after pushing their carts
past to make sure what they had seen was correct.

You know, it's one thing to have a girl in a bathing suit
down on the beach, where what with the glare nobody can look
at each other much anyway, and another thing in the cool of the
A & P, under the fluorescent lights, against all those stacked
packages, with her feet paddling along naked over our checker-
board green-and-cream rubber-tile floor.

"Oh Daddy," Stokesie said beside me. "I feel so faint."

"Darling," I said. "Hold me tight." Stokesie's married, with two babies chalked up on his fuselage already, but as far as I can tell that's the only difference. He's twenty-two, and I was nineteen this April.

"Is it done?" he asks, the responsible married man finding his voice. I forgot to say he thinks he's going to be manager some sunny day, maybe in 1990 when it's called the Great Alexandrov and Petrooshki Tea Company or something.

What he meant was, our town is five miles from a beach, with a big summer colony out on the Point, but we're right in the middle of town, and the women generally put on a shirt or shorts or something before they get out of the car into the street. And anyway these are usually women with six children and varicose veins mapping their legs and nobody, including them, could care less. As I say, we're right in the middle of town, and if you stand at our front doors you can see two banks and the Congregational church and the newspaper store and three real-estate offices and about twenty-seven old freeloaders tearing up Central Street because the sewer broke again. It's not as if we're on the Cape; we're north of Boston and there's people in this town haven't seen the ocean for twenty years.

The girls had reached the meat counter and were asking McMahon something. He pointed, they pointed, and they shuffled out of sight behind a pyramid of Diet Delight peaches. All that was left for us to see was old McMahon patting his mouth and looking after them sizing up their joints. Poor kids; I began to feel sorry for them, they couldn't help it.

.　　.　　.

Now here comes the sad part of the story, at least my family says it's sad, but I don't think it's so sad myself. The store's pretty empty, it being Thursday afternoon, so there was nothing much to do except lean on the register and wait for the girls to show up again. The whole store was like a pinball machine and I didn't know which tunnel they'd come out of. After a while they come around out of the far aisle, around the light bulbs, records at discount of the Caribbean Six or Tony Martin Sings or some such gunk you wonder they waste the wax on, sixpacks of candy bars, and plastic toys done up in cellophane that fall apart when a kid looks at them anyway. Around they come, Queenie still leading the way, and holding a little gray jar in her hand. Slots Three through Seven are unmanned and I could see her wondering between Stokes and me, but Stokesie with his usual luck draws an old party in baggy gray pants who stumbles up with four giant cans of pineapple juice (what do these bums *do* with all that pineapple juice? I've often asked myself) so the girls come to me. Queenie puts down the jar and I take it into my fingers icy cold. Kingfish Fancy Herring Snacks in Pure Sour Cream: 49¢. Now her hands are empty, not a ring or a bracelet, bare as God made them, and I wonder where the money's coming from. Still with that prim look she lifts a folded dollar bill out of the hollow at the center of her nubbled pink top. The jar went heavy in my hand. Really, I thought that was so cute.

Then everybody's luck begins to run out. Lengel comes in from haggling with a truck full of cabbages on the lot and is about to scuttle into that door marked MANAGER behind which he hides all day when the girls touch his eye. Lengel's pretty dreary, teaches Sunday school and the rest, but he doesn't miss that much. He comes over and says, "Girls, this isn't the beach."

Queenie blushes, though maybe it's just a brush of sun-burn I was noticing for the first time, now that she was so close. "My mother asked me to pick up a jar of herring snacks." Her voice kind of startled me, the way voices do when you see the people first, coming out so flat and dumb yet kind of tony, too, the way it ticked over "pick up" and "snacks." All of a sudden I slid right down her voice into her living room. Her father and the other men were standing around in ice-cream coats and bow ties and the women were in sandals picking up herring snacks on toothpicks off a big glass plate and they were all holding drinks the color of water with olives and sprigs of mint in them. When my parents have somebody over they get lemonade and if it's a real racy affair Schlitz in tall glasses with "They'll Do It Every Time" cartoons stencilled on.

"That's all right," Lengel said. "But this isn't the beach." His repeating this struck me as funny, as if it had just occurred to him, and he had been thinking all these years the A & P was a great big dune and he was the head lifeguard. He didn't like my smiling—as I say he doesn't miss much—but he concentrates on giving the girls that sad Sunday-school-superintendent stare.

Queenie's blush is no sunburn now, and the plump one in plaid, that I liked better from the back—a really sweet can—pipes up, "We weren't doing any shopping. We just came in for the one thing."

"That makes no difference," Lengel tells her, and I could see from the way his eyes went that he hadn't noticed she was wearing a two-piece before. "We want you decently dressed when you come in here."

"We *are* decent," Queenie says suddenly, her lower lip pushing, getting sore now that she remembers her place, a place from which the crowd that runs the A & P must look pretty crummy. Fancy Herring Snacks flashed in her very blue eyes.

"Girls, I don't want to argue with you. After this come in here with your shoulders covered. It's our policy." He turns his back. That's policy for you. Policy is what the kingpins want. What the others want is juvenile delinquency.

All this while, the customers had been showing up with their carts but, you know, sheep, seeing a scene, they had all bunched up on Stokesie, who shook open a paper bag as gently as peeling a peach, not wanting to miss a word. I could feel in the silence everybody getting nervous, most of all Lengel, who asks me, "Sammy, have you rung up their purchase?"

I thought and said "No" but it wasn't about that I was thinking. I go through the punches, 4, 9, GROC, TOT—it's more complicated than you think, and after you do it often enough, it begins to make a little song, that you hear words to, in my case "Hello (*bing*) there, you (*gung*) hap-py pee-pul (*splat*)!"—the *splat* being the drawer flying out. I uncrease the bill, tenderly as you may imagine, it just having come from between the two smoothest scoops of vanilla I had ever known were there, and pass a half and a penny into her narrow pink palm, and nestle the herrings in a bag and twist its neck and hand it over, all the time thinking.

The girls, and who'd blame them, are in a hurry to get out, so I say "I quit" to Lengel quick enough for them to hear, hoping they'll stop and watch me, their unsuspected hero. They keep right on going, into the electric eye; the door flies open and they flicker across the lot to their car, Queenie and Plaid and Big Tall Goony-Goony (not that as raw material she was so bad), leaving me with Lengel and a kink in his eyebrow.

"Did you say something, Sammy?"

"I said I quit."

"I thought you did."

"You didn't have to embarrass them."

"It was they who were embarrassing us."

I started to say something that came out "Fiddle-de-doo." It's a saying of my grandmother's, and I know she would have been pleased.

"I don't think you know what you're saying," Lengel said.

"I know you don't," I said. "But I do." I pull the bow at the back of my apron and start shrugging it off my shoulders. A couple customers that had been heading for my slot begin to knock against each other, like scared pigs in a chute.

Lengel sighs and begins to look very patient and old and gray. He's been a friend of my parents for years. "Sammy, you don't want to do this to your Mom and Dad," he tells me. It's true, I don't. But it seems to me that once you begin a gesture it's fatal not to go through with it. I fold the apron, "Sammy" stitched in red on the pocket, and put it on the counter, and drop the bow tie on top of it. The bow tie is theirs, if you've ever wondered. "You'll feel this for the rest of your life," Lengel says, and I know that's true, too, but remembering how he made that pretty girl blush makes me so scrunchy inside I punch the No Sale tab and the machine whirs "pee-pul" and the drawer spats out. One advantage to this scene taking place in summer, I can follow this up with a clean exit, there's no fumbling around getting your coat and galoshes, I just saunter into the electric eye in my white shirt that my mother ironed the night before, and the door heaves itself open, and outside the sunshine is skating around on the asphalt.

I look around for my girls, but they're gone, of course. There wasn't anybody but some young married screaming with her children about some candy they didn't get by the door of a powder-blue Falcon station wagon. Looking back in the big windows, over the bags of peat moss and aluminum lawn furniture stacked on the pavement, I could see Lengel in my place in the slot, checking the sheep through. His face was dark gray and his back stiff, as if he'd just had an injection of iron, and my stomach kind of fell as I felt how hard the world was going to be to me hereafter.

JOHN UPDIKE was born in Shillington, Pennsylvania, in 1932. He received his education at Harvard and the Ruskin School of Drawing and Fine Arts and later was on the staff of the *New Yorker* magazine. He writes poetry as well as novels and short stories, most of which deal with the ordinary lives of smalltown people. He lives with his family in Ipswich, Massachusetts. His novels include *Poorhouse Fair; Rabbit, Run; The Centaur; Couples;* and *Bech: A Book.* His short stories are collected in *The Same Door, Pigeon Feathers,* and *The Music School.*

Kristin Hunter

What can a girl learn about boys that would give her a great power over them?

Notice how Judy comes out into the world of society when she makes her

DEBUT

"Hold *still*, Judy," Mrs. Simmons said around the spray of pins that protruded dangerously from her mouth. She gave the thirtieth tug to the tight sash at the waist of the dress. "Now walk over there and turn around slowly."

The dress, Judy's first long one, was white organdy over taffeta, with spaghetti straps that bared her round brown shoulders and a floating skirt and a wide sash that cascaded in a butterfly effect behind. It was a dream, but Judy was sick and tired of the endless fittings she had endured so that she might wear it at the Debutantes' Ball. Her thoughts leaped ahead to the Ball itself....

"*Slowly*, I said!" Mrs. Simmons' dark, angular face was always grim, but now it was screwed into an expression resembling a prune. Judy, starting nervously, began to revolve by moving her feet an inch at a time.

147

Her mother watched her critically. "No, it's still not right. I'll just have to rip out that waistline seam again."

"Oh, Mother!" Judy's impatience slipped out at last. "Nobody's going to notice all those little details."

"They will too. They'll be watching you every minute, hoping to see something wrong. You've got to be the *best*. Can't you get that through your head?" Mrs. Simmons gave a sigh of despair. "You better start noticin' 'all those little details' yourself. I can't do it for you all your life. Now turn around and stand up straight."

"Oh, Mother," Judy said, close to tears from being made to turn and pose while her feet itched to be dancing, "I can't stand it any more!"

"You can't stand it, huh? How do you think *I* feel?" Mrs. Simmons said in her harshest tone.

Judy was immediately ashamed, remembering the weeks her mother had spent at the sewing machine, picking her already tattered fingers with needles and pins, and the great weight of sacrifice that had been borne on Mrs. Simmons' shoulders for the past two years so that Judy might bare hers at the Ball.

"All right, take it off," her mother said. "I'm going to take it up the street to Mrs. Luby and let her help me. It's got to be right or I won't let you leave the house."

"Can't we just leave it the way it is, Mother?" Judy pleaded without hope of success. "I think it's perfect."

"You would," Mrs. Simmons said tartly as she folded the dress and prepared to bear it out of the room. "Sometimes I think I'll never get it through your head. You got to look just right and act just right. That Rose Griffin and those other girls can afford to be careless, maybe, but you can't. You're gonna be the darkest, poorest one there."

Judy shivered in her new lace strapless bra and her old, childish knit snuggies. "You make it sound like a battle I'm going to instead of just a dance."

"It is a battle," her mother said firmly. "It starts tonight and it goes on for the rest of your life. The battle to hold your head up and get someplace and be somebody. We've done all we can for you, your father and I. Now you've got to start fighting some on your own." She gave Judy a slight smile; her voice softened a little. "You'll do all right, don't worry. Try and get some rest this afternoon. Just don't mess up your hair."

"All right, Mother," Judy said listlessly.

She did not really think her father had much to do with anything that happened to her. It was her mother who had in-gratiated her way into the Gay Charmers two years ago, taking all sorts of humiliation from the better-dressed, better-off, lighter-skinned women, humbly making and mending their dresses, fixing food for their meetings, addressing more mail and selling more tickets than anyone else. The club had put it off as long as they could, but finally they had to admit Mrs. Simmons to membership because she worked so hard. And that meant, of course, that Judy would be on the list for this year's Ball.

Her father, a quiet carpenter who had given up any other ambitions years ago, did not think much of Negro society or his wife's fierce determination to launch Judy into it. "Just keep clean and be decent," he would say. "That's all anybody has to do."

Her mother always answered, "If that's all *I* did we'd still be on relief," and he would shut up with shame over the years he had been laid off repeatedly and her days' work and sewing had kept them going. Now he had steady work but she refused to quit, as if she expected it to end at any moment. The intense energy that burned in Mrs. Simmons' large dark eyes had scorched her features into permanent irony. She worked day and night and spent her spare time scheming and planning. Whatever her per-sonal ambitions had been, Judy knew she blamed Mr. Simmons for their failure; now all her schemes revolved around their only child.

Judy went to her mother's window and watched her stride down the street with the dress until she was hidden by the high brick wall that went around two sides of their house. Then she returned to her own room. She did not get dressed because she was afraid of pulling a sweater over her hair—her mother would notice the difference even if it looked all right to Judy—and be-cause she was afraid that doing anything, even getting dressed, might precipitate her into the battle. She drew a stool up to her window and looked out. She had no real view, but she liked her room. The wall hid the crowded tenement houses beyond the alley, and from its cracks and bumps and depressions she could construct any imaginary landscape she chose. It was how she had spent most of the free hours of her dreamy adolescence.

"Hey, can I go?"

It was the voice of an invisible boy in the alley. As another boy chuckled, Judy recognized the familiar ritual; if you said yes, they said, "Can I go with you?" It had been tried on her dozens of times. She always walked past, head in the air, as if she had not heard. Her mother said that was the only thing to do; if they knew she was a lady, they wouldn't dare bother her. But this time a girl's voice, cool and assured, answered.

"If you think you're big enough," it said.

It was Lucy Mae Watkins; Judy could picture her standing there in a tight dress with bright, brazen eyes.

"I'm big enough to give you a baby," the boy answered.

Judy would die if a boy ever spoke to her like that, but she knew Lucy Mae could handle it. Lucy Mae could handle all the boys, even if they ganged up on her, because she had been born knowing something other girls had to learn.

"Aw, you ain't big enough to give me a shoe-shine," she told him.

"Come here and I'll show you how big I am," the boy said.

"Yeah, Lucy Mae, what's happenin'?" another, younger boy said. "Come here and tell us."

Lucy Mae laughed. "What I'm puttin' down is too strong for little boys like you."

"Come here a minute, baby," the first boy said. "I got a cigarette for you."

"Aw, I ain't studyin' your cigarettes," Lucy Mae answered. But her voice was closer, directly below Judy. There were the sounds of a scuffle and Lucy Mae's muffled laughter. When she spoke her voice sounded raw and cross. "Come on now, boy. Cut it out and give me the damn cigarette." There was more scuffling, and the sharp crack of a slap, and then Lucy Mae said, "Cut it out, I said. Just for that I'm gonna take 'em all." The clack of high heels rang down the sidewalk with a boy's clumsy shoes in pursuit.

Judy realized that there were three of them down there. "Let her go, Buster," one said. "You can't catch her now."

"Aw, hell, man, she took the whole damn pack," the one called Buster complained.

"That'll learn you!" Lucy Mae voice mocked from down the street. "Don't mess with nothin' you can't handle."

"Hey, Lucy Mae. Hey, I heard Rudy Grant already gave you a baby," a second boy called out.

"Yeah. Is that true, Lucy Mae?" the youngest one yelled. There was no answer. She must be a block away by now.

For a moment the hidden boys were silent; then one of them guffawed directly below Judy, and the other two joined in the secret male laughter that was oddly high-pitched and feminine.

"Aw man, I don't know what you all laughin' about," Buster finally grumbled. "That girl took all my cigarettes. You got some, Leroy?"

"Naw," the second boy said.

"Me neither," the third one said.

"What we gonna do? I ain't got but fifteen cent. Hell, man, I want more than a feel for a pack of cigarettes." There was an unpleasant whine in Buster's voice. "Hell, for a pack of cigarettes I want a bitch to come across."

"She will next time, man," the boy called Leroy said.

"She better," Buster said. "You know she better. If she pass by here again, we gonna jump her, you hear?"

"Sure, man," Leroy said. "The three of us can grab her easy."

"Then we can all three of us have some fun. Oh, *yeah,* man," the youngest boy said. He sounded as if he might be about 14.

Leroy said, "We oughta get Roland and J. T. too. For a whole pack of cigarttes she oughta treat all five of us."

"Aw, man, why tell Roland and J. T.?" the youngest voice whined. "They ain't in it. Them was *our* cigarettes."

"They was *my* cigarettes, you mean," Buster said with authority. "You guys better quit it before I decide to cut you out."

"Oh, man, don't do that. We with you, you know that."

"Sure, Buster, we your aces, man."

"All right, that's better." There was a minute of silence.

Then, "What we gonna do with the girl, Buster?" the youngest one wanted to know.

"When she come back we gonna pump the bitch, man. We gonna jump her and grab her. Then we gonna turn her every way but loose." He went on, spinning a crude fantasy that got wilder each time he retold it, until it became so secretive that their voices dropped to a low indistinct murmur punctuated by guffaws. Now and then Judy could distinguish the word "girl" or the other word they used for it; these words always produced the loudest guffaws of all. She shook off her fear with the thought that Lucy Mae was too smart to pass there again today. She had heard them at their dirty talk in the alley before and had always been successful in ignoring it; it had nothing to do with her, the wall protected her from their kind. All the ugliness was on their side of it, and this was hers to fill with beauty.

She turned on her radio to shut them out completely and began to weave her tapestry to its music. More for practice than anything else, she started by picturing the maps of the places to which she intended to travel, then went on to the faces of her friends. Rose Griffin's sharp, Indian profile appeared on the wall. Her coloring was like an Indian's too and her hair was straight and black and glossy. Judy's hair, naturally none of these things, had been "done" four days ago so that tonight it would be "old" enough to have a gloss as natural-looking as Rose's. But Rose, despite her handsome looks, was silly; her voice broke constantly into high-pitched giggles and she became even sillier and more nervous around boys.

Judy was not sure that she knew how to act around boys either. The sisters kept boys and girls apart at the Catholic high school where her parents sent her to keep her away from low-class kids. But she felt that she knew a secret: tonight, in that dress, with her hair in a sophisticated upsweep, she would be transformed into a poised princess. Tonight all the college boys her mother described so eagerly would rush to dance with her, and then from somewhere *the boy* would appear. She did not know his name; she neither knew nor cared whether he went to college, but she imagined that he would be as dark as she was, and that there would be awe and diffidence in his manner as he bent to kiss her hand . . .

A waltz swelled from the radio; the wall, turning blue in deepening twilight, came alive with whirling figures. Judy rose and began to go through the steps she had rehearsed for so many weeks. She swirled with a practiced smile on her face, holding an imaginary skirt at her side; turned, dipped, and flicked on her bedside lamp without missing a fraction of the beat. Faster and faster she danced with her imaginary partner, to an inner music that was better than the sounds on the radio. She was "coming out," and tonight the world would discover what it had been waiting for all these years.

"Aw, git it, baby." She ignored it as she would ignore the crowds that lined the streets to watch her pass on her way to the Ball.

"Aw, do your number." She waltzed on, safe and secure on her side of the wall.

"Can I come up there and do it with you?"

At this she stopped, paralyzed. Somehow they had come over the wall or around it and into her room.

"Man, I sure like the view from here," the youngest boy said. "How come we never tried this view before?"

She came to life, ran quickly to the lamp and turned it off, but not before Buster said, "Yeah, and the back view is fine, too."

"Aw, she turned off the light," a voice complained.

"Put it on again, baby, we don't mean no harm."

"Let us see you dance some more. I bet you can really do it."

"Yeah, I bet she can shimmy on down."

"You know it, man."

"Come on down here, baby," Buster's voice urged softly dangerously. "I got a cigarette for you."

"Yeah, and he got something else for you, too."

Judy, flattened against her closet door, gradually lost her urge to scream. She realized that she was shivering in her underwear. Taking a deep breath, she opened the closet door and found her robe. She thought of going to the window and yelling down, "You don't have a thing I want. Do you understand?" But she had more important things to do.

Wrapping her hair in protective plastic, she ran a full steaming tub and dumped in half a bottle of her mother's favorite cologne. At first she scrubbed herself furiously, irritating her skin. But finally she stopped, knowing she would never be able to get cleaner than this again. She could not wash away the thing they considered dirty, the thing that made them pronounce "girl" in the same way as the other four-letter words they wrote on the wall in the alley; it was part of her, just as it was part of her mother and Rose Griffin and Lucy Mae. She relaxed then because it was true that the boys in the alley did not have a thing she wanted. She had what they wanted, and the knowledge replaced her shame with a strange, calm feeling of power.

After her bath she splashed on more cologne and spent 40 minutes on her makeup, erasing and retracing her eyebrows six times until she was satisfied. She went to her mother's room then and found the dress, finished and freshly pressed, on its hanger.

When Mrs. Simmons came upstairs to help her daughter she found her sitting on the bench before the vanity mirror as if it were a throne. She looked young and arrogant and beautiful and perfect and cold.

"Why, you're dressed already," Mrs. Simmons said in surprise. While she stared, Judy rose with perfect, icy grace and glided to the center of the room. She stood there motionless as a mannequin.

"I want you to fix the hem, Mother," she directed. "It's still uneven in back."

Her mother went down obediently on her knees, muttering, "It looks all right to me." She put in a couple of pins. "That better?"

"Yes," Judy said with a brief glance at the mirror. "You'll have to sew it on me, Mother. I can't take it off now. I'd ruin my hair."

Mrs. Simmons went to fetch her sewing things, returned, and surveyed her daughter. "You sure did a good job on yourself, I must say," she admitted grudgingly. "Can't find a thing to complain about. You'll look as good as anybody there."

"Of course, Mother," Judy said as Mrs. Simmons knelt and sewed. "I don't know what you were so worried about." Her secret feeling of confidence had returned, stronger than ever, but the evening ahead was no longer the vague girlish fantasy she had pictured on the wall; it had hard, clear outlines leading up to a definite goal. She would be the belle of the Ball because she knew more than Rose Griffin and her silly friends; more than her mother; more, even, than Lucy Mae, because she knew better than to settle for a mere pack of cigarettes.

"There," her mother said, breaking the thread. She got up. "I never expected to get you ready this early. Ernest Lee won't be here for another hour."

"That silly Ernest Lee," Judy said, with a new contempt in her young voice. Until tonight she had been pleased by the thought of going to the dance with Ernest Lee; he was nice, she felt comfortable with him, and he might even be the awe-struck boy of her dream. He was a dark, serious neighborhood boy who could not afford to go to college; Mrs. Simmons had reluctantly selected him to take Judy to the dance because all the Gay Charmers' sons were spoken for. Now, with an undertone of excitement, Judy said, "I'm going to ditch him after the first dance, Mother. You'll see. I'm going to come home with one of the college boys."

"It's very nice, Ernest Lee," she told him an hour later when he handed her the white orchid, "but it's rather small. I'm going to wear it on my wrist, if you don't mind." And dazzling him with a smile of sweetest cruelty, she stepped back and waited while he fumbled with the door.

"You know, Edward, I'm not worried about her any more," Mrs. Simmons said to her husband after the children were gone. Her voice became harsh and grating. "Put down that paper and listen to me! Aren't you interested in your child?—That's better," she said as he complied meekly. "I was saying, I do believe she's learned what I've been trying to teach her, after all."

KRISTIN HUNTER is one of the most promising of today's young black novelists and short-story writers. She was born in Philadelphia in 1931 and was educated at the University of Pennsylvania. She has successfully worked at a variety of writing jobs —newspaper columnist, feature writer, advertising copywriter, and freelance writer. Her television documentary (1956) *Minority of One* earned her the Fund for the Republic Prize. Her two novels are *God Bless the Child* and *The Landlord*.

Carson McCullers

What causes siblings to quarrel and have disagreements?

Why is friendship both strong and delicate?

One boy regrets the loss of his cousin's friendship, even though the cousin is a

SUCKER

It was always like I had a room to myself. Sucker slept in my bed with me but that didn't interfere with anything. The room was mine and I used it as I wanted to. Once I remember sawing a trap door in the floor. Last year when I was a sophomore in high school I tacked on my wall some pictures of girls from magazines and one of them was just in her underwear. My mother never bothered me because she had the younger kids to look after. And Sucker thought anything I did was always swell.

Whenever I would bring any of my friends back to my room all I had to do was just glance once at Sucker and he would get up from whatever he was busy with and maybe half smile at me, and leave without saying a word. He never brought kids back there. He's twelve, four years younger than I am, and he always knew without me even telling him that I didn't want kids that age meddling with my things.

Half the time I used to forget that Sucker isn't my brother. He's my first cousin but practically ever since I remember he's been in our family. You see his folks were killed in a wreck when he was a baby. To me and my kid sisters he was like our brother.

Sucker used to always remember and believe every word I said. That's how he got his nick-name. Once a couple of years ago I told him that if he'd jump off our garage with an umbrella it would act as a parachute and he wouldn't fall hard. He did it and busted his knee. That's just one instance. And the funny thing was that no matter how many times he got fooled he would still believe me. Not that he was dumb in other ways—it was just the way he acted with me. He would look at everything I did and quietly take it in.

There is one thing I have learned, but it makes me feel guilty and is hard to figure out. If a person admires you a lot you despise him and don't care—and it is the person who doesn't notice you that you are apt to admire. This is not easy to realize. Maybelle Watts, this senior at school, acted like she was the Queen of Sheba and even humiliated me. Yet at this same time I would have done anything in the world to get her attentions. All I could think about day and night was Maybelle until I was nearly crazy. When Sucker was a little kid and on up until the time he was twelve I guess I treated him as bad as Maybelle did me.

Now that Sucker had changed so much it is a little hard to remember him as he used to be. I never imagined anything would suddenly happen that would make us both very different. I never knew that in order to get what has happened straight in my mind I would want to think back on him as he used to be and compare and try to get things settled. If I could have seen ahead maybe I would have acted different.

I never noticed him much or thought about him and when you consider how long we have had the same room together it is funny the few things I remember. He used to talk to himself a lot when he'd think he was alone—all about him fighting gangsters and being on ranches and that sort of kids' stuff. He'd get in the bathroom and stay as long as an hour and sometimes his voice would go up high and excited and you could hear him all over the house. Usually, though, he was very quiet. He didn't have many boys in the neighborhood to buddy with and his face had the look of a kid who is watching a game and waiting to be asked to play. He didn't mind wearing the sweaters and coats that I outgrew, even if the sleeves did flop down too big and make his wrists look as thin and white as a little girl's. That is how I remember him—getting a little bigger every year but still being the same. That was Sucker up until a few months ago when all this trouble began.

Maybelle was somehow mixed up in what happened so I guess I ought to start with her. Until I knew her I hadn't given much time to girls. Last fall she sat next to me in General Science class and that was when I first began to notice her. Her hair is the brightest yellow I ever saw and occasionally she will wear it set into curls with some sort of gluey stuff. Her fingernails are pointed and manicured and painted a shiny red. All during class I used to watch Maybelle, nearly all the time except when I thought she was going to look my way or when the teacher called on me. I couldn't keep my eyes off her hands, for one thing. They are very little and white except for that red stuff, and when she would turn the pages of her book she always licked her thumb and held out her little finger and turned very slowly. It is impossible to describe Maybelle. All the boys are crazy about her but she didn't even notice me. For one thing she's almost two years older than I am. Between periods I used to try and pass very close to her in the halls but she would hardly ever smile at me. All I could do was sit and look at her in class—and sometimes it was like the whole room could hear my heart beating and I wanted to holler or light out and run for Hell.

At night, in bed, I would imagine about Maybelle. Often this would keep me from sleeping until as late as one or two o'clock. Sometimes Sucker would wake up and ask me why I couldn't get settled and I'd tell him to hush his mouth. I suppose I was mean to him lots of times. I guess I wanted to ignore somebody like Maybelle did me. You could always tell by Sucker's face when his feelings were hurt. I don't remember all the ugly remarks I must have made because even when I was saying them my mind was on Maybelle.

That went on for nearly three months and then somehow she began to change. In the halls she would speak to me and every morning she copied my homework. At lunch time once I danced with her in the gym. One afternoon I got up nerve and went to her house with a carton of cigarettes. I knew she smoked in the girls' basement and sometimes outside of school—and I didn't want to take her candy because I think that's been run into the ground. She was very nice and it seemed to me everything was going to change.

It was that night when this trouble really started. I had come into my room late and Sucker was already asleep. I felt too happy and keyed up to get in a comfortable position and I was awake thinking about Maybelle a long time. Then I dreamed about her and it seemed I kissed her. It was a surprise to wake up and see the dark. I lay still and a little while passed before I could come to and understand where I was. The house was quiet and it was a very dark night.

Sucker's voice was a shock to me. "Pete? . . ."

I didn't answer anything or even move.

"You do like me as much as if I was your own brother, don't you Pete?"

I couldn't get over the surprise of everything and it was like this was the real dream instead of the other.

"You have liked me all the time like I was your own brother, haven't you?"

"Sure," I said.

Then I got up for a few minutes. It was cold and I was glad to come back to bed. Sucker hung on to my back. He felt little and warm and I could feel his warm breathing on my shoulder.

"No matter what you did I always knew you liked me."

I was wide awake and my mind seemed mixed up in a strange way. There was this happiness about Maybelle and all that —but at the same time something about Sucker and his voice when he said these things made me take notice. Anyway I guess you understand people better when you are happy than when something is worrying you. It was like I had never really thought about Sucker until then. I felt I had always been mean to him. One night a few weeks before I had heard him crying in the dark. He said he had lost a boy's beebee gun and was scared to let anybody know. He wanted me to tell him what to do. I was sleepy and tried to make him hush and when he wouldn't I kicked at him. That was just one of the things I remembered. It seemed to me he had always been a lonesome kid. I felt bad.

There is something about a dark cold night that makes you feel close to someone you're sleeping with. When you talk together it is like you are the only people awake in the town.

"You're a swell kid, Sucker," I said.

It seemed to me suddenly that I did like him more than anybody else I knew—more than any other boy, more than my sisters, more in a certain way even than Maybelle. I felt good all over and it was like when they play sad music in the movies. I wanted to show Sucker how much I really thought of him and make up for the way I had always treated him.

We talked for a good while that night. His voice was fast and it was like he had been saving up these things to tell me for a long time. He mentioned that he was going to try to build a canoe and that the kids down the block wouldn't let him in on their football team and I don't know what all. I talked some too and it was a hard feeling to think of him taking in everything I said so seriously. I even spoke of Maybelle a little, only I made out like it was her who had been running after me all this time. He asked questions about high school and so forth. His voice was excited and he kept on talking fast like he could never get the words out in time. When I went to sleep he was still talking and I could still feel his breathing on my shoulder, warm and close.

During the next couple of weeks I saw a lot of Maybelle. She acted as though she really cared for me a little. Half the time I felt so good I hardly knew what to do with myself.

But I didn't forget about Sucker. There were a lot of old things in my bureau drawer I'd been saving—boxing gloves and Tom Swift books and second rate fishing tackle. All this I turned over to him. We had some more talks together and it was really like I was knowing him for first time. When there was a long cut on his cheek I knew he had been monkeying around with this new first razor set of mine, but I didn't say anything. His face seemed different now. He used to look timid and sort of like he was afraid of a whack over the head. That expression was gone. His face, with those wide-open eyes and ears sticking out and his mouth never quite shut, had the look of a person who is surprised and expecting something swell.

Once I started to point him out to Maybelle and tell her he was my kid brother. It was an afternoon when a murder mystery was on at the movie. I had earned a dollar working for my Dad and I gave Sucker a quarter to go and get candy and so forth. With the rest I took Maybelle. We were sitting near the back and I saw Sucker come in. He began to stare at the screen the minute he stepped past the ticket man and he stumbled down the aisle without noticing where he was going. I started to punch Maybelle but couldn't quite make up my mind. Sucker looked a little silly— walking like a drunk with his eyes glued to the movie. He was wiping his reading glasses on his shirt tail and his knickers flopped down. He went on until he got to the first few rows where the kids usually sit. I never did punch Maybelle. But I got to thinking it was good to have both of them at the movie with the money I earned.

I guess things went on like this for about a month or six weeks. I felt so good I couldn't settle down to study or put my mind on anything. I wanted to be friendly with everybody. There were times when I just had to talk to some person. And usually that would be Sucker. He felt as good as I did. Once he said: "Pete, I am gladder that you are like my brother than anything else in the world."

Then something happened between Maybelle and me. I never have figured out just what it was. Girls like her are hard to understand. She began to act different toward me. At first I wouldn't let myself believe this and tried to think it was just my imagination. She didn't act glad to see me any more. Often she went out riding with this fellow on the football team who owns this yellow roadster. The car was the color of her hair and after school she would ride off with him, laughing and looking into his face. I couldn't think of anything to do about it and she was on my mind all day and night. When I did get a chance to go out with her she was snippy and didn't seem to notice me. This made me feel like something was the matter—I would worry about my shoes clopping too loud on the floor, or the fly of my pants, or the bumps on my chin. Sometimes when Maybelle was around, a devil would get into me and I'd hold my face stiff and call grown men by their last names without the Mister and say rough things. In the night I would wonder what made me do all this until I was too tired for sleep.

At first I was so worried I just forgot about Sucker. Then later he began to get on my nerves. He was always hanging around until I would get back from high school, always looking like he had something to say to me or wanted me to tell him. He made me a magazine rack in his Manual Training class and one week he saved his lunch money and bought me three packs of cigarettes. He couldn't seem to take it in that I had things on my mind and didn't want to fool with him. Every afternoon it would be the same—him in my room with this waiting expression on his face. Then I wouldn't say anything or I'd maybe answer him rough-like and he would finally go on out.

I can't divide that time up and say this happened one day and that the next. For one thing I was so mixed up the weeks just slid along into each other and I felt like Hell and didn't care. Nothing definite was said or done. Maybelle still rode around with this fellow in his yellow roadster and sometimes she would smile at me and sometimes not. Every afternoon I went from one place to another where I thought she would be. Either she would act almost nice and I would begin thinking how things would finally clear up and she would care for me—or else she'd behave so that if she hadn't been a girl I'd have wanted to grab her by that white little neck and choke her. The more ashamed I felt for making a fool of myself the more I ran after her.

Sucker kept getting on my nerves more and more. He would look at me as though he sort of blamed me for something, but at the same time knew that it wouldn't last long. He was growing fast and for some reason began to stutter when he talked. Sometimes he had nightmares or would throw up his breakfast. Mom got him a bottle of cod liver oil.

Then the finish came between Maybelle and me. I met her going to the drug store and asked for a date. When she said no I remarked something sarcastic. She told me she was sick and tired of my being around and that she had never cared a rap about me. She said all that, I just stood there and didn't answer anything. I walked home very slowly.

For several afternoons I stayed in my room by myself. I didn't want to go anywhere or talk to anyone. When Sucker would come in and look at me sort of funny I'd yell at him to get out. I didn't want to think of Maybelle and I sat at my desk reading *Popular Mechanics* or whittling at a toothbrush rack I was making. It seemed to me I was putting that girl out of my mind pretty well.

But you can't help what happens to you at night. That is what make things how they are now.

You see a few nights after Maybelle said those words to me I dreamed about her again. It was like that first time and I was squeezing Sucker's arm so tight I woke him up. He reached for my hand.

"Pete, what's the matter with you?"

All of a sudden I felt so mad my throat choked—at myself and the dream and Maybelle and Sucker and every single person I knew. I remembered all the times Maybelle had humiliated me and everything bad that had ever happened. It seemed to me for a second that nobody would ever like me but a sap like Sucker.

"Why is it we aren't buddies like we were before? Why—?"

"Shut your damn trap!" I threw off the cover and got up and turned on the light. He sat in the middle of the bed, his eyes blinking and scared.

There was something in me and I couldn't help myself. I don't think anybody ever gets that mad but once. Words came without me knowing what they would be. It was only afterward that I could remember each thing I said and see it all in a clear way.

"Why aren't we buddies? Because you're the dumbest slob I ever saw! Nobody cares anything about you! And just because I felt sorry for you sometimes and tried to act decent don't think I give a damn about a dumb-bunny like you!"

If I talked loud or hit him it wouldn't have been so bad. But my voice was slow and like I was very calm. Sucker's mouth was part way open and he looked as though he'd knocked his funny bone. His face was white and sweat came out on his forehead. He wiped it away with the back of his hand and for a minute his arm stayed raised that way as though he was holding something away from him.

"Don't you know a single thing? Haven't you even been around at all? Why don't you get a girl friend instead of me? What kind of a sissy do you want to grow up to be anyway?"

I didn't know what was coming next. I couldn't help myself or think.

Sucker didn't move. He had on one of my pajama jackets and his neck stuck out skinny and small. His hair was damp on his forehead.

"Why do you always hang around me? Don't you know when you're not wanted?"

Afterward I could remember the change in Sucker's face. Slowly that blank look went away and he closed his mouth. His eyes got narrow and his fists shut. There had never been such a look on him before. It was like every second he was getting older. There was a hard look to his eyes you don't see usually in a kid. A drop of sweat rolled down his chin and he didn't notice. He just sat there with those eyes on me and he didn't speak and his face was hard and didn't move.

"No you don't know when you're not wanted. You're too dumb. Just like your name—a dumb Sucker."

It was like something had busted inside me. I turned off the light and sat down in the chair by the window. My legs were shaking and I was so tired I could have bawled. The room was cold and dark. I sat there for a long time and smoked a squashed cigarette I had saved. Outside the yard was black and quiet. After a while I heard Sucker lie down.

I wasn't mad any more, only tired. It seemed awful to me that I had talked like that to a kid only twelve. I couldn't take it all in. I told myself I would go over to him and try to make it up. But I just sat there in the cold until a long time had passed. I planned how I could straighten it out in the morning. Then, trying not to squeak the springs, I got back in bed.

Sucker was gone when I woke up the next day. And later when I wanted to apologize as I had planned he looked at me in this new hard way so that I couldn't say a word.

All of that was two or three months ago. Since then Sucker has grown faster than any boy I ever saw. He's almost as tall as I am and his bones have gotten heavier and bigger. He won't wear any of my old clothes any more and has bought his first pair of long pants—with some leather suspenders to hold them up. Those are just the changes that are easy to see and put into words.

Our room isn't mine at all any more. He's gotten up this gang of kids and they have a club. When they aren't digging trenches in some vacant lot and fighting they are always in my room. On the door there is some foolishness written in Mercurochrome saying "Woe to the Outsider who Enters" and signed with crossed bones and their secret initials. They have rigged up a radio and every afternoon it blares out music. Once as I was coming in I heard a boy telling something in a low voice about what he saw in the back of his big brother's automobile. I could guess what I didn't hear. *That's what her and my brother do. It's the truth— parked in the car.* For a minute Sucker looked surprised and his face was almost like it used to be. Then he got hard and tough again. "Sure, dumbell. We know all that." They didn't notice me. Sucker began telling them how in two years he was planning to be a trapper in Alaska.

But most of the time Sucker stays by himself. It is worse when we are alone together in the room. He sprawls across the bed in those long corduroy pants with the suspenders and just stares at me with that hard, half sneering look. I fiddle around my desk and can't get settled because of those eyes of his. And the thing is I just have to study because I've gotten three bad cards this term already. If I flunk English I can't graduate next year. I don't want to be a bum and I just have to get my mind on it. I don't care a flip for Maybelle or any particular girl any more and it's only this thing between Sucker and me that is the trouble now. We never speak except when we have to before the family. I don't even want to call him Sucker any more and unless I forget I call him by his real name, Richard. At night I can't study with him in the room and I have to hang around the drug store, smoking and doing nothing, with the fellows who loaf there.

More than anything I want to be easy in my mind again. And I miss the way Sucker and I were for a while in a funny, sad way that before this I never would have believed. But everything is so different that there seems to be nothing I can do to get it right. I've sometimes thought if we could have it out in a big fight that would help. But I can't fight him because he's four years younger. And another thing—sometimes this look in his eyes makes me almost believe that if Sucker could he would kill me.

CARSON McCULLERS, who was born in Columbus, Georgia, in 1917, began to write at age sixteen, while she was in high school. She intended to further her education at the Julliard School of Music and Columbia University, but she accidentally lost her tuition money on a subway and so quit school. Her famous novels include *The Heart Is a Lonely Hunter, The Member of the Wedding,* and *Reflections in a Golden Eye,* all of which were made into movies. She also wrote *Clock Without Hands* and *Ballad of the Sad Cafe.*

Langston Hughes

Should a church be open at all times so that anyone who wants to may go inside for rest and sanctuary, or should the doors be kept locked to strangers?

Have you ever been so insulted and enraged that you felt you were strong enough to destroy something—even pull down a building?

Observe what happens to a bum during the Great Depression when he finds himself

ON THE ROAD

He was not interested in the snow. When he got off the freight, one early evening during the depression, Sargeant never even noticed the snow. But he must have felt it seeping down his neck, cold, wet, sopping in his shoes. But if you had asked him, he wouldn't have known it was snowing. Sargeant didn't see the snow, not even under the bright lights of the main street, falling white and flaky against the night. He was too hungry, too sleepy, too tired.

The Reverend Mr. Dorset, however, saw the snow when he switched on his porch light, opened the front door of his parsonage, and found standing there before him a big black man with snow on his face, a human piece of night with snow on his face—obviously unemployed.

Said the Reverend Mr. Dorset before Sargeant even realized he'd opened his mouth: "I'm sorry. No! Go right on down

167

this street four blocks and turn to your left, walk up seven and you'll see the Relief Shelter. I'm sorry. No!" He shut the door.

Sargeant wanted to tell the holy man that he had already been to the Relief Shelter, been to hundreds of relief shelters during the depression years, the beds were always gone and supper was over, the place was full, and they drew the color line anyhow. But the minister said, "No," and shut the door. Evidently he didn't want to hear about it. And he *had* a door to shut.

The big black man turned away. And even yet he didn't see the snow, walking right into it. Maybe he sensed it, cold, wet, sticking to his jaws, wet on his black hands, sopping in his shoes. He stopped and stood on the sidewalk hunched over—hungry, sleepy, cold—looking up and down. Then he looked right where he was—in front of a church. Of course! A church! Sure, right next to a parsonage, certainly a church.

It had *two* doors.

Broad white steps in the night all snowy white. Two high arched doors with slender stone pillars on either side. And way up, a round lacy window with a stone crucifix in the middle and Christ on the crucifix in stone. All this was pale in the street lights, solid and stony pale in the snow.

Sargeant blinked. When he looked up, the snow fell into his eyes. For the first time that night he *saw* the snow. He shook his head. He shook the snow from his coat sleeves, felt hungry, felt lost, felt not lost, felt cold. He walked up the steps of the church. He knocked at the door. No answer. He tried the handle. Locked. He put his shoulder against the door and his long black body slanted like a ramrod. He pushed. With loud rhythmic grunts, like the grunts in a chain-gang song, he pushed against the door.

"I'm tired . . . Huh! . . . Hongry . . . Uh! . . . I'm sleepy . . . Huh! I'm cold . . . I got to sleep somewheres," Sargeant said. "This here is a church, ain't it? Well, uh!"

He pushed against the door.

Suddenly, with an undue cracking and screaking, the door began to give way to the tall black Negro who pushed ferociously against it.

By now two or three white people had stopped in the

street, and Sargeant was vaguely aware of some of them yelling at him concerning the door. Three or four more came running, yelling at him.

"Hey!" they said. "Hey!"

"Uh-huh," answered the big tall Negro, "I know it's a white folks' church, but I got to sleep somewhere." He gave another lunge at the door. "Huh!"

And the door broke open.

But just when the door gave way, two white cops arrived in a car, ran up the steps with their clubs, and grabbed Sargeant. But Sargeant for once had no intention of being pulled or pushed away from the door.

Sargeant grabbed, but not for anything so weak as a broken door. He grabbed for one of the tall stone pillars beside the door, grabbed at it and caught it. And held it. The cops pulled and Sargeant pulled. Most of the people in the street got behind the cops and helped them pull.

"A big black unemployed Negro holding onto our church!" thought the people. "The idea!"

The cops began to beat Sargeant over the head, and nobody protested. But he held on.

And then the church fell down.

Gradually, the big stone front of the church fell down, the walls and the rafters, the crucifix and the Christ. Then the whole thing fell down, covering the cops and the people with bricks and stones and debris. The whole church fell down in the snow.

Sargeant got out from under the church and went walking on up the street with the stone pillar on his shoulder. He was under the impression that he had buried the parsonage and the Reverend Mr. Dorset who said, "No!" So he laughed, and threw the pillar six blocks up the street and went on.

Sargeant thought he was alone, but listening to the *crunch, crunch, crunch* on the snow of his own footsteps, he heard other footsteps, too, doubling his own. He looked around, and there was Christ walking along beside him, the same Christ that had been on the cross on the church—still stone with a rough stone surface, walking along beside him just like he was broken off the cross when the church fell down.

"Well, I'll be dogged," said Sargeant. "This here's the first time I ever seed you off the cross."

"Yes," said Christ, crunching his feet in the snow. "You had to pull the church down to get me off the cross."

"You glad?" said Sargeant.

"I sure am," said Christ.

They both laughed.

"I'm a hell of a fellow, ain't I?" said Sargeant. "Done pulled the church down!"

"You did a good job," said Christ. "They have kept me nailed on a cross for nearly two thousand years."

"Whee-ee-e!" said Sargeant. "I know you are glad to get off."

"I sure am," said Christ.

They walked on in the snow. Sargeant looked at the man of stone.

"And you have been up there two thousand years?"

"I sure have," Christ said.

"Well, if I had a little cash," said Sargeant, "I'd show you around a bit."

"I been around," said Christ.

"Yeah, but that was a long time ago."

"All the same," said Christ, "I've been around."

They walked on in the snow until they came to the railroad yards. Sargeant was tired, sweating and tired.

"Where you goin'?" Sargeant said, stopping by the tracks. He looked at Christ. Sargeant said, "I'm just a bum on the road. How about you? Where you goin'?"

"God knows," Christ said, "but I'm leavin' here."

They saw the red and green lights of the railroad yard half veiled by the snow that fell out of the night. Away down the track they saw a fire in a hobo jungle.

"I can go there and sleep," Sargeant said.

"You can?"

"Sure," said Sargeant. "That place ain't got no doors."

Outside the town, along the tracks, there were barren trees and bushes below the embankment, snow-gray in the dark. And down among the trees and bushes there were makeshift houses made out of boxes and tin and old pieces of wood and canvas. You couldn't see them in the dark, but you knew they were there if you'd ever been on the road, if you had ever lived with the homeless and hungry in a depression.

"I'm side-tracking," Sargeant said. "I'm tired."

"I'm gonna make it on to Kansas City," said Christ.

"O.K.," Sargeant said. "So long!"

He went into the hobo jungle and found himself a place to sleep. He never did see Christ no more. About 6:00 a.m. a freight came by. Sargeant scrambled out of the jungle with a dozen or so more hobos and ran along the track, grabbing at the freight. It was dawn, early dawn, cold and gray.

"Wonder where Christ is by now?" Sargeant thought. "He musta gone on way down the road. He didn't sleep in this jungle."

Sargeant grabbed the train and started to pull himself up into a moving coal car, over the edge of a wheeling coal car. But strangely enough, the car was full of cops. The nearest cop rapped Sargeant soundly across the knuckles with his night stick. Wham! Rapped his big black hands for clinging to the top of the car. Wham! But Sargeant did not turn loose. He clung on and tried to pull himself into the car. He hollered at the top of his voice, "Damn it, lemme in this car!"

"Shut up," barked the cop. "You crazy coon!" He rapped Sargeant across the knuckles and punched him in the stomach. "You ain't out in no jungle now. This ain't no train. You in jail."

Wham! across his bare black fingers clinging to the bars of his cell. Wham! between the steel bars low down against his shins.

Suddenly Sargeant realized that he really was in jail. He wasn't on no train. The blood of the night before had dried on his face, his head hurt terribly, and a cop outside in the corridor was hitting him across the knuckles for holding onto the door, yelling and shaking the cell door.

"They musta took me to jail for breaking down the door last night," Sargeant thought, "that church door."

Sargeant went over and sat on a wooden bench against the cold stone wall. He was emptier than ever. His clothes were wet, clammy cold wet, and shoes sloppy with snow water. It was just about dawn. There he was, locked up behind a cell door, nursing his bruised fingers.

The bruised fingers were his, but not the *door.*

Not the *club,* but the fingers.

"You wait," mumbled Sargeant, black against the jail wall. "I'm gonna break down this door, too."

"Shut up—or I'll paste you one," said the cop.

"I'm gonna break down this door," yelled Sargeant as he stood up in his cell.

Then he must have been talking to himself because he said, "I wonder where Christ's gone? I wonder if he's gone to Kansas City?"

LANGSTON HUGHES, one of the most important and prolific Negro writers in America, has written numerous poems, plays, essays, novels, and short stories. He was born in Joplin, Missouri in 1902 and died in 1967. During his action-filled life, he traveled all over the world and worked at a variety of jobs; dishwasher in Paris, busboy in a New York hotel, farmer and delivery boy in Manhattan, student, messboy on freighters, and he once almost starved as a beachcomber in Genoa, Italy. Some of his famous books include *The Big Sea, Not Without Laughter, Simple Speaks His Mind* (and others about Simple), and *Laughing To Keep From Crying.* He has also edited *An African Treasury* and *The Best Short Stories By Negro Writers.*

Jesse Hill Ford

Do hospitals admit patients who may not pay their bills?

   Could a patient die while the hospital is busy collecting a down payment for admission?

   In this story a poor black in the South must taste

THE BITTER BREAD

It was after Christmas, towards the end of December. There had come a sudden thaw. The roads got soft—the Devil was baking his bread, as the saying is, getting ready to pass out the hard luck for the New Year.

"Yes, yes," said the midwife, coming behind Robert in the narrow lane, toting her black suitcase. "It happen this way every year."

Maybe, thought Robert, maybe not. The damp cold tugged at his hands. Tonight the roads would freeze again. He looked back. "Can't you walk no faster?" he said.

"The first chile always slow," she replied.

"She alone by herself though," Robert said. "Lemme tote that bag—"

"Don't nobody tote this bag but me."

He waited up until she came alongside him and then,

reluctantly, he matched his pace with her own. A hawk went hunting rabbits above the dun-colored fields to the left, patiently tracing back and forth, hovering along the shaggy fence rows. Woods already dark with the cold shadows of winter lay to the right of the lane.

He smelled woodsmoke. His dog, a little brown fice, yapped three times, nervously, like a fox, and ran under the house.

"He won't bite," Robert said leading the way across the porch and entering the little room ahead of the midwife. On the bed beside the fireplace, Jeannie had not raised up.

"It's just me," said the midwife. Jeannie stirred. "How old is she?"

"She's seventeen," Robert said. He squatted down and set two hickory logs into the fire. The logs hissed. Flame flickered from the red and yellow embers. It fluttered above the logs in the smoke. "How you feeling, Jeannie?" He asked without looking at the bed.

"No, no, *no*," said the midwife. Robert stood up. He looked around. The midwife had opened her suitcase. "We must take her to the hospital. Wrap her up warm. See how drowsy she is? Feel her?"

"Yes'm."

"Fever," said the midwife. "You ain't got a truck?"

"No."

"Wagon?"

"No."

"Then we have to tote her. Down to the main road we can flag somebody." The midwife leaned over the bed. "We got to get you to town, understand me? Can you hear me? You too drowsy—hear?"

"Yes," Jeannie said. She did not open her eyes.

"How you feel?" Robert said.

"I hurt some," Jeannie said in a sleepy voice.

Robert got her shoes from the hearth.

"Don't bother with that. We'll wrap her up like a baby, see here? Now, lift her," said the midwife. "That's the time."

"She feel hot," Robert said.

The midwife was ahead of him, out the door and across

the bare yard. "Makase," she said, going ahead of him almost at a trot now. Carrying Jeannie held close against his chest, his powerful arms under her knees and her shoulders, Robert followed the midwife down the lane. The mud was already beginning to freeze crisp. Sunset made a dark red glow in the sky beyond soft fields of dead grass. Ahead and above him he saw the stars of evening.

Dark had come swiftly down by the time they reached the embankment to the highway. The midwife took off her scarf and waved at the first approaching headlights. A pickup truck stopped. The midwife opened the door. "This girl need to go to the hospital. . . ."

"Get in," said the white man.

Robert climbed into the warm cab, holding Jeannie on his lap like a child. The midwife closed the door and waved good-bye. The truck moved down the highway.

"Has she got anything catching?" said the white man.

"She's having a baby."

"Oh." The white man turned the heater up and stepped harder on the gas pedal. Robert's feet began to tingle and get warm. The lights of Somerton appeared. At the Negro entrance to the hospital, down a narrow drive at the rear of the flat wooden building, the white man stopped the truck. He climbed out and came around to Robert's side. He opened the door.

"How much I owe you?" Robert said, climbing down with Jeannie in his arms.

"Nothing," the man said. "I was coming in town anyhow." He walked ahead and opened the door to the hospital.

"I'm much obliged to you," Robert said.

"You're welcome," said the man. "Good luck." And he was gone.

In one corner of the waiting room there was a statue of Lord Jesus, standing on a pedestal. Beside the Coca-Cola machine in the hall stood another statue, Mary, dressed in blue robes. "Yes, can I help you?" The white nurse came from behind a counter.

"We need the white doctor," Robert said.

"What's her trouble?"

"Baby," said Robert.

The nurse turned and walked up the corridor. She came back rolling a narrow hospital cart.

Now it's going to be all right, Robert thought. He put Jeannie on the cart.

"Straight down that hall to the front office. You'll see a window. The sign says 'Hospital Admissions.' "

"What about the doctor, please ma'am?"

"After she's admitted to the hospital we'll call the doctor. Meanwhile she can lie here in the hall. She seems to be resting."

"Yes'm," Robert said.

He went down the strange corridor. The woman behind the admissions window was a Sister in black robes. Robert answered her questions one after the other while she filled in a white form.

"Fifty dollars," the Sister said.

"Yes'm. Put it on the book. I'll pay it."

"Cash, now," she said.

He reached into the pocket of his denim jacket and brought out the bills and the change, six dollars and forty-seven cents. He laid it out for her. "I can put this here down."

"Didn't you hear me just explain to you a while ago? We have rules. Your wife can't be admitted until you've paid fifty dollars cash in advance."

"Fifty dollars," Robert said.

"Fifty dollars," the Sister said. "I didn't make the rule."

"She need the white doctor," Robert said.

"I'm sure she does, and we'll call the doctor as soon as we can get her into a hospital bed. The doctor can't deliver babies out in the hall. I'll hold these papers while you go for the money."

"Yes'm. I don't have it."

"Then you'll have to borrow it, won't you?"

"Yes'm."

She turned away in the bright, silent room beyond the glass, bent about other business. Robert went out the front door and walked quickly down the road. For the first time he knew he had been sweating in the warm corridor because the cold came through his clothes. The sweat combined with it to chill him. He pushed his hands into the pockets of his coat and set off walking. Fear caught at him then. He began suddenly to run down the side of the road. He turned and waved at the lights of a car. It passed him slowly by, its exhaust making a steaming white plume in the air that was freezing him. He began running again. He ran down towards the intersection, past a row of neat white houses. Dogs rushed down the lawns and leaped the ditch, barking. He walked then. The dogs backed nervously away, whining at the strange smell of him.

At the corner he stopped. There was a filling station on his right, well lit, and painted blue and red. Inside the station two white men warmed themselves beside a kerosene heater. He crossed the street. A sidewalk took up on the other side and he began running again. He had a glimpse of white faces peering at him from the passing cars. He ran doggedly on, sweating again, breathing through his mouth, and tasting the bite of the cold air. By now, he thought, the land would be frozen—nearly hard as this sidewalk, by now.

He passed the last houses in the white section of town. He saw the cotton gin and the railroad crossing. He stopped running and walked long enough for his heart to stop pounding so, long enough for the ache inside to ease a bit. Beyond the rail crossing and up a side street he saw Joe-Thell's barbecue stand and the beer hall.

Robert had passed some time in the place on Saturday evenings at strawberry harvest and during cotton season. He ran up the street and pushed through the flimsy door. Joe-Thell looked up, frightened. "What's wrong?" he said. "Say, Robert?" There were no customers in the place.

"I need to borrow fifty dollars," Robert said.

"That quick," said Joe-Thell. He was an old man, wise in the ways of the world and never at a loss for words. He listened as Robert explained, nodding to let Robert know he had heard the same story six dozen times before. Joe-Thell nodded, sadly amused. He struck a kitchen match and lit his cigarette. He wiped his hands on his apron.

"*This* time of year though," said Joe-Thell, "peoples ain't got any work. Peoples ain't got any money, and you got nothing to hock."

"If it was another time of year I wouldn't need to borrow," Robert said. "I can pay back."

"If I had it you could have it," said Joe-Thell. "But I don't have it. Here it is already after dark."

"Then who does have it?" Robert said. "Jeannie up there laying in the hall."

"You got to have a lender, Robert. Mama Lavorn about the only one I know that might go that high with you this time of year."

"Mama Lavorn?"

"Sure," Joe-Thell said. "Over to the Cafe and Tourist. Don't you know the Cafe and Tourist?" Joe-Thell was smiling a weary smile. "Look here, Robert. Go back to the crossing and then follow the dirt street by the tracks, that's south on a dirt street that angles and slants off. Mama Lavorn got a red light that winks on and off above her front entrance. It's up that road on the right-hand side."

"Mama Lavorn," Robert said.

"Tell her I sent you. Say to her Joe-Thell said she might go that high."

Robert was already backing away to the door. He turned suddenly out into the cold again, running back the way he had come, crossing the railroad and running; running then up the dark dirt side street. He suddenly sprawled. He fell, crashing through thin ice into a puddle of freezing water. He leaped up, the front of him wet through. He was stung by the cold water. Almost without knowing it he was running again, but carefully now, watching for the pale gleam of the frozen puddles. His thin clothes began to stiffen in front where the puddle had wet them. His hands burned.

He crossed the porch beneath the blinking red light bulb and opened the front door. He saw Mama Lavorn smiling at him. She sat in a high chair behind the cash register. She was a fat, dark woman in a purple dress. She wore earbobs that glittered like ice when she moved her head.

"Lord, look here!" said Mama Lavorn. "I mean *somebody's* in a hurry!"

Her smile disappeared as he began talking. "So you need fifty dollars," she said. "You know anyplace else you can get it?"

She didn't wait for him to say no, but went on: "Because if you do I'm going to give you good advice. Go there and get it. I'm a lender. If you get it here it's going to cost you money—*if you get it.*"

"Please . . ." he said.

"The interest on a dollar for one week is two bits—twenty-five cents," she said. "In a week this fifty dollars gonna come to sixty-two fifty. Put it another week, you can bring me twelve and a half dollars every Saturday to take care of the interest and keep the fifty dollars until strawberry season if you have to."

Robert nodded. "Sign here, on this line." She pushed him a check on the Farmers and Merchants Bank. She handed him her fountain pen. He signed the check. "If you come up and don't pay, or if you miss a payment, all I have to do is take this check to court and they'll come after you. It mean jail then, don't you know?"

"Yes'm."

She counted the money out of the cash drawer and into his big hand. "How come you so wet?"

"I fell," he said. Clutching the money, he made himself walk out the door. Then he ran.

Now, he was thinking, it *will* be all right. Running was easier now. The way back seemed shorter. The sidewalk started again. Almost before he knew it he saw the blue-and-red filling station, then the two white men, standing inside as before, beside the heater. Again the dogs rushed down at him but he hardly minded them. They drew back as though astonished and let him pass. Lightly he bounded over the dead short grass on the hospital lawn and took his time then, opening the front door and approaching the admissions window. He laid the five bills on the black marble shelf.

Silently, the Sister took the money, counted it, and pushed him a receipt. "Take this to the nurse."

"The doctor?"

"The doctor will be called."

He went down to the Negro waiting room. The nurse took the receipt. "Do you have a regular doctor?"

"No," he said. "No, ma'am."

The nurse picked up the phone. Robert walked around

the corner and into the hall to the cart. The hallway was dim. It didn't seem proper to touch his wife, not here.

"What took me so long," he said softly. "I had to go after the money."

Jeannie made no answer. Resting, he thought.

He walked back to the waiting room. It was deserted. Only Christ and Mary looked at him from pale, hard eyes. The red eye in the cold-drink machine said "Nickels Only." The doctor came briskly up the hall, nodded in Robert's direction and muttered something to the nurse.

The two of them went into the dim hallway. Presently they come back.

"Should have called me at once!" the doctor said. "How long ago did you bring her in?"

"I think. . . ."

"You *think?*" The doctor came slowly from behind the counter. "Robert?" The doctor's white face had a smooth powdered look. His eyes were soft and blue.

"Sir?"

"Your wife's dead. She's been dead maybe half an hour. Sister will refund your fifty dollars. There'll be no fee for my services. There's the body to be taken care of—I usually call the L. B. Jones Funeral Parlor for Colored."

"And they bury her?"

"Well, they fix her and arrange a burial for her, yes. You have a burial policy?"

"I don't have one," Robert said.

"Doctor?" It was the nurse. The doctor went to the counter. He took out his fountain pen. In a moment he returned, holding a slip of paper. He handed the paper to Robert.

"That's the death certificate. However you decide about handling the burial will be all right. Whoever does it will need this."

"Thank you, sir," Robert said. He sat down on the yellow patterned sofa. The doctor went away.

Presently a priest appeared. "I'm sorry about your wife, my son. She's in the arms of God now. She's with God. Are you a Catholic?"

"No, sir."

"We always ask. Not many Negroes are Catholics. We've a few converts among the Negro personnel who work here at the hospital."

"Yes, sir."

"Can I help you in any way? With arrangements?"

The nurse handed something to the priest, who then handed it to Robert—the fifty dollars. Robert put the bills in the damp, cold pocket of his cloth jacket. He carefully folded the death certificate then. The embarrassment of grief had begun to blind him a little—to make him dizzy. He stood up and pushed the slip of white paper into the watch pocket of his overalls.

A big man, taller than the white people, he felt better standing up.

"We can't keep the body here," the nurse was saying.

Robert walked down the hall to the cart. He pulled the white sheet away. Then he wrapped Jeannie carefully in her quilt. He lifted her in his arms.

"If I can help in any way," the priest was saying. "If there's anyone I can call. . . ."

"Just open the door, please sir," Robert said.

The priest looked at the nurse. "Oh, this happens, it happens," the nurse said. "Wait till you've been here long as I have."

The priest opened the door. "God love you," he said.

Robert stepped into the cold. He walked slowly at first, until he reached the road, then he shifted his burden to his shoulder. It rested lightly. He walked at a quick steady pace and was soon out of town, beyond the last yellow street lamp. He chose the longer way, by the old road, a hard, narrow winding road that soon played out to gravel wending between the frozen fields.

At last he crossed the highway, climbed the embankment, and entered the lane. His shoulder was numb. His side had begun to ache. As he had known it would be, the earth in the lane was frozen hard. The ground everywhere would be hard this night. Like a taste of sudden sickness, grief welled up inside him again, bone-hard and hard as the frozen ground, yet after the first few strokes of the pick the crust finally would give way. He knew the spade would bite and bite again, deeper and deeper still.

JESSE HILL FORD, a native Southerner, was born in Troy, Alabama, in 1928, grew up in Nashville, Tennessee, and then graduated from Vanderbilt University in 1951. He served in the Korean War as a Navy officer. In 1955 he studied fiction writing at the University of Florida, where he earned a Master of Arts degree. He has written three novels, *Mountains of Gilead, Liberation of Lord Byron Jones,* and *The Feast of St. Barnabas.* His stage play, *The Conversion of Buster Drumwright,* was originally produced on CBS television. He lives with his wife, four children, and their St. Bernard dog in Humboldt, Tennessee.

Ralph Ellison

*Under what circumstances would you play a game
that would result in either a better life for you or
your immediate death?*

    *Why has life—that is, the business of living
—often been called a game?*

    See what one player does when he becomes

KING OF THE
BINGO GAME

    The woman in front of him was eating roasted peanuts
that smelled so good that he could barely contain his hunger. He
could not even sleep and wished they'd hurry and begin the bingo
game. There, on his right, two fellows were drinking wine out of
a bottle wrapped in a paper bag, and he could hear soft gurgling
in the dark. His stomach gave a low, gnarling growl. "If this was
down South," he thought, "all I'd have to do is lean over and say,
'Lady, gimme a few of those peanuts, please ma'am,' and she'd
pass me the bag and never think nothing of it." Or he could ask
the fellows for a drink in the same way. Folks down South stuck
together that way; they didn't even have to know you. But up here
it was different. Ask somebody for something, and they'd think
you were crazy. Well, I ain't crazy. I'm just broke, 'cause I got
no birth certificate to get a job, and Laura 'bout to die 'cause we
got no money for a doctor. But I ain't crazy. And yet a pinpoint

of doubt was focused in his mind as he glanced toward the screen and saw the hero stealthily entering a dark room and sending the beam of a flashlight along a wall of bookcases. This is where he finds the trapdoor, he remembered. The man would pass abruptly through the wall and find the girl tied to a bed, her legs and arms spread wide, and her clothing torn to rags. He laughed softly to himself. He had seen the picture three times, and this was one of the best scenes.

On his right the fellow whispered wide-eyed to his companion, "Man, look a-yonder!"

"Damn!"

"Wouldn't I like to have her tied up like that . . ."

"Hey! That fool's letting her loose!"

"Aw, man, he loves her."

"Love or no love!"

The man moved impatiently beside him, and he tried to involve himself in the scene. But Laura was on his mind. Tiring quickly of watching the picture he looked back to where the white beam filtered from the projection room above the balcony. It started small and grew large, specks of dust dancing in its whiteness as it reached the screen. It was strange how the beam always landed right on the screen and didn't mess up and fall somewhere else. But they had it all fixed. Everything was fixed. Now suppose when they showed that girl with her dress torn and the girl started taking off the rest of her clothes, and when the guy came in he didn't untie her but kept her there and went to taking off his own clothes? *That* would be something to see. If a picture got out of hand like that those guys up there would go nuts. Yeah, and there'd be so many folks in here you couldn't find a seat for nine months! A strange sensation played over his skin. He shuddered. Yesterday he'd seen a bedbug on a woman's neck as they walked out into the bright street. But exploring his thigh through a hole in his pocket he found only goose pimples and old scars.

The bottle gurgled again. He closed his eyes. Now a dreamy music was accompanying the film and train whistles were sounding in the distance, and he was a boy again walking along a railroad trestle down South, and seeing the train coming, and running back as fast as he could go, and hearing the whistle blowing, and getting off the trestle to solid ground just in time, with the earth trembling beneath his feet, and feeling relieved as he ran down the cinder-strewn embankment onto the highway, and looking back and seeing with terror that the train had left the track and was following him right down the middle of the street, and all the white people laughing as he ran screaming . . .

"Wake up there, buddy! What the hell do you mean hollering like that? Can't you see we trying to enjoy this here picture?"

He stared at the man with gratitude.

"I'm sorry, old man," he said. "I musta been dreaming."

"Well, here, have a drink. And don't be making no noise like that, damn!"

His hands trembled as he tilted his head. It was not wine, but whiskey. Cold rye whiskey. He took a deep swoller, decided it was better not to take another, and handed the bottle back to its owner.

"Thanks, old man," he said.

Now he felt the cold whiskey breaking a warm path straight through the middle of him, growing hotter and sharper as it moved. He had not eaten all day, and it made him light-headed. The smell of the peanuts stabbed him like a knife, and he got up and found a seat in the middle aisle. But no sooner did he sit than he saw a row of intense-faced young girls, and got up again, thinking, "You chicks musta been Lindy-hopping somewhere." He found a seat several rows ahead as the lights came on, and he saw the screen disappear behind a heavy red and gold curtain; then the curtain rising, and the man with the microphone and a uniformed attendant coming on the stage.

He felt for his bingo cards, smiling. The guy at the door wouldn't like it if he knew about his having *five* cards. Well, not everyone played the bingo game; and even with five cards he didn't have much of a chance. For Laura, though, he had to have faith. He studied the cards, each with its different numerals, punching the free center hole in each and spreading them neatly across his lap; and when the lights faded he sat slouched in his seat so that he could look from his cards to the bingo wheel with but a quick shifting of his eyes.

Ahead, at the end of the darkness, the man with the

microphone was pressing a button attached to a long cord and spinning the bingo wheel and calling out the number each time the wheel came to rest. And each time the voice rang out his finger raced over the cards for the number. With five cards he had to move fast. He became nervous; there were too many cards, and the man went too fast with his grating voice. Perhaps he should just select one and throw the others away. But he was afraid. He became warm. Wonder how much Laura's doctor would cost? Damn that, watch the cards! And with despair he heard the man call three in a row which he missed on all five cards. This way he'd never win . . .

When he saw the row of holes punched across the third card, he sat paralyzed and heard the man call three more numbers before he stumbled forward, screaming,

"Bingo! Bingo!"

"Let that fool up there," someone called.

"Get up there, man!"

He stumbled down the aisle and up the steps to the stage into a light so sharp and bright that for a moment it blinded him, and he felt that he had moved into the spell of some strange, mysterious power. Yet it was as familiar as the sun, and he knew it was the perfectly familiar bingo.

The man with the microphone was saying something to the audience as he held out his card. A cold light flashed from the man's finger as the card left his hand. His knees trembled. The man stepped closer, checking the card against the numbers chalked on the board. Suppose he had made a mistake? The pomade on the man's hair made him feel faint, and he backed away. But the man was checking the card over the microphone now, and he had to stay. He stood tense, listening.

"Under the O, forty-four," the man chanted. "Under the I, seven. Under the G, three. Under the B, ninety-six. Under the N, thirteen!"

His breath came easier as the man smiled at the audience.

"Yessir, ladies and gentlemen, he's one of the chosen people!"

The audience rippled with laughter and applause.

"Step right up to the front of the stage."

He moved slowly forward, wishing that the light was not so bright.

"To win tonight's jackpot of $36.90 the wheel must stop between the double zero, understand?"

He nodded, knowing the ritual from the many days and nights he had watched the winners march across the stage to press the button that controlled the spinning wheel and receive the prizes. And now he followed the instructions as though he'd crossed the slippery stage a million prize-winning times.

The man was making some kind of a joke, and he nodded vacantly. So tense had he become that he felt a sudden desire to cry and shook it away. He felt vaguely that his whole life was determined by the bingo wheel; not only that which would happen now that he was at last before it, but all that had gone before, since his birth, and his mother's birth and the birth of his father. It had always been there, even though he had not been aware of it, handing out the unlucky cards and numbers of his days. The feeling persisted, and he started quickly away. I better get down from here before I make a fool of myself, he thought.

"Here, boy," the man called. "You haven't started yet."

Someone laughed as he went hesitantly back.

"Are you all reet?"

He grinned at the man's jive talk, but no words would come, and he knew it was not a convincing grin. For suddenly he knew that he stood on the slippery brink of some terrible embarrassment.

"Where are you from, boy?" the man asked.

"Down South."

"He's from down South, ladies and gentlemen," the man said. "Where from? Speak right into the mike."

"Rocky Mont," he said. "Rock' Mont, North Car'lina."

"So you decided to come down off that mountain to the U.S.," the man laughed. He felt that the man was making a fool of him, but then something cold was placed in his hand, and the lights were no longer behind him.

Standing before the wheel he felt alone, but that was somehow right, and he remembered his plan. He would give the wheel a short quick twirl. Just a touch of the button. He had watched it many times, and always it came close to double zero when it was short and quick. He steeled himself; the fear had left, and he felt a profound sense of promise, as though he were about to be repaid for all the things he'd suffered all his life. Trembling, he pressed the button. There was a whirl of lights, and in a second he realized with finality that though he wanted to, he could not stop. It was as though he held a high-powered line in his naked hand. His nerves tightened. As the wheel increased its speed it seemed to draw him more and more into its power, as though it held his fate; and with it came a deep need to submit, to whirl, to lose himself in its swirl of color. He could not stop it now, he knew. So let it be.

The button rested snugly in his palm where the man had placed it. And now he became aware of the man beside him, advising him through the microphone, while behind the shadowy audience hummed with noisy voices. He shifted his feet. There was still that feeling of helplessness within him, making part of him desire to turn back, even now that the jackpot was right in his hand. He squeezed the button until his fist ached. Then, like the sudden shriek of a subway whistle, a doubt tore through his head. Suppose he did not spin the wheel long enough? What could he do, and how could he tell? And then he knew, even as he wondered, that as long as he pressed the button, he could control the jackpot. He and only he could determine whether or not it was to be his. Not even the man with the microphone could do anything about it now. He felt drunk. Then, as though he had come down from a high hill into a valley of people, he heard the audience yelling.

"Come down from there, you jerk!"

"Let somebody else have a chance . . ."

"Ole Jack thinks he done found the end of the rainbow..."

The last voice was not unfriendly, and he turned and smiled dreamily into the yelling mouths. Then he turned his back squarely on them.

"Don't take too long, boy," a voice said.

He nodded. They were yelling behind him. Those folks did not understand what had happened to him. They had been playing the bingo game day in and night out for years, trying to win rent money or hamburger change. But not one of those wise guys had discovered this wonderful thing. He watched the wheel whirling past the numbers and experienced a burst of exhaltation: This is God! This is the really truly God! He said it aloud, "This *is* God!"

He said it with such absolute conviction that he feared he would fall fainting into the footlights. But the crowd yelled so loud that they could not hear. Those fools, he thought. I'm here trying to tell them the most wonderful secret in the world, and they're yelling like they gone crazy. A hand fell upon his shoulder.

"You'll have to make a choice now, boy. You've taken too long."

He brushed the hand violently away.

"Leave me alone, man. I know what I'm doing!"

The man looked surprised and held on to the microphone for support. And because he did not wish to hurt the man's feelings he smiled, realizing with a sudden pang that there was no way of explaining to the man just why he had to stand there pressing the button forever.

"Come here," he called tiredly.

The man approached, rolling the heavy microphone across the stage.

"Anybody can play this bingo game, right?" he said.

"Sure, but . . ."

He smiled, feeling inclined to be patient with this slick looking white man with his blue sport shirt and his sharp gabardine suit.

"That's what I thought," he said. "Anybody can win the jackpot as long as they get the lucky number, right?"

"That's the rule, but after all . . ."

"That's what I thought," he said. "And the big prize goes to the man who knows how to win it?"

The man nodded speechlessly.

"Well then, go on over there and watch me win like I want to. I ain't going to hurt nobody," he said, "and I'll show you how to win. I mean to show the whole world how it's got to be done."

And because he understood, he smiled again to let the man know that he held nothing against him for being white and impatient. Then he refused to see the man any longer and stood pressing the button, the voices of the crowd reaching him like sounds in distant streets. Let them yell. All the Negroes down there were just ashamed because he was black like them. He smiled inwardly, knowing how it was. Most of the time he was ashamed of what Negroes did himself. Well, let them be ashamed for something this time. Like him. He was like a long thin black wire that was being stretched and wound upon the bingo wheel; wound until he wanted to scream; wound, but this time himself controlling the winding and the sadness and the shame, and because he did, Laura would be all right. Suddenly the lights flickered. He staggered backwards. Had something gone wrong? All this noise. Didn't they know that although he controlled the wheel, it also controlled him, and unless he pressed the button forever and forever and ever it would stop, leaving him high and dry, dry and high on this hard high slippery hill and Laura dead? There was only one chance; he had to do whatever the wheel demanded. And gripping the button in despair, he discovered with surprise that it imparted a nervous energy. His spine tingled. He felt a certain power.

Now he faced the raging crowd with defiance, its screams penetrating his eardrums like trumpets shrieking from a juke-box. The vague faces glowing in the bingo lights gave him a sense of himself that he had never know before. He was running the show, by God! They had to react to him, for he was their luck. This is *me*, he thought. Let the bastards yell. Then someone was laughing inside him, and he realized that somehow he had forgotten his own name. It was a sad, lost feeling to lose your name, and a crazy thing to do. That name had been given him by the white man who had owned his grandfather a long lost time ago down South. But maybe those wise guys knew his name.

"Who am I?" he screamed.

"Hurry up and bingo, you jerk!"

They didn't know either, he thought sadly. They didn't even know their own names, they were all poor nameless bastards. Well, he didn't need that old name; he was reborn. For as long as he pressed the button he was The-man-who-pressed-the-button-who-held-the-prize-who-was-the-King-of-Bingo. That was the way it was, and he'd have to press the button even if nobody understood, even though Laura did not understand.

"Live!" he shouted.

The audience quieted like the dying of a huge fan.

"Live, Laura, baby. I got holt of it now, sugar. Live!"

He screamed it, tears streaming down his face. "I got nobody but YOU!"

The screams tore from his very guts. He felt as though the rush of blood to his head would burst out in baseball seams of small red droplets, like a head beaten by police clubs. Bending over he saw a trickle of blood splashing the toe of his shoe. With his free hand he searched his head. It was his nose. God, suppose something has gone wrong? He felt that the whole audience had somehow entered him and was stamping its feet in his stomach and he was unable to throw them out. They wanted the prize, that was it. They wanted the secret for themselves. But they'd never get it; he would keep the bingo wheel whirling forever, and Laura would be safe in the wheel. But would she? It had to be, because if she were not safe the wheel would cease to turn; it could not go on. He had to get away, *vomit* all, and his mind formed an image of himself running with Laura in his arms down the tracks of the subway just ahead of an A train, running desperately *vomit* with people screaming for him to come out but knowing no way of leaving the tracks because to stop would bring the train crushing down upon him and to attempt to leave across the other tracks would mean to run into a hot third rail as high as his waist which threw blue sparks that blinded his eyes until he could hardly see.

He heard singing and the audience was clapping its hands.

> *Shoot the liquor to him, Jim, boy!*
> *Clap-clap-clap*
> *Well a-calla the cop*
> *He's blowing his top!*
> *Shoot the liquor to him, Jim, boy!*

Bitter anger grew within him at the singing. They think I'm crazy. Well let 'em laugh. I'll do what I got to do.

He was standing in an attitude of intense listening when he saw that they were watching something on the stage behind him. He felt weak. But when he turned he saw no one. If only his thumb did not ache so. Now they were applauding. And for a moment he thought that the wheel had stopped. But that was impossible, his thumb still pressed the button. Then he saw them. Two men in uniform beckoned from the end of the stage. They were coming toward him, walking in step, slowly, like a tap-dance team returning for a third encore. But their shoulders shot forward, and he backed away, looking wildly about. There was nothing to fight them with. He had only the long black cord which led to a plug somewhere back stage, and he couldn't use that because it operated the bingo wheel. He backed slowly, fixing the men with his eyes as his lips stretched over his teeth in a tight, fixed grin; moved toward the end of the stage and realizing that he couldn't go much further, for suddenly the cord became taut and he couldn't afford to break the cord. But he had to do something. The audience was howling. Suddenly he stopped dead, seeing the men halt, their legs lifted as in an interrupted step of a slow-motion dance. There was nothing to do but run in the other direction and he dashed forward, slipping and sliding. The men fell back, surprised. He struck out violently going past.

"Grab him!"

He ran, but all too quickly the cord tightened, resistingly, and he turned and ran back again. This time he slipped them, and discovered by running in a circle before the wheel he could keep the cord from tightening. But this way he had to flail his arms to keep the men away. Why couldn't they leave a man alone? He ran, circling.

"Ring down the curtain," someone yelled. But they couldn't do that. If they did the wheel flashing from the projection room would be cut off. But they had him before he could tell them so, trying to pry open his fist, and he was wrestling and trying to bring his knees into the fight and holding on to the button, for it was his life. And now he was down, seeing a foot coming down, crushing his wrist cruelly, down, as he saw the wheel whirling serenely above.

"I can't give it up," he screamed. Then quietly, in a confidential tone, "Boys, I really can't give it up."

It landed hard against his head. And in the blank moment they had it away from him, completely now. He fought them trying to pull him up from the stage as he watched the wheel spin slowly to a stop. Without surprise he saw it rest at double-zero.

"You see," he pointed bitterly.

"Sure, boy, sure, it's O.K.," one of the men said smiling.

And seeing the man bow his head to someone he could not see, he felt very, very happy; he would receive what all the winners received.

But as he warmed in the justice of the man's tight smile he did not see the man's slow wink, nor see the bow-legged man behind him step clear of the swiftly descending curtain and set himself for a blow. He only felt the dull pain exploding in his skull, and he knew even as it slipped out of him that his luck had run out on the stage.

RALPH ELLISON, an extremely popular contemporary black novelist, was born in 1914 in Oklahoma City, Oklahoma, where he grew up. He attended Tuskegee Institute and planned to become a composer of symphonic music. However, after meeting Richard Wright, another black writer, in New York in 1937, he turned to writing. His famous novel *Invisible Man* received the National Book Award in 1953. He has also written numerous short stories.

Roald Dahl

What would you do if you awoke in bed and found a poisonous snake curled up on your stomach?

Do you believe there are poisons more deadly to man than the venom of a snake?

See what happens in India, where there is more than one kind of

POISON

It must have been around midnight when I drove home, and as I approached the gates of the bungalow I switched off the head-lamps of the car so the beam wouldn't swing in through the window of the side bedroom and wake Harry Pope. But I needn't have bothered. Coming up the drive I noticed his light was still on, so he was awake anyway—unless perhaps he'd dropped off while reading.

I parked the car and went up the five steps to the balcony, counting each step carefully in the dark so I wouldn't take an extra one which wasn't there when I got to the top. I crossed the balcony, pushed through the screen doors into the house itself and switched on the light in the hall. I went across to the door of Harry's room, opened it quietly, and looked in.

He was lying on the bed and I could see he was awake.

But he didn't move. He didn't even turn his head toward me, but I heard him say, "Timber, Timber, come here."

He spoke slowly, whispering each word carefully, separately, and I pushed the door right open and started to go quickly across the room.

"Stop. Wait a moment, Timber." I could hardly hear what he was saying. He seemed to be straining enormously to get the words out.

"What's the matter, Harry?"

"Sshhh!" he whispered. "Sshhh! For God's sake don't make a noise. Take your shoes off before you come nearer. *Please* do as I say, Timber."

The way he was speaking reminded me of George Barling after he got shot in the stomach when he stood leaning against a crate containing a spare airplane engine, holding both hands on his stomach and saying things about the German pilot in just the same hoarse, straining half whisper Harry was using now.

"Quickly, Timber, but take your shoes off first."

I couldn't understand about taking off the shoes but I figured that if he was as ill as he sounded I'd better humor him, so I bent down and removed the shoes and left them in the middle of the floor. Then I went over to his bed.

"Don't touch the bed! For God's sake don't touch the bed!" He was still speaking like he'd been shot in the stomach and I could see him lying there on his back with a single sheet covering three quarters of his body. He was wearing a pair of pajamas with blue, brown, and white stripes, and he was sweating terribly. It was a hot night and I was sweating a little myself, but not like Harry. His whole face was wet and the pillow around his head was sodden with moisture. It looked like a bad go of malaria to me.

"What is it, Harry?"

"A krait," he said.

"A *krait!* Oh, my God! Where'd it bite you? How long ago?"

"Shut up," he whispered.

"Listen, Harry," I said, and I leaned forward and touched his shoulder. "We've got to be quick. Come on now, quickly, tell me where it bit you." He was lying there very still and tense as though he were holding on to himself hard because of sharp pain.

"I haven't been bitten," he whispered. "Not yet. It's on my stomach. Lying there asleep."

I took a quick pace backward; I couldn't help it, and I stared at his stomach or rather at the sheet that covered it. The sheet was rumpled in several places and it was impossible to tell if there was anything underneath.

"You don't really mean there's a krait lying on your stomach now?"

"I swear it."

"How did it get there?" I shouldn't have asked the question because it was easy to see he wasn't fooling. I should have told him to keep quiet.

"I was reading," Harry said, and he spoke very slowly, taking each word in turn and speaking it carefully so as not to move the muscles of his stomach. "Lying on my back reading and I felt something on my chest, behind the book. Sort of tickling. Then out of the corner of my eye saw this little krait sliding over my pajamas. Small, about ten inches. Knew I mustn't move. Couldn't have, anyway. Lay there watching it. Thought it would go over top of the sheet." Harry paused and was silent for a few moments. His eyes looked down along his body toward the place where the sheet covered his stomach, and I could see he was watching to make sure his whispering wasn't disturbing the thing that lay there.

"There was a fold in the sheet," he said, speaking more slowly than ever now and so softly I had to lean close to hear him. "See it, it's still there. It went under that. I could feel it through my pajamas, moving on my stomach. Then it stopped moving and now it's lying there in the warmth. Probably asleep. I've been waiting for you." He raised his eyes and looked at me.

"How long ago?"

"Hours," he whispered. "Hours and bloody hours and hours. I can't keep still much longer. I've been wanting to cough."

There was not much doubt about the truth of Harry's story. As a matter of fact it wasn't a surprising thing for a krait to do. They hang around people's houses and they go for the warm places. The surprising thing was that Harry hadn't been bitten. The bite is quite deadly except sometimes when you catch it at once and they kill a fair number of people each year in Bengal, mostly in the villages.

"All right, Harry," I said, and now I was whispering too. "Don't move and don't talk any more unless you have to. You know it won't bite unless it's frightened. We'll fix it in no time."

I went softly out of the room in my stocking feet and fetched a small sharp knife from the kitchen. I put it in my trouser pocket ready to use instantly in case something went wrong while we were still thinking out a plan. If Harry coughed or moved or did something to frighten the krait and got bitten, I was going to be ready to cut the bitten place and try to suck the venom out. I came back to the bedroom and Harry was still lying there very quiet and sweating all over his face. His eyes followed me as I moved across the room to his bed and I could see he was wondering what I'd been up to. I stood beside him, trying to think of the best thing to do.

"Harry," I said, and now when I spoke I put my mouth almost on his ear so I wouldn't have to raise my voice above the softest whisper, "I think the best thing to do is for me to draw the sheet back very, very gently. Then we could have a look first. I think I could do that without disturbing it."

"Don't be a damn fool." There was no expression in his voice. He spoke each word too slowly, too carefully, and too softly for that. The expression was in the eyes and around the corners of the mouth.

"Why not?"

"The light would frighten him. It's dark under there now."

"Then how about whipping the sheet back quick and brushing it off before it has time to strike?"

"Why don't you get a doctor?" Harry said. The way he looked at me told me I should have thought of that myself in the first place.

"A doctor. Of course. That's it. I'll get Ganderbai."

I tiptoed out to the hall, looked up Ganderbai's number in the book, lifted the phone and told the operator to hurry.

"Doctor Ganderbai," I said. "This is Timber Woods."

"Hello, Mr. Woods. You not in bed yet?"

"Look, could you come round at once? And bring serum —for a krait bite."

"Who's been bitten?" The question came so sharply it was like a small explosion in my ear.

"No one. No one yet. But Harry Pope's in bed and he's got one lying on his stomach—asleep under the sheet on his stomach."

For about three seconds there was silence on the line. Then speaking slowly, not like an explosion now but slowly, precisely, Ganderbai said, "Tell him to keep quite still. He is not to move or to talk. Do you understand?"

"Of course."

"I'll come at once!" He rang off and I went back to the bedroom. Harry's eyes watched me as I walked across to his bed.

"Ganderbai's coming. He said for you to lie still."

"What in God's name does he think I'm doing!"

"Look, Harry, he said no talking. Absolutely no talking. Either of us."

"Why don't you shut up then?" When he said this, one side of his mouth started twitching with rapid little downward movements that continued for a while after he finished speaking. I took out my handkerchief and very gently I wiped the sweat off his face and neck, and I could feel the slight twitching of the muscle—the one he used for smiling—as my fingers passed over it with the handkerchief.

I slipped out to the kitchen, got some ice from the icebox, rolled it up in a napkin, and began to crush it small. That business of the mouth, I didn't like that. Or the way he talked, either. I carried the ice pack back to the bedroom and laid it across Harry's forehead.

"Keep you cool."

He screwed up his eyes and drew breath sharply through his teeth. "Take it away," he whispered. "Make me cough." His smiling-muscle began to twitch again.

The beam of a head-lamp shone through the window as Ganderbai's car swung around to the front of the bungalow. I went out to meet him, holding the ice pack with both hands.

"How is it?" Ganderbai asked, but he didn't stop to talk; he walked on past me across the balcony and through the screen doors into the hall. "Where is he? Which room?"

He put his bag down on a chair in the hall and followed me into Harry's room. He was wearing soft-soled bedroom slippers and he walked across the floor noiselessly, delicately, like a careful cat. Harry watched him out of the sides of his eyes. When Ganderbai reached the bed he looked down at Harry and smiled, confident and reassuring, nodding his head to tell Harry it was a simple matter and he was not to worry but just to leave it to Doctor Ganderbai. Then he turned and went back to the hall and I followed him.

"First thing is to try to get some serum into him," he said, and he opened his bag and started to make preparations. "Intravenously. But I must do it neatly. Don't want to make him flinch."

We went into the kitchen and he sterilized a needle. He had a hypodermic syringe in one hand and a small bottle in the other and he stuck the needle through the rubber top of the bottle and began drawing a pale yellow liquid up into the syringe by pulling out the plunger. Then he handed the syringe to me.

"Hold that till I ask for it."

He picked up the bag and together we returned to the room. Harry's eyes were bright now and wide open. Ganderbai bent over Harry and very cautiously, like a man handling sixteenth-century lace, he rolled up the pajama sleeve to the elbow without moving the arm. I noticed he stood well away from the bed.

He whispered, "I'm going to give you an injection. Serum. Just a prick but try not to move. Don't tighten your stomach muscles. Let them go limp."

Harry looked at the syringe.

Ganderbai took a piece of red rubber tubing from his bag and slid one end under and up and around Harry's bicep; then he tied the tubing tight with a knot. He sponged a small area of the bare forearm with alcohol, handed the swab to me and took the syringe from my hand. He held it up to the light, squinting at the calibrations, squirting out some of the yellow fluid. I stood still beside him, watching. Harry was watching too and sweating all over his face so it shone like it was smeared thick with face cream melting on his skin and running down onto the pillow.

I could see the blue vein on the inside of Harry's forearm, swollen now because of the tourniquet, and then I saw the needle above the vein, Ganderbai holding the syringe almost flat against the arm, sliding the needle in sideways through the skin into the blue vein, sliding it slowly but so firmly it went in smooth as into cheese. Harry looked at the ceiling and closed his eyes and opened them again but he didn't move.

When it was finished Ganderbai leaned forward putting his mouth close to Harry's ear. "Now you'll be all right even if you *are* bitten. But don't move. Please don't move. I'll be back in a moment."

He picked up his bag and went out to the hall and I followed.

"Is he safe now?" I asked.

"No."

"How safe is he?"

The little Indian doctor stood there in the hall rubbing his lower lip.

"It must give some protection, mustn't it?" I asked.

He turned away and walked to the screen doors that led onto the veranda. I thought he was going through them but he stopped this side of the doors and stood looking out into the night.

"Isn't the serum very good?" I asked.

"Unfortunately not," he answered without turning round. "It might save him. It might not. I am trying to think of something else to do."

"Shall we draw the sheet back quick and brush it off before it has time to strike?"

"Never! We are not entitled to take a risk." He spoke sharply and his voice was pitched a little higher than usual.

"We can't very well leave him lying there," I said. "He's getting nervous."

"Please! Please!" he said, turning round, holding both hands up in the air. "Not so fast, please. This is not a matter to rush into bald-headed." He wiped his forehead with his handkerchief and stood there, frowning, nibbling his lip.

"You see," he said at last. "There is a way to do this. You know what we must do—we must administer an anesthetic to the creature where it lies."

It was a splendid idea.

"It is not safe," he continued, "because a snake is cold-blooded and anesthetic does not work so well or so quick with such animals, but it is better than any other thing to do. We could use ether...chloroform..." He was speaking slowly and trying to think the thing out while he talked.

"Which shall we use?"

"Chloroform," he said suddenly. "Ordinary chloroform. That is best. Now quick!" He took my arm and pulled me toward the balcony. "Drive to my house! By the time you get there I will have waked up my boy on the telephone and he will show you my poisons cupboard. Here is the key of the cupboard. Take a bottle of chloroform. It has an orange label and the name is printed on it. I stay here in case anything happens. Be quick now, hurry! No, no, you don't need your shoes!"

I drove fast and in about fifteen minutes I was back with the bottle of chloroform. Ganderbai came out of Harry's room and met me in the hall. "You got it?" he said. "Good, good. I just been telling him what we are going to do. But now we must hurry. It is not easy for him in there like that all this time. I am afraid he might move."

He went back to the bedroom and I followed, carrying the bottle carefully with both hands. Harry was lying on the bed in precisely the same position as before with the sweat pouring down his cheeks. His face was white and wet. He turned his eyes toward me and I smiled at him and nodded confidently. He continued to look at me. I raised my thumb, giving him the okay signal. He closed his eyes. Ganderbai was squatting down by the bed, and on the floor beside him was the hollow rubber tube that he had previously used as a tourniquet, and he'd got a small paper funnel fitted into one end of the tube.

He began to pull a little piece of the sheet out from under the mattress. He was working directly in line with Harry's stomach, about eighteen inches from it, and I watched his fingers as they tugged gently at the edge of the sheet. He worked so slowly it was almost impossible to discern any movement either in his fingers or in the sheet that was being pulled.

Finally he succeeded in making an opening under the sheet and he took the rubber tube and inserted one end of it in the opening so that it would slide under the sheet along the mattress toward Harry's body. I do not know how long it took him to slide that tube in a few inches. It may have been twenty minutes, it may have been forty. I never once saw the tube move. I knew it was going in because the visible part of it grew gradually shorter, but I doubted that the krait could have felt even the faintest vibration. Ganderbai himself was sweating now, large pearls of sweat standing out all over his forehead and along his upper lip. But his hands were steady and I noticed that his eyes were watching, not the tube in his hands, but the area of crumpled sheet above Harry's stomach.

Without looking up, he held out a hand to me for the chloroform. I twisted out the ground-glass stopper and put the bottle right into his hand, not letting go till I was sure he had a good hold on it. Then he jerked his head for me to come closer and he whispered, "Tell him I'm going to soak the mattress and that it will be very cold under his body. He must be ready for that and he must not move. Tell him now."

I bent over Harry and passed on the message.

"Why doesn't he get on with it?" Harry said.

"He's going to now, Harry. But it'll feel very cold, so be ready for it."

"Oh, God Almighty, get on, get on!" For the first time he raised his voice, and Ganderbai glanced up sharply, watched him for a few seconds, then went back to his business.

Ganderbai poured a few drops of chloroform into the paper funnel and waited while it ran down the tube. Then he poured some more. Then he waited again, and the heavy sickening smell of chloroform spread out over the room bringing with it faint unpleasant memories of white-coated nurses and white surgeons standing in a white room around a long white table. Ganderbai was pouring steadily now and I could see the heavy vapor of the chloroform swirling slowly like smoke above the paper funnel. He paused, held the bottle up to the light, poured one more funnelful and handed the bottle back to me. Slowly he drew out the rubber tube from under the sheet; then he stood up.

The strain of inserting the tube and pouring the chloroform must have been great, and I recollect that when Ganderbai turned and whispered to me, his voice was small and tired. "We'll give it fifteen minutes. Just to be safe."

I leaned over to tell Harry. "We're going to give it fifteen minutes, just to be safe. But it's probably done for already."

"Then why for God's sake don't you look and see!"

Again he spoke loudly and Ganderbai sprang round, his small brown face suddenly very angry. He had almost pure black eyes and he stared at Harry and Harry's smiling-muscle started to twitch. I took my handkerchief and wiped his wet face, trying to stroke his forehead a little for comfort as I did so.

Then we stood and waited beside the bed, Ganderbai watching Harry's face all the time in a curious intense manner. The little Indian was concentrating all his will power on keeping Harry quiet. He never once took his eyes from the patient and although he made no sound, he seemed somehow to be shouting at him all the time, saying: Now listen, you've got to listen, you're not going to go spoiling this now, d'you hear me; and Harry lay there twitching his mouth, sweating, closing his eyes, opening them, looking at me, at the sheet, at the ceiling, at me again, but never at Ganderbai. Yet somehow Ganderbai was holding him. The smell of chloroform was oppressive and it made me feel sick, but I couldn't leave the room now. I had the feeling someone was blowing up a huge balloon and I could see it was going to burst but I couldn't look away.

At length Ganderbai turned and nodded and I knew he was ready to proceed. "You go over to the other side of the bed," he said. "We will each take one side of the sheet and draw it back together, but very slowly please, and very quietly."

"Keep still now, Harry," I said and I went around to the other side of the bed and took hold of the sheet. Ganderbai stood opposite me, and together we began to draw back the sheet, lifting it up clear of Harry's body, taking it back very slowly, both of us standing well away but at the same time bending forward, trying to peer underneath it. The smell of chloroform was awful. I remember trying to hold my breath and when I couldn't do that any longer I tried to breathe shallow so the stuff wouldn't get into my lungs.

The whole of Harry's chest was visible now, or rather the striped pajama top which covered it, and then I saw the white cord of his pajama trousers, neatly tied in a bow. A little farther and I saw a button, a mother-of-pearl button, and that was something I had never had on my pajamas, a fly button, let alone a mother-of-pearl one. This Harry, I thought, he is very refined. It is odd how one sometimes has frivolous thoughts at exciting moments, and I distinctly remember thinking about Harry being very refined when I saw that button.

Apart from the button there was nothing on his stomach.

We pulled the sheet back faster then, and when we had uncovered his legs and feet we let the sheet drop over the end of the bed onto the floor.

"Don't move," Ganderbai said, "don't move, Mr. Pope"; and he began to peer around along the side of Harry's body and under his legs.

"We must be careful," he said. "It may be anywhere. It could be up the leg of his pajamas."

When Ganderbai said this, Harry quickly raised his head from the pillow and looked down at his legs. It was the first time he had moved. Then suddenly he jumped up, stood on his bed and shook his legs one after the other violently in the air. At that moment we both thought he had been bitten and Ganderbai was already reaching down into his bag for a scalpel and a tourniquet when Harry ceased his caperings and stood still and looked at the mattress he was standing on and shouted, "It's not there!"

Ganderbai straightened up and for a moment he too looked at the mattress; then he looked up at Harry. Harry was all right. He hadn't been bitten and now he wasn't going to get bitten and he wasn't going to be killed and everything was fine. But that didn't seem to make anyone feel any better.

"Mr. Pope, you are of course *quite* sure you saw it in the first place?" There was a note of sarcasm in Ganderbai's voice that he would never have employed in ordinary circumstances.

"You don't think you might possibly have been dreaming, do you, Mr. Pope?" The way Ganderbai was looking at Harry, I realized that the sarcasm was not seriously intended. He was only easing up a bit after the strain.

Harry stood on his bed in his striped pajamas, glaring at Ganderbai, and the color began to spread out over his cheeks.

"Are you telling me I'm a liar?" he shouted.

Ganderbai remained absolutely still, watching Harry. Harry took a pace forward on the bed and there was a shining look in his eyes.

"Why, you dirty little Hindu sewer rat!"

"Shut up, Harry!" I said.

"You dirty black—"

"Harry!" I called. "Shut up, Harry!" It was terrible, the things he was saying.

Ganderbai went out of the room as though neither of us was there and I followed him and put my arm around his shoulder as he walked across the hall and out onto the balcony.

"Don't you listen to Harry," I said. "This thing's made him so he doesn't know what he's saying."

We went down the steps from the balcony to the drive and across the drive in the darkness to where his old Morris car was parked. He opened the door and got in.

"You did a wonderful job," I said. "Thank you so very much for coming."

"All he needs is a good holiday," he said quietly, without looking at me, then he started the engine and drove off.

ROALD DAHL was born in Llandaff, South Wales, England, in 1916. He was educated in English public schools and served in the Royal Air Force from 1939 to 1945, attaining the rank of wing commander. He is married to actress Patricia Neal, and they have three children. In addition to his suspenseful short stories, for which he has received the Edgar Allan Poe Award, he has written books for children.

Jack Cady

What kind of accidental death would be the most horrible and painful?

How could you help if your best friend were trapped inside the burning cab of a truck?

See what one truck driver does in

THE BURNING

Sunlight gleamed as Singleton and I walked down the hill to the charred wreckage of what had been a truck. Gates was dead, and the breeze lifted sooty material that mixed with the valley smells of weeds, flowers, and diesel stink. Manny was in jail. Nothing more could be done for Gates, but now Manny was sitting in his own fire, burning because he was kind, because he was gentle.

Traffic was moving as usual on the long slopes; only an occasional car slowed, its occupants looking over the scene of last night's fire. The truck drivers would know all about the trouble, and they did not want to see. Besides, there was a hill to climb on either side of the valley. They could not afford to lose speed. I knew that by now the word of the burning had spread at least a hundred miles. As far as Lexington, drivers would be leaning against counters listening, with wildness spreading in them. Singleton and I had not slept through the long night. We revisited the scene because we felt it was the final thing we could do for both men.

Close-up the sunlight played on bright runs of metal where someone had pulled the cab apart hoping to recover enough of Gates's remains for burial. An oil fire, when the oil is pouring on a man, doesn't leave much. Only the frame and other heavy structural members of the truck remained.

"If he had only been knocked out or killed before the fire got to him . . ." We were both thinking the words. Either might have said them.

"His company's sending an investigator." Singleton told me. "But since we're here, let's go over it. They'll be sure to ask."

"Are you going to pull?"

"No." He shook his head and ran his hand across his face. "No. Next week maybe or the week after. I'm not steady. I called for three drivers. That's one for your rig too."

"Thanks. I've got vacation coming. I'm taking it."

The road surface along the wreck was blackened, and the asphalt waved and sagged. It was a bad spot. The state should have put up signs. Forty-seven feet of power and pay-load; now it seemed little there in the ditch, its unimportance turning my stomach. I wanted to retch. I felt lonely and useless.

We walked to the far hill to look at the tire marks. Narrow little lines which swung wide across the other lane and then back in, suddenly breaking and spinning up the roadway. Heavy black lines were laid beside them where the driver of the car being passed had ridden his brakes and then gone on up the hill. Coming down were the marks Gates made, and they showed that he had done what a trucker is supposed to do. He had avoided at all costs. The marks ran off the road.

I never knew him. Manny, tall, sandy-haired, and laughing, was my good friend, but I did not know Gates. I did not know until later that Singleton knew him.

We had picked Gates up twenty miles back on the narrow two-lane that ran through the Kentucky hills. We rode behind him figuring to pass when he got a chance to let us around. It was early, around 3 a.m., but there was still heavy vacation-season traffic. Manny was out front behind Gates. My rig was second behind him, and Singleton was behind me. Our three freights were grossing less than fifty thousand so we could go.

Gates's tanker must have scaled at around sixty thousand. Even with that weight you can usually go, but his gas-powered tractor was too light.

It slowed us to be laying back, but there was no reason to dog it. He was making the best time he could. He topped the hill by June's Stop and ran fast after he crested on the long slope down. He had Manny by maybe two hundred yards because Manny had signaled into June's.

When he signaled I checked my mirrors. Singleton kept pulling so I kept pulling. When he saw us coming on, Manny cancelled the signal and went over the top behind Gates. It allowed enough of a lag for Gates to get out front, and it kept Manny from being killed.

We took the hill fast. You have to climb out the other side. I was a quarter mile back, running at forty-five and gaining speed, when I saw the headlights of the little car swing into the lane ahead of Gates's tanker. The driver had incorrectly estimated the truck's speed or the car's passing power.

It was quick and not bad at first. The tanker went into the ditch. The car cut back in, broke traction, and spun directly up the roadway. It came to a stop next to Manny's rig, almost brushing against his drive axle and not even bending sheet metal, a fluke. The car it had passed went onto the shoulder and recovered. The driver took it on up the hill to get away from the wreck and involvement.

Manny was closer. He had perhaps a second more to anticipate the wreck. He had stopped quicker than I believed possible. It was about a minute before the fire started. I was running with my extinguisher when I saw it, and I knew I would be too late.

"I wish he'd exploded," Singleton said. He kicked up dust along the roadway. He was too old for this, and he was beat-out and shaken. The calmness of resignation was trying to take him, and I hoped it would. I wondered to myself if those clear eyes that had looked down a million and a half miles of road had ever looked at anything like this.

"Exploded? Yes, either that or got out."

"He was hurt. I think he was hurt bad." He looked at me almost helplessly. "No sense wishing; let's go back up."

After the wreck Singleton had backed his rig over the narrow two-lane, following the gradual bend of the road in the dark. He had taken the two girls from the small car into his cab.

I had stayed a little longer until Gates's burning got really bad. Then I brought the little car in, feeling the way I feel in any car: naked, unprotected, and nearly blind. I was shaking from weakness. The road was blocked above. There was no oncoming beyond the pot flares. The cop with the flashlight had arrived ten or fifteen minutes after the wreck. Behind me the fire rose against the summer blackness and blanketed the valley with the acrid smell of number-two diesel. Because of the distance, Manny's rig seemed almost in the middle of the fire and silhouetted against the burning, though I knew he had stopped nearly fifty yards up the roadway. My own rig was pulled in behind him; its markers stood pale beside the bigger glow. As I was about to go past the cop, he waved me over.

"Where you taking it?"

"Just to the top," I told him. "The girls were pretty shaken up. Don't worry, they won't go anywhere."

"Think they need an ambulance?" He paused, uncertain. "Christ," he said. "Will that other cruiser ever get here?"

"What about Manny?" I asked.

"In there." He nodded to where Manny sat in the cruiser. The lights were out inside. He could not be seen. "I'll take a statement at the top. You'll see him at the top."

I wanted to call to Manny, but there was nothing I could do. I took the car on to June's Stop. Rigs were starting to pile in, even stacking up along the roadway. Cars were parked around and between them, blacked out and gleaming small and dull in the lights from the truck markers. Most of the guys had cut their engines. It would be a long wait.

Singleton's truck was down by the restaurant. Inside around the counter, which formed a kind of box, drivers were sitting and talking. A few were standing around. They were excited and walked back and forth. I wanted coffee, needed it, but I could not go in. At least not then. A driver came up behind me.

"You Wakefield?" he asked. He meant did I drive for Wakefield. My name is Arnold.

I told him yes.

"Your buddy took the girls to Number Twelve. He said to come."

"As if we didn't have enough trouble . . ."

"He's got the door open." The guy grinned. He was short with a light build and was in too good a mood. I disliked him right away. "Listen," he said. "They say there's going to be a shakedown."

"Who says?"

"Who knows? That's just the word. If you left anything back there, you'd better get it out. Check it with June."

He meant guns and pills. A lot of companies require them in spite of the law. A lot of guys carry them on their own, the guns I mean. Pills are Benzedrine, Bennies, or a stronger kind called footballs. Only drivers who don't know any better use them to stay awake or get high on.

"I've got it right here," I told him, and patted my side pocket. "I'll hang onto it myself."

"Your funeral," he said, grinning. He gave me a sick feeling. He was a guy with nose trouble, one who spreads his manure up and down the road, a show-off to impress waitresses. "Thanks," I said, and turned to go to the motel room.

"Hey," he yelled, "what do you think will happen to him?"

"You figure it out." I went over to the motel, found Twelve, and went inside.

The room had twin beds. Singleton was sitting on one, facing the two girls on the other. One was kind of curled up. The other was leaning forward still crying. Vassar, I thought. No, nothing like that on 25 south; University of Kentucky likely, but the same sorry type. I edged down beside Singleton. "Why do you bother?" I asked him. "To hell with them." The girl bawling looked up hard for a moment and started bawling worse.

"I had room," she bawled.

We were all under a strain. The diesel smell was bad, but the other smell that I would never forget had been worse. Even away from the fire I seemed still to smell it.

"You thought you had room!" I yelled at her.

"No, really. I was all right. I had room." She was convinced, almost righteous. At some other time she might have been pretty. Both were twenty or twenty-one. The curled-up one was sort of mousy-looking. The one who was bawling was tall with long hair. I thought of her as a thing.

"No—really," I yelled at her; "you had no room, but keep lying to yourself. Pretty soon that'll make everything OK."

"Leave it, Arn," Singleton told me. "You're not doing any good."

He went to the sink to wet a towel, bringing it to the girl. "Wipe your face," he told her. Then he turned to me. "Did you bring their car?"

"I brought it—just a minute. You can have them in just a minute." I was still blind angry. "Old, young, men, women, we've seen too many of their kind. I just want to say it once." I looked directly at her. "How much have you driven?"

For a moment it didn't take; then she understood.

"Five years."

"Not years. Miles."

"Why—I guess—I don't know. Five years."

"Five thousand a year? Ten thousand? That would be plenty; you haven't driven that much. Five years times ten is fifty thousand. That's six to eight months' work for those guys down there. *You had no room!*" I bit it out at her. She just looked confused, and I felt weak. "I'm ready to leave it now," I told Singleton. "I should have known. Remember, we've got a friend down there."

"I've got two."

He looked different than ever before. He sat slouched on the bed and leaned forward a little. His hands were in his lap, and the lines and creases in his face were shadowed in the half-light from the floor lamp.

"Who was he?" I asked.

He looked at me. I realized with a shock that he had been

fighting back tears, but his eyes were gray and clear as always. The silver hair that had been crossed with dark streaks as long as I had known him now seemed a dull gray. The hands in his lap were steady. He reached into a pocket.

"Get coffee." He looked at the girls. "Get two apiece for everybody."

"Who was it, Singleton?"

"Get the coffee. We'll talk later." He looked at the girl who was curled up. "She's not good."

"Shock?"

"Real light. If it was going to get worse, I think it would have. Maybe you'd better bring June." He got up again and tried to straighten the curled-up girl. He asked her to turn on her back. She looked OK. She tried to fight him. "Help him," I told the one who had been bawling.

The restaurant was better than a hundred yards off. A hillbilly voice was deviling a truck song. June was in the kitchen. I told her I needed help, and she came right away. Business is one thing, people are another. She has always been that way. She brought a Silex with her, and we walked back across the lot. In the distance there was the sound of two sirens crossing against each other.

"The other police car."

"That and a fire truck," she told me.

June is a fine woman, once very pretty but now careless of her appearance and too heavy. It is always sad and a little strange to see a nice-looking woman allow herself to slide. There must be reasons, but not the kind that bear thinking about. She had a good hand with people, a good way. She ran a straight business. When we came to the room, she asked us to leave and started mothering the girls. We went outside with the coffee and sat on the step.

"I'm sorry," I told him. "I shouldn't have blown up, but for a minute I could have killed them. I hate every fool like them."

"It's their road too."

"I know."

"Everybody makes mistakes. You—me—nobody has perfect judgment."

"But not like that."

"No. No, we're not like that, but she won't ever be again either. She has to live with that."

I understood a little more about him. He was good in his judgments. It was suddenly not a matter for us to forgive. There was the law. It had nothing to do with us.

We sat listening to the muffled sounds from the room behind us. Soon, off at the downhill corner of the lot, headlights appeared coming from the wreck. The state car cruised across the lot. It stopped at the end of the motel row. Singleton stood up and motioned to him. The car moved toward us, rolling in gently. The cop got out. Manny was sitting in the back seat. He was slumped over and quiet. When the cop slammed the door, he did not look up.

He was an older cop, too old to be riding a cruiser. In the darkness and excitement there had been no way to tell much about him. He was tired and walked to us unofficially. We made room for him on the step. He sat between us, letdown, his hands shaking with either fatigue or nervousness.

"Charles," he said to Singleton, "who was he?"

"You'd better have some coffee," Singleton told him. He reached over and put his hand on the cop's shoulder. I poured coffee from the Silex, and he drank it fast.

"Gates," said Singleton. "Island Oil. When Haber went broke, I pulled tanks for two years." He stopped as if reflecting. "He was pretty good. I broke him in."

The cop pointed to the car. "Him?"

"Manley, Johnny Manley."

"You're taking him in," I said. "What's the charge?"

"I don't know," the cop told me. "I wouldn't even know what would stick. His rig's half in one lane. If you're going to say I need a charge, then I'll take him in for obstructing the road."

"I didn't mean that. I'm not trying to push you. I just wanted to see how you felt."

"Then ask straight out. I don't know what I think myself till I get the whole story."

Singleton walked to the car. He leaned through the window to call softly to Manny. Manny did not move, and Singleton leaned against the car for a little while as the cop and I sat and watched. A couple of drivers came by, curious but respectfully silent, and the cop ran them off. June came out with a chair and sat beside the steps. The two girls came out and stood quietly. I looked at them. They were both young, pretty, and in the present circumstances useless and destructively ignorant. I could no longer hate them.

"Is that him?" one of them whispered.

"Yes." I felt like whispering myself. It seemed wrong to be talking about him when he was no more than ten yards off, but I doubted that he was listening to anyone. He was looking down, his face, which was never very good-looking, was drawn tight around his fixed eyes, and his hands were not visible. Perhaps he held them in his lap.

"They can't prove nothing," the cop said. "I bet he gets off." He stood up. "Let's get it over with; we've wasted time."

Singleton came back then. "Tell me," the cop said to him.

"He won't be driving again. I don't know what the law will do, but I know what Manny can't do. He won't take another one out. You can take her statement on the accident"—he pointed at one of the girls—"and his"—he pointed at me. "I was just over the crest—couldn't see it very well. What I can tell you about is afterward, but"—he turned to the girls—"I want to tell you something first maybe you ought to know. I've known that man yonder seven, eight years. He's a quiet guy. Doesn't say much; really not hard to get to know. He likes people, has patience with them. Sometimes you think he'd be more sociable if he just knew how to start." He hesitated as if searching for words.

"I don't know exactly how to tell it. Instead of talking, he does nice things. Always has extra equipment to spare if the scales are open and the ICC's checking, or maybe puts a bag of apples in your cab before you leave out. Kid stuff—yes, that's it, kid stuff a lot of the time. Sometimes guys don't understand and joke him.

"When he finally got married, it was to a girl who started the whole thing, not him. She was wild. Silly, you know, not especially bad but not the best either. She worked at a stop in Tennessee and quit work after she married instead of going back like she planned. The guy has something. He did good for that girl. I don't know what's going to happen to them now, and it's none of our business I guess, but I just thought you ought to know."

He turned back to the cop. "I came over the crest and saw Manny's and Arnie's stoplights and saw Arnie's trailer jump and pitch sideways till he corrected and got it stopped. I pulled in behind them, and they were both already out and running. Before I got there, I saw the fire. He could tell you more about how it started." He looked at me. I was thinking about it. I nodded for him to go on because it was very real to me, still happening. I wondered if maybe I could get out of having to describe it. I knew there would have to be a corroborative statement, so as Singleton told it I thought along with him.

He did a good job of the telling. He had gotten there only a minute or so after Manny and I were on the scene. Manny jumped from his cab, dodged around the car with the girls in it, and ran to the wreck. I took only enough time to grab my extinguisher. When I got there, Manny was on top of the wreck trying to pull Gates out and holding the door up at the same time.

The tanker had gone in hitting the ditch fast but stretching out the way you want to try to hit a ditch. It had made no motion to jackknife. The ditch had been too deep, and instead it had lain over on its side. All along there—for that matter, all through those hills—the roadside is usually an outcropping of limestone, slate, and coal. In the cuts and even in the valleys there is rock. Until the truck was pulled off, there would be no way to know. It was likely that the tank and maybe his saddle tank had been opened up on an outcrop of rock. There was a little flicker of fire forward of the cab. Gasoline, I had thought, but it did not grow quick like gasoline. The diesel from his tank was running down the ditch and muffled it some at first.

I went for it with the extinguisher, but it was growing and the extinguisher was a popgun. Manny started yelling to come help him, and I whirled and climbed up over the jutting wheel. Singleton was suddenly there, grabbing me, boosting me up. I took the cab door and held it up, and Gates started to yell.

Manny had him under the shoulders pulling hard, had him about halfway out, but he was hung up. I believe Gates's leg was pinched or held by the wheel. Otherwise Manny would not have gotten him out that far. Manny knew though. He knelt down beside him staring into the wrecked cab.

The fire was getting big behind me, building with a roar.

It was flowing down the ditch but gaining backward over the surface rapidly. I gave Manny a little shove and closed the door over Gates's head so we could both reach him through the window. He was a small chunky man—hard to grasp. We got him under the arms and pulled hard, and he screamed again. The heat was close now. I was terrified, confused. We could not pull harder. There was no way to get him out.

Then I was suddenly alone. Manny jumped down, stumbling against Singleton, who tried to climb up and was driven back, his face lined and desperate in the fire glow. Manny disappeared running into the darkness. Where I was above the cab, the air was getting unbearably hot. The fire had not yet worked in under the wreck. I tugged hopelessly until I could no longer bear the heat and jumped down and rolled away. Singleton helped me up and pulled me back just as the screams changed from hurt to fear; high weeping, desperate and unbelieving cries as the heat but not the fire got to him.

I was held in horrified disbelief of what was happening. Outside the cab and in front of it were heavy oil flames. Gates, his head and neck and one hand outside the window, was leaning back away from them, screaming another kind of cry because the fire that had been getting close had arrived. The muscles of his neck and face were cast bronze in the fire glow, and his mouth was a wide black circle issuing cries. His eyes were closed tight, and his straining hand tried to pull himself away.

Then there was a noise, and he fell back and disappeared into the fire, quietly sinking to cremation with no further sound, and we turned to look behind us. Manny was standing helplessly, his pistol dropping from his shaking hand to the ground, and then he too was falling to the ground, covering his eyes with his hands and rolling on his side away from us.

"If I'd known, I wouldn't have stopped him," Singleton told the cop. "Of all the men I know, he's the only one who could have done that much."

He hestitated, running his hand through his graying hair. "I didn't help, you understand—didn't help." He looked pleading. "Nothing I could do, no use—Arn didn't help. Only Manny."

The girls and June were sobbing. The sky to the eastward was coming alive with light. The cop who was too old to be riding a cruiser looked blanched and even older in the beginning dawn. I felt as I had once felt at sea after battling an all-night storm. Only Singleton seemed capable of further speech, his almost ancient features passive but alive.

He looked at the patrol car where Manny still slumped. "They can't prove he killed a man. There's nothing to prove it with. They can't even prove the bullet didn't miss, and in a way that's the worst thing that can happen. You see, I know him. You think maybe he'll change after a while—maybe it will dull down and let him live normal. It won't. I sat with him before you came and did what I could, and it was nothing. Do they electrocute in this state or use gas? If they were kind, the way he is kind, they'd do one or the other."

JACK CADY knows well the ways of truckers, for he has been a truck driver himself over many years, operating his own rig out of Louisville, Kentucky. He was born in Columbus, Ohio, in 1932, worked in his family's auctioneering business as a boy in Louisville, served four years in the U.S. Coast Guard, and worked for a time in the Social Security Administration. He graduated from the University of Louisville in 1961 with a B.S. in sociology.

Lawrence Sargent Hall

How would you try to save yourself if you were trapped on a rock in the ocean and the tide began to rise?

Would dying on Christmas Day be any more significant than dying on some other day?

Observe a fisherman whose life hangs in the balance as he stands on

THE LEDGE

On Christmas morning before sunup the fisherman embraced his warm wife and left his close bed. She did not want him to go. It was Christmas morning. He was a big, raw man, with too much strength, whose delight in winter was to hunt the sea ducks that flew in to feed by the outer ledges, bare at low tide.

As his bare feet touched the cold floor and the frosty air struck his nude flesh, he might have changed his mind in the dark of this special day. It was a home day, which made it seem natural to think of the outer ledges merely as some place he had shot ducks in the past. But he had promised his son, thirteen, and his nephew, fifteen, who came from inland. That was why he had given them his present of an automatic shotgun each the night before, on Christmas Eve. Rough man though he was known to be, and no spoiler of boys, he kept his promises when he understood what they meant. And to the boys, as to him, home meant where you came for rest after you had your Christmas fill of action and excitement.

His legs astride, his arms raised, the fisherman stretched as high as he could in the dim privacy of his bedroom. Above the snug murmer of his wife's protest he heard the wind in the pines and knew it was easterly as the boys had hoped and he had surmised the night before. Conditions would be ideal, and when they were, anybody ought to take advantage of them. The birds would be flying. The boys would get a man's sport their first time outside on the ledges.

His son at thirteen, small but steady and experienced, was fierce to grow up in hunting, to graduate from sheltered waters and the blinds along the shores of the inner bay. His nephew at fifteen, an overgrown farm boy, had a farm boy's love of the sea, though he could not swim a stroke and was often sick in choppy weather. That was the reason his father, the fisherman's brother, was a farmer and chose to sleep in on the holiday morning at his brother's house. Many of the ones the farmer had grown up with were regularly seasick and could not swim, but they were unafraid of the water. They could not have dreamed of being anything but fishermen. The fisherman himself could swim like a seal and was never sick, and he would sooner die than be anything else.

He dressed in the cold and dark, and woke the boys gruffly. They tumbled out of bed, their instincts instantly awake while their thoughts still fumbled slumbrously. The fisherman's wife in the adjacent bedroom heard them apparently trying to find their clothes, mumbling sleepily and happily to each other, while her husband went down to the hot kitchen to fry eggs— sunny-side up, she knew, because that was how they all liked them.

Always in winter she hated to have them go outside, the weather was so treacherous and there were so few others out in case of trouble. To the fisherman these were no more than woman's fears, to be taken for granted and laughed off. When they were first married, they fought miserably every fall because she was after him constantly to put his boat up until spring. The fishing was all outside in winter, and though prices were high the storms made the rate of attrition high on gear. Nevertheless he did well. So she could do nothing with him.

People thought him a hard man, and gave him the reputation of being all out for himself because he was inclined to brag and be disdainful. If it was true, and his own brother was one of those who strongly felt it was, they lived better than others, and his brother had small right to criticize. There had been times when in her loneliness she had yearned to leave him for another man. But it would have been dangerous. So over the years she had learned to shut her mind to his hard-driving, and take what comfort she might from his unsympathetic competence. Only once or twice, perhaps, had she gone so far as to dwell guiltily on what it would be like to be a widow.

The thought that her boy, possibly because he was small, would not be insensitive like his father, and the rattle of dishes and smell of frying bacon downstairs in the kitchen shut off from the rest of the chilly house, restored the cozy feeling she had had before she was alone in bed. She heard them after a while go out and shut the back door.

Under her window she heard the snow grind drily beneath their boots, and her husband's sharp, exasperated commands to the boys. She shivered slightly in the envelope of her own warmth. She listened to the noise of her son and nephew talking elatedly. Twice she caught the glimmer of their lights on the white ceiling above the window as they went down the path to the shore. There would be frost on the skiff and freezing suds at the water's edge. She herself used to go gunning when she was younger; now, it seemed to her, anyone going out like that on Christmas morning had to be incurably male. They would none of them think about her until they returned and piled the birds they had shot on top of the sink for her to dress.

Ripping into the quiet pre-dawn cold she heard the hot snarl of the outboard taking them out to the boat. It died as abruptly as it had burst into life. Two or three or four or five minutes later the big engine broke into a warm reassuring roar. He had the best of equipment, and he kept it in the best of condition. She closed her eyes. It would not be too long before the others would be up for Christmas. The summer drone of the exhaust deepened. Then gradually it faded in the wind until it was lost at sea, or she slept.

The engine had started immediately in spite of the temperature. This put the fisherman in a good mood. He was proud of his boat. Together he and the two boys heaved the skiff and outboard onto the stern and secured it athwartships. His son went forward along the deck, iridescent in the ray of the light the nephew shone through the windshield, and cast the mooring pennant loose into darkness. The fisherman swung to starboard, glanced at his compass, and headed seaward down the obscure bay.

There would be just enough visibility by the time they reached the headland to navigate the crooked channel between the islands. It was the only nasty stretch of water. The fisherman had done it often in fog or at night—he always swore he could go anywhere in the bay blindfolded—but there was no sense in taking chances if you didn't have to. From the mouth of the channel he could lay a straight course for Brown Cow Island, anchor the boat out of sight behind it, and from the skiff set their tollers off Devil's Hump three hundred yards to seaward. By then the tide would be clearing the ledge and they could land and be ready to shoot around half-tide.

It was early, it was Christmas, and it was farther out than most hunters cared to go in this season of the closing year, so that he felt sure no one would be taking possession ahead of them. He had shot thousands of ducks there in his day. The Hump was by far the best hunting. Only thing was you had to plan for the right conditions because you didn't have too much time. About four hours was all, and you had to get it before three in the afternoon when the birds left and went out to sea ahead of nightfall.

They had it figured exactly right for today. The ledge would not be going under until after the gunning was over, and they would be home for supper in good season. With a little luck the boys would have a skiff-load of birds to show for their first time outside. Well beyond the legal limit, which was no matter. You took what you could get in this life, or the next man made out and you didn't.

The fisherman had never failed to make out gunning from Devil's Hump. And this trip, he had a hunch, would be above the ordinary. The westerly wind would come up just stiff enough, the tide was right, and it was going to storm by tomorrow morning so the birds would be moving. Things were perfect.

The old fierceness was in his bones. Keeping a weather eye to the murk out front and a hand on the wheel, he reached over and cuffed both boys playfully as they stood together close to the heat of the exhaust pipe running up through the center of the house. They poked back at him and shouted above the drumming engine, making bets as they always did on who would shoot the most birds. This trip they had the thrill of new guns, the best money could buy, and a man's hunting ground. The black retriever wagged at them and barked. He was too old and arthritic to be allowed in December water, but he was jaunty anyway at being brought along.

Groping in his pocket for his pipe, the fisherman suddenly had his high spirits rocked by the discovery that he had left his tobacco at home. He swore. Anticipation of a day out with nothing to smoke made him incredulous. He searched his clothes, and then he searched them again, unable to believe the tobacco was not somewhere. When the boys inquired what was wrong he spoke angrily to them, blaming them for being in some devious way at fault. They were instantly crestfallen and willing to put back after the tobacco, though they could appreciate what it meant only through his irritation. But he bitterly refused. That would throw everything out of phase. He was a man who did things the way he set out to do.

He clamped his pipe between his teeth, and twice more during the next few minutes he ransacked his clothes in disbelief. He was no stoic. For one relaxed moment he considered putting about gunning somewhere nearer home. Instead he held his course and sucked the empty pipe, consoling himself with the reflection that at least he had whiskey enough if it got too uncomfortable on the ledge. Peremptorily he made the boys check to make certain the bottle was really in the knapsack with the lunches where he thought he had taken care to put it. When they reassured him, he despised his fate a little less.

The fisherman's judgment was as usual accurate. By the time they were abreast of the headland there was sufficient light so that he could wind his way among the reefs without slackening speed. At last he turned his bow toward open ocean, and as the winter dawn filtered upward through long layers of smoky cloud on the eastern rim his spirits rose again with it.

He opened the throttle, steadied on his course, and settled down to the two-hour run. The wind was stronger but seemed less cold coming from the sea. The boys had withdrawn from the fisherman and were talking together while they watched the sky through the windows. The boat churned solidly through a light chop, flinging spray off her flaring bow. Astern the headland thinned rapidly till it lay like a blackened sill on the grey water. No other boats were aboard.

The boys fondled their new guns, sighted along the barrels, worked the mechanisms, compared notes, boasted, and gave each other contradictory advice. The fisherman got their attention once and pointed at the horizon. They peered through the windows and saw what looked like a black scum floating on top of gently agitated water. It wheeled and tilted, rippled, curled, then rose, strung itself out and became a huge raft of ducks escaping over the sea. A good sign.

The boys rushed out and leaned over the washboards in the wind and spray to see the flock curl below the horizon. Then they went and hovered around the hot engine, bewailing their lot. If only they had been already out and waiting. Maybe these ducks would be crazy enough to return later and be slaughtered. Ducks were known to be foolish.

In due course and right on schedule they anchored at mid-morning in the lee of Brown Cow Island. They put the skiff overboard and loaded it with guns, knapsacks, and tollers. The boys showed their eagerness by being clumsy. The fisherman showed his in bad temper and abuse which they silently accepted in the absorbed tolerance of being boys. No doubt they laid it to lack of tobacco.

By outboard they rounded the island and pointed due east in the direction of a ridge of foam which could be seen whitening the surface three hundred yards away. They set the decoys in a broad, straddling vee opening wide into the ocean. The fisherman warned them not to get their hands wet, and when they did he made them carry on with red and painful fingers, in order to teach them. Once they got their numbed fingers inside their oilskins and hugged their warm crotches. In the meantime the fisherman had turned the skiff toward the patch of foam where as if by magic, like a black glossy rib of earth, the ledge had broken through the belly of the sea.

Carefully they inhabited their slippery nub of the North American continent, while the unresting Atlantic swelled and swirled as it had for eons round the indomitable edges. They hauled the skiff after them, established themselves as comfortably as they could in a shallow sump on top, lay on their sides a foot or so above the water, and waited, guns in hand.

In time the fisherman took a thermos bottle from the knapsack and they drank steaming coffee, and waited for the nodding decoys to lure in the first flight to the rock. Eventually the boys got hungry and restless. The fisherman let them open the picnic lunch and eat one sandwich apiece, which they both shared with the dog. Having no tobacco the fisherman himself would not eat.

Actually the day was relatively mild, and they were warm enough at present in their woollen clothes and socks underneath oilskins and hip boots. After a while, however, the boys began to feel cramped. Their nerves were agonized by inactivity. The nephew complained and was severely told by the fisherman—who pointed to the dog, crouched unmoving except for his white-rimmed eyes—that part of doing a man's hunting was learning how to wait. But he was beginning to have misgivings of his own. This could be one of those days where all the right conditions masked an incalculable flaw.

If the fisherman had been alone, as he often was, stopping off when the necessary coincidence of tide and time occurred on his way home from hauling trawls, and had plenty of tobacco, he would not have fidgeted. The boys' being nervous made him nervous. He growled at them again. When it came it was likely to come all at once, and then in a few moments be over. He warned them not to slack off, never to slack off, to be always ready. Under his rebuke they kept their tortured peace, though they could not help shifting and twisting until he lost what patience he had left and bullied them into lying still. A duck could see an eyelid twitch. If the dog could go without moving so could they.

"Here it comes!" the fisherman said tersely at last.

The boys quivered with quick relief. The flock came in downwind, quartering slightly, myriad, black, and swift.

"Beautiful—" breathed the fisherman's son.

"All right," said the fisherman, intense and precise. "Aim at singles in the thickest part of the flock. Wait for me to fire and then don't stop shooting till your gun's empty." He rolled up onto his left elbow and spread his legs to brace himself. The flock bore down, arrowy and vibrant, then a hundred yards beyond the decoys it veered off.

"They're going away!" the boys cried, sighting in.

"Not yet!" snapped the fisherman. "They're coming round."

The flock changed shape, folded over itself, and drove into the wind in a tight arc. "Thousands—" the boys hissed through their teeth. All at once a whistling storm of black and white broke over the decoys.

"Now!" the fisherman shouted. "Perfect!" And he opened fire at the flock just as it hung suspended in momentary chaos above the tollers. The three pulled at their triggers and the birds splashed into the water, until the last report went off unheard, the last smoking shell flew unheeded over their shoulders, and the last of the routed flock scattered diminishing, diminishing in every direction.

Exultantly the boys dropped their guns, jumped up and scrambled for the skiff.

"I'll handle that skiff!" the fisherman shouted at them. They stopped. Gripping the painter and balancing himself he eased the skiff into the water stern first and held the bow hard against the side of the rock shelf the skiff had rested on. "You stay here," he said to his nephew. "No sense in all three of us going in, the boat."

The boy on the reef gazed at the grey water rising and falling hypnotically along the glistening edge. It had dropped about a foot since their arrival. "I want to go with you," he said in a sullen tone, his eyes on the streaming eddies.

"You want to do what I tell you if you want to gun with me," answered the fisherman harshly. The boy couldn't swim, and he wasn't going to have him climbing in and out of the skiff any more than necessary. Besides, he was too big.

The fisherman took his son in the skiff and cruised round

and round among the decoys picking up dead birds. Meanwhile the other boy stared unmoving after them from the highest part of the ledge. Before they had quite finished gathering the dead birds, the fisherman cut the outboard and dropped to his knees in the skiff. "Down!" he yelled. "Get down!" About a dozen birds came tolling in. "Shoot—shoot!" his son hollered from the bottom of the boat to the boy on the ledge.

The dog, who had been running back and forth whining, sank to his belly, his muzzle on his forepaws. But the boy on the ledge never stirred. The ducks took late alarm at the skiff, swerved aside and into the air, passing with a whirr no more than fifty feet over the head of the boy, who remained on the ledge like a statue, without his gun, watching the two crouching in the boat.

The fisherman's son climbed onto the ledge and held the painter. The bottom of the skiff was covered with feathery black and white bodies with feet upturned and necks lolling. He was jubilant. "We got twenty-seven!" he told his cousin. "How's that? Nine apiece. Boy—" he added, "what a cool Christmas!"

The fisherman pulled the skiff onto its shelf and all three went and lay down again in anticipation of the next flight. The son, reloading, patted his gun affectionately. "I'm going to get me ten next time," he said. Then he asked his cousin, "Whatsamatter —didn't you see the strays?"

"Yeah," the boy said.

"How come you didn't shoot at 'em?"

"Didn't feel like it," replied the boy, still with a trace of sullenness.

"You stupid or something?" The fisherman's son was astounded. "What a highlander!" But the fisherman, though he said nothing, knew that the older boy had had an attack of ledge fever.

"Cripes!" his son kept at it. "I'd at least of tried."

"Shut up," the fisherman finally told him, "and leave him be."

At slack water three more flocks came in, one right after the other, and when it was over, the skiff was half full of clean, dead birds. During the subsequent lull they broke out the lunch and ate it all and finished the hot coffee. For a while the fisherman sucked away on his cold pipe. Then he had himself a swig of whiskey.

The boys passed the time contentedly jabbering about who shot the most—there were ninety-two all told—which of their friends they would show the biggest ones to, how many each could eat at a meal provided they didn't have to eat any vegetables. Now and then they heard sporadic distant gunfire on the mainland, at its nearest point about two miles to the north. Once far off they saw a fishing boat making in the direction of home.

At length the fisherman got a hand inside his oilskins and produced his watch.

"Do we have to go now?" asked his son.

"Not just yet," he replied. "Pretty soon." Everything had been perfect. As good as he had ever had it. Because he was getting tired of the boys' chatter he got up, heavily in his hip boots, and stretched. The tide had turned and was coming in, the sky was more ashen, and the wind had freshened enough so that whitecaps were beginning to blossom. It would be a good hour before they had to leave the ledge and pick up the tollers. However, he guessed they would leave a little early. On account of the rising wind he doubted there would be much more shooting. He stepped carefully along the back of the ledge, to work his kinks out. It was also getting a little colder.

The whiskey had begun to warm him, but he was unprepared for the sudden blaze that flashed upward inside him from belly to head. He was standing at the shelf where the skiff was. Only the foolish skiff was not there!

For the second time that day the fisherman felt the deep vacuity of disbelief. He gaped, seeing nothing but the flat shelf of rock. He whirled, started toward the boys, slipped, recovered himself, fetched a complete circle, and stared at the unimaginably empty shelf. Its emptiness made him feel as if everything he had done that day so far, his life so far, he had dreamed. What could have happened? The tide was still nearly a foot below. There had been no sea to speak of. The skiff could hardly have slid off by itself. For the life of him, consciously careful as he inveterately was, he could not now remember hauling it up the last time. Perhaps in the heat of hunting, he had left it to the boy. Perhaps he could not remember which was the last time.

"Christ—" he exclaimed loudly, without realizing it because he was so entranced by the invisible event.

"What's wrong, Dad?" asked his son, getting to his feet.

The fisherman went blind with uncontainable rage. "Get back down there where you belong!" he screamed. He scarcely noticed the boy sink back in amazement. In a frenzy he ran along the ledge thinking the skiff might have been drawn up at another place, though he knew better. There was no other place.

He stumbled, half falling, back to the boys who were gawking at him in consternation, as though he had gone insane. "God damn it!" he yelled savagely, grabbing both of them and yanking them to their knees. "Get on your feet!"

"What's wrong?" his son repeated in a stifled voice.

"Never mind what's wrong," he snarled. "Look for the skiff—it's adrift!" When they peered around he gripped their shoulders, brutally facing them about. "Downwind—" He slammed his fist against his thigh. "Jesus!" he cried, struck to madness by their stupidity.

At last he sighted the skiff himself, magically bobbing along the grim sea like a toller, a quarter of a mile to leeward on a direct course for home. The impulse to strip himself naked was succeeded instantly by a queer calm. He simply sat down on the ledge and forgot everything except the marvelous mystery.

As his awareness partially returned he glanced toward the boys. They were still observing the skiff speechlessly. Then he was gazing into the clear young eyes of his son.

"Dad," asked the boy steadily, "what do we do now?"

That brought the fisherman upright. "The first thing we have to do," he heard himself saying with infinite tenderness as if he were making love, "is think."

"Could you swim it?" asked his son.

He shook his head and smiled at them. They smiled quickly back, too quickly. "A hundred yards maybe, in this water. I wish I could," he added. It was the most intimate and pitiful thing he had ever said. He walked in circles round them, trying to break the stall his mind was left in.

He gauged the level of the water. To the eye it was quite stationary, six inches from the shelf at this second. The fisherman did not have to mark it on the side of the rock against the passing of time to prove to his reason that it was rising, always rising. Already it was over the brink of reason, beyond the margins of thought—a senseless measurement. No sense to it.

All his life the fisherman had tried to lick the element of

time, by getting up earlier and going to bed later, owning a faster boat, planning more than the day would hold, and tackling just one other job before the deadline fell. If, as on rare occasions he had the grand illusion, he ever really had beaten the game, he would need to call on all his reserves of practice and cunning now.

He sized up the scant but unforgivable three hundred yards to Brown Cow Island. Another hundred yards behind it his boat rode at anchor, where, had he been aboard, he could have cut in a fathometer to plumb the profound and occult seas, or a ship-to-shore radio on which in an interminably short time he would have heard his wife's voice talking to him over the air about homecoming.

"Couldn't we wave something so somebody would see us?" his nephew suggested.

The fisherman spun around. "Load your guns!" he ordered. They loaded as if the air had suddenly gone frantic with birds. "I'll fire once and count to five. Then you fire. Count to five. That way they won't just think it's only somebody gunning ducks. We'll keep doing that."

"We've only got just two-and-a-half boxes left," said his son.

The fisherman nodded, understanding that from beginning to end their situation was purely mathematical, like the ticking of the alarm clock in his silent bedroom. Then he fired. The dog, who had been keeping watch over the decoys, leaped forward and yelped in confusion. They all counted off, fired the first five rounds by threes, and reloaded. The fisherman scanned first the horizon, then the contracting borders of the ledge, which was the sole place the water appeared to be climbing. Soon it would be over the shelf.

They counted off and fired the second five rounds. "We'll hold off a while on the last one," the fisherman told the boys. He sat down and pondered what a trivial thing was a skiff. This one he and the boy had knocked together in a day. Was a gun, manufactured for killing.

His son tallied up the remaining shells, grouping them symmetrically in threes on the rock when the wet box fell apart. "Two short," he announced. They reloaded and laid the guns on their knees.

Behind thickening clouds they could not see the sun going

down. The water, coming up, was growing blacker. The fisherman thought he might have told his wife they would be home before dark since it was Christmas day. He realized he had forgotten about its being any particular day. The tide would not be high until two hours after sunset. When they did not get in by nightfall, and could not be raised by radio, she might send somebody to hunt for them right away. He rejected this arithmetic immediately, with a sickening shock, recollecting it was a two-and-a-half hour run at best. Then it occurred to him that she might send somebody on the mainland who was nearer. She would think he had engine trouble.

He rose and searched the shoreline, barely visible. Then his glance dropped to the toy shoreline at the edges of the reef. The shrinking ledge, so sinister from a boat, grew dearer minute by minute as though the whole wide world he gazed on from horizon to horizon balanced on its contracting rim. He checked the water level and found the shelf awash.

Some of what went through his mind the fisherman told to the boys. They accepted it without comment. If he caught their eyes they looked away to spare him or because they were not yet old enough to face what they saw. Mostly they watched the rising water. The fisherman was unable to initiate a word of encouragement. He wanted one of them to ask him whether somebody would reach them ahead of the tide. He would have found it possible to say. But they did not inquire.

The fisherman was not sure how much, at their age, they were able to imagine. Both of them had seen from the docks drowned bodies put ashore out of boats. Sometimes they grasped things, and sometimes not. He supposed they might be longing for the comfort of their mothers, and was astonished, as much as he was capable of any astonishment except the supreme one, to discover himself wishing he had not left his wife's dark, close, naked bed that morning.

"Is it time to shoot now?" asked his nephew.

"Pretty soon," he said, as if he were putting off making good on a promise. "Not yet."

His own boy cried softly for a brief moment, like a man, his face averted in an effort neither to give nor show pain.

"Before school starts," the fisherman said, wonderfully

detached, "we'll go to town and I'll buy you boys anything you want."

With great difficulty, in a dull tone as though he did not in the least desire it, his son said after a pause, "I'd like one of those new thirty-horse outboards."

"All right," said the fisherman. And to his nephew, "How about you?"

The nephew shook his head desolately. "I don't want anything," he said.

After another pause the fisherman's son said, "Yes he does, Dad. He wants one too."

"All right—" the fisherman said again, and said no more.

The dog whined in uncertainty and licked the boys' faces where they sat together. Each threw an arm over his back and hugged him. Three strays flew in and sat companionably down among the stiff-necked decoys. The dog crouched, obedient to his training. The boys observed them listlessly. Presently, sensing something untoward, the ducks took off, splashing the wave tops with feet and wingtips, into the dusky waste.

The sea began to make up in the mountain wind, and the wind bore a new and deadly chill. The fisherman, scouring the somber, dwindling shadow of the mainland for a sign, hoped it would not snow. But it did. First a few flakes, then a flurry, then storming past horizontally. The fisherman took one long, bewildered look at Brown Cow Island three hundred yards dead to leeward, and got to his feet.

Then it shut in, as if what was happening on the ledge was too private even for the last wan light of the expiring day.

"Last round," the fisherman said austerely.

The boys rose and shouldered their tacit guns. The fisherman fired into the flying snow. He counted methodically to five. His son fired and counted. His nephew. All three fired and counted. Four rounds.

"You've got one left, Dad," his son said.

The fisherman hesitated another second, then he fired the final shell. Its pathetic report, like the spat of a popgun, whipped away on the wind and was instantly blanketed in falling snow.

Night fell all in a moment to meet the ascending sea. They were now barely able to make one another out through driving snowflakes, dim as ghosts in their yellow oilskins. The fisherman heard a sea break and glanced down where his feet were. They seemed to be wound in a snowy sheet. Gently he took the boys by the shoulders and pushed them in front of him, feeling with his feet along the shallow sump to the place where it triangulated into a sharp crevice at the highest point of the ledge. "Face ahead," he told them. "Put the guns down."

"I'd like to hold mine, Dad," begged his son.

"Put it down," said the fisherman. "The tide won't hurt it. Now brace your feet against both sides and stay there."

They felt the dog, who was pitch black, running up and down in perplexity between their straddled legs. "Dad," said his son, "what about the pooch?"

If he had called the dog by name it would have been too personal. The fisherman would have wept. As it was he had all he could do to keep from laughing. He bent his knees, and when he touched the dog hoisted him under one arm. The dog's belly was soaking wet.

So they waited, marooned in their consciousness, surrounded by a monstrous tidal space which was slowly, slowly closing them out. In this space the periwinkle beneath the fisherman's boots was king. While hovering airborne in his mind he had an inward glimpse of his house as curiously separate, like a June mirage.

Snow, rocks, seas, wind the fisherman had lived by all his life. Now he thought he had never comprehended what they were, and he hated them. Though they had not changed. He was deadly chilled. He set out to ask the boys if they were cold. There was no sense. He thought of the whiskey, and sidled backward, still holding the awkward dog, till he located the bottle under water with his toe. He picked it up squeamishly as though afraid of getting his sleeve wet, worked his way forward and bent over his son. "Drink it," he said, holding the bottle against the boy's ribs. The boy tipped his head back, drank, coughed hotly, then vomited.

"I can't," he told his father wretchedly.

"Try—try—" the fisherman pleaded, as if it meant the difference between life and death.

The boy obediently drank, and again he vomited hotly.

He shook his head against his father's chest and passed the bottle forward to his cousin, who drank and vomited also. Passing the bottle back, the boys dropped it in the frigid water between them.

When the waves reached his knees the fisherman set the warm dog loose and said to his son, "Turn around and get up on my shoulders." The boy obeyed. The fisherman opened his oil-skin jacket and twisted his hands behind him through his suspenders, clamping the boy's booted ankles with his elbows.

"What about the dog?" the boy asked.

"He'll make his own way all right," the fisherman said. "He can take the cold water." His knees were trembling. Every instinct shrieked for gymnastics. He ground his teeth and braced like a colossus against the sides of the submerged crevice.

The dog, having lived faithfully as though one of them for eleven years, swam a few minutes in and out around the fisherman's legs, not knowing what was happening, and left them without a whimper. He would swim and swim at random by himself, round and round in the blinding night, and when he had swum routinely through the paralyzing water all he could, he would simply, in one incomprehensible moment, drown. Almost the fisherman, waiting out infinity, envied him his pattern.

Freezing seas swept by, flooding inexorably up and up as the earth sank away imperceptibly beneath them. The boy called out once to his cousin. There was no answer. The fisherman, marveling on a terror without voice, was dumbly glad when the boy did not call again. His own boots were long full of water. With no sensation left in his straddling legs he dared not move them. So long as the seas came sidewise against his hips, and then sidewise against his shoulders, he might balance—no telling how long. The upper half of him was what felt frozen. His legs, disengaged from his nerves and his will, he came to regard quite scientifically. They were the absurd, precarious axis around which reeled the surged universal tumult. The waves would come on; he could not visualize how many tossing reinforcements lurked in the night beyond—inexhaustible numbers, and he wept in supernatural fury at each because it was higher, till he transcended hate and took them, swaying like a convert, one by one as they lunged against him and away aimlessly into their own undisputed, wild realm.

From his hips upward the fisherman stretched to his utmost as a man does whose spirit reaches out of dead sleep. The boy's head, none too high, must be at least seven feet above the ledge. Though growing larger every minute, it was a small light life. The fisherman meant to hold it there, if need be, through a thousand tides.

By and by the boy, slumped on the head of his father, asked, "Is it over your boots, Dad?"

"Not yet," the fisherman said. Then through his teeth he added, "If I fall—kick your boots off—swim for it—downwind—to the island...."

"You...?" the boy finally asked.

The fisherman nodded against the boy's belly. "—Won't see each other," he said.

The boy did for the fisherman the greatest thing that can be done. He may have been too young for perfect terror, but he was old enough to know there were things beyond the power of any man. All he could do he did, trusting his father to do all he could, and asking nothing more.

The fisherman, rocked to his soul by a sea, held his eyes shut upon the interminable night.

"Is it time now?" the boy said.

The fisherman could hardly speak. "Not yet," he said. "Not just yet...."

As the land mass pivoted toward sunlight the day after Christmas, a tiny fleet of small craft converged off shore like iron filings to a magnet. At daybreak they found the skiff floating unscathed off the headland, half full of ducks and snow. The shooting *had* been good, as someone hearing on the mainland the previous afternoon had supposed. Two hours afterward they found the unharmed boat adrift five miles at sea. At high noon they found the fisherman at ebb tide, his right foot jammed cruelly into a glacial crevice of the ledge beside three shotguns, his hands tangled behind him in his suspenders, and under his right elbow a rubber boot with a sock and a live starfish in it. After dragging unlit depth all day for the boys, they towed the fisherman home in his own boat at sundown, and in the frost of evening, mute with discovering purgatory, laid him on his wharf for his wife to see.

She, somehow, standing on the dock as in her frequent dream, gazing at the fisherman pure as crystal on the icy boards, a small rubber boot still frozen under one clenched arm saw him exaggerated beyond remorse or grief, absolved of his mortality.

LAWRENCE SARGENT HALL, who was born in Haverhill, Massachusetts, in 1915, served in the Navy during World War II. He was educated at Bowdoin College and at Yale and now teaches at Bowdoin, in New Brunswick, Maine.

Flannery O'Connor

Do you think murderers kill in cold blood without any feeling whatsoever for their victims, or do they feel pity but hide it?

Is it possible for a family outing to turn into tragedy and death for no real reason?

In this story a family trip turns sour from the beginning just because

A GOOD MAN IS HARD TO FIND

The grandmother didn't want to go to Florida. She wanted to visit some of her connections in east Tennessee and she was seizing at every chance to change Bailey's mind. Bailey was the son she lived with, her only boy. He was sitting on the edge of his chair at the table, bent over the orange sports section of the *Journal*. "Now look here, Bailey," she said, "see here, read this," and she stood with one hand on her thin hip and the other rattling the newspaper at his bald head. "Here this fellow that calls himself The Misfit is aloose from the Federal Pen and headed toward Florida and you read here what it says he did to these people. Just you read it. I wouldn't take my children in any direction with a criminal like that aloose in it. I couldn't answer to my conscience if I did."

Bailey didn't look up from his reading so she wheeled around then and faced the children's mother, a young woman in slacks, whose face was as broad and innocent as a cabbage and was tied round with a green head-kerchief that had two points on the top like rabbit's ears. She was sitting on the sofa, feeding the baby his apricots out of a jar. "The children have been to Florida before," the old lady said. "You all ought to take them somewhere else for a change so they would see different parts of the world and be broad. They never have been to east Tennessee."

The children's mother didn't seem to hear her but the eight-year-old boy, John Wesley, a stocky child with glasses, said, "If you don't want to go to Florida, why dontcha stay at home?" He and the little girl, June Star, were reading the funny papers on the floor.

"She wouldn't stay at home to be queen for a day," June Star said without raising her yellow head.

"Yes, and what would you do if this fellow, The Misfit, caught you?" the grandmother asked.

"I'd smack his face," John Wesley said.

"She wouldn't stay at home for a million bucks," June Star said. "Afraid she'd miss something. She has to go everywhere we go."

"All right, Miss," the grandmother said. "Just remember that the next time you want me to curl your hair."

June Star said her hair was naturally curly.

The next morning the grandmother was the first one in the car, ready to go. She had her big black valise that looked like the head of a hippopotamus in one corner, and underneath it she was hiding a basket with Pitty Sing, the cat, in it. She didn't intend for the cat to be left alone in the house for three days because he would miss her too much and she was afraid he might brush against one of the gas burners and accidentally asphyxiate himself. Her son, Bailey, didn't like to arrive at a motel with a cat.

She sat in the middle of the back seat with John Wesley and June Star on either side of her. Bailey and the children's mother and the baby sat in front and they left Atlanta at eight forty-five with the mileage on the car at 55890. The grandmother wrote this down because she thought it would be interesting to say how many miles they had been when they got back. It took them twenty minutes to reach the outskirts of the city.

The old lady settled herself comfortably, removing her

white cotton gloves and putting them up with her purse on the shelf in front of the back window. The children's mother still had on slacks and still had her head tied up in a green kerchief, but the grandmother had on a navy blue straw sailor hat with a bunch of white violets on the brim and a navy blue dress with a small white dot in the print. Her collars and cuffs were white organdy trimmed with lace and at her neckline she had pinned a purple spray of cloth violets containing a sachet. In case of an accident, anyone seeing her dead on the highway would know at once that she was a lady.

She said she thought it was going to be a good day for driving, neither too hot nor too cold, and she cautioned Bailey that the speed limit was fifty-five miles an hour and that the patrolmen hid themselves behind billboards and small clumps of trees and sped out after you before you had a chance to slow down. She pointed out interesting details of the scenery: Stone Mountain; the blue granite that in some places came up to both sides of the highway; the brilliant red clay banks slightly streaked with purple; and the various crops that made rows of green lace-work on the ground. The trees were full of silver-white sunlight and the meanest of them sparkled. The children were reading comic magazines and their mother had gone back to sleep.

"Let's go through Georgia fast so we won't have to look at it much," John Wesley said.

"If I were a little boy," said the grandmother, "I wouldn't talk about my native state that way. Tennessee has the mountains and Georgia has the hills."

"Tennessee is just a hillbilly dumping ground," John Wesley said, "and Georgia is a lousy state too."

"You said it," June Star said.

"In my time," said the grandmother, folding her thin veined fingers, "children were more respectful of their native states and their parents and everything else. People did right then. Oh look at the cute little pickaninny!" she said and pointed to a Negro child standing in the door of a shack. "Wouldn't that make a picture, now?" she asked and they all turned and looked at the little Negro out of the back window. He waved.

"He didn't have any britches on," June Star said.

"He probably didn't have any," the grandmother explained. "Little niggers in the country don't have things like we do. If I could paint, I'd paint that picture," she said.

The children exchanged comic books.

The grandmother offered to hold the baby and the children's mother passed him over the front seat to her. She set him on her knee and bounced him and told him about the things they were passing. She rolled her eyes and screwed up her mouth and stuck her leathery thin face into his smooth bland one. Occasionally he gave her a faraway smile. They passed a large cotton field with five or six graves fenced in the middle of it, like a small island. "Look at the graveyard!" the grandmother said, pointing it out. "That was the old family burying ground. That belonged to the plantation."

"Where's the plantation?" John Wesley asked.

"Gone With the Wind," said the grandmother. "Ha. Ha."

When the children finished all the comic books they had brought, they opened the lunch and ate it. The grandmother ate a peanut butter sandwich and an olive and would not let the children throw the box and the paper napkins out the window. When there was nothing else to do they played a game by choosing a cloud and making the other two guess what shape it suggested. John Wesley took one the shape of a cow and June Star guessed a cow and John Wesley said, no, an automobile, and June Star said he didn't play fair, and they began to slap each other over the grandmother.

The grandmother said she would tell them a story if they would keep quiet. When she told a story, she rolled her eyes and waved her head and was very dramatic. She said once when she was a maiden lady she had been courted by a Mr. Edgar Atkins Teagarden from Jasper, Georgia. She said he was a very good-looking man and a gentleman and that he brought her a watermelon every Saturday afternoon with his initials cut in it, E. A. T. Well, one Saturday, she said, Mr. Teagarden brought the watermelon and there was nobody at home and he left it on the front porch and returned in his buggy to Jasper, but she never got the watermelon, she said, because a nigger boy ate it when he saw the initials, E. A. T.! This story tickled John Wesley's funny bone and he giggled and giggled but June Star didn't think it was any good. She said she wouldn't marry a man that just brought her a watermelon on Saturday. The grandmother said she would have done well to marry Mr. Teagarden because he was a gentleman and had bought Coca-Cola stock when it first came out and that he had died only a few years ago, a very wealthy man.

They stopped at The Tower for barbecued sandwiches. The Tower was a part stucco and part wood filling station and dance hall set in a clearing outside of Timothy. A fat man named Red Sammy Butts ran it and there were signs stuck here and there on the building and for miles up and down the highway saying, TRY RED SAMMY'S FAMOUS BARBEQUE. NONE LIKE FAMOUS RED SAMMY'S! RED SAM! THE FAT BOY WITH THE HAPPY LAUGH. A VETERAN! RED SAMMY'S YOUR MAN!

Red Sammy was lying on the bare ground outside The Tower with his head under a truck while a gray monkey about a foot high, chained to a small chinaberry tree, chattered nearby. The monkey sprang back into the tree and got on the highest limb as soon as he saw the children jump out of the car and run toward him.

Inside, The Tower was a long dark room with a counter at one end and tables at the other and dancing space in the middle. They all sat down at a board table next to the nickel-odeon and Red Sam's wife, a tall burnt-brown woman with hair and eyes lighter than her skin, came and took their order. The children's mother put a dime in the machine and played "The Tennessee Waltz," and the grandmother said that tune always made her want to dance. She asked Bailey if he would like to dance but he only glared at her. He didn't have a naturally sunny disposition like she did and trips made him nervous. The grand-mother's brown eyes were very bright. She swayed her head from side to side and pretended she was dancing in her chair. June Star said play something she could tap to so the children's mother put in another dime and played a fast number and June Star stepped out onto the dance floor and did her tap routine.

"Ain't she cute?" Red Sam's wife said, leaning over the counter. "Would you like to come be my little girl?"

"No I certainly wouldn't," June Star said. "I wouldn't live in a broken-down place like this for a million bucks!" and she ran back to the table.

"Ain't she cute?" the woman repeated, stretching her mouth politely.

"Aren't you ashamed?" hissed the grandmother.

Red Sam came in and told his wife to quit lounging on the counter and hurry with these people's order. His khaki trousers reached just to his hip bones and his stomach hung over them like a sack of meal swaying under his shirt. He came over and sat down at a table nearby and let out a combination sigh and yodel. "You can't win," he said. "You can't win," and he wiped his sweating red face off with a gray handkerchief. "These days you don't know who to trust," he said. "Ain't that the truth?"

"People are certainly not nice like they used to be," said the grandmother.

"Two fellers came in here last week," Red Sammy said, "driving a Chrysler. It was a old beat-up car but it was a good one and these boys looked all right to me. Said they worked at the mill and you know I let them fellers charge the gas they bought? Now why did I do that?"

"Because you're a good man!" the grandmother said at once.

"Yes'm, I suppose so," Red Sam said as if he were struck with the answer.

His wife brought the orders, carrying the five plates all at once without a tray, two in each hand and one balanced on her arm. "It isn't a soul in this green world of God's that you can trust," she said. "And I don't count nobody out of that, not nobody," she repeated, looking at Red Sammy.

"Did you read about that criminal, The Misfit, that's escaped?" asked the grandmother.

"I wouldn't be a bit surprised if he didn't attack this place right here," said the woman. "If he hears about it being here, I wouldn't be none surprised to see him. If he hears it's two cent in the cash register, I wouldn't be a tall surprised if he..."

"That'll do," Red Sam said. "Go bring these people their Co'Colas," and the woman went off to get the rest of the order.

"A good man is hard to find," Red Sammy said. "Everything is getting terrible. I remember the day you could go off and leave your screen door unlatched. Not no more."

He and the grandmother discussed better times. The old lady said that in her opinion Europe was entirely to blame for the way things were now. She said the way Europe acted you would think we were made of money and Red Sam said it was no use talking about it, she was exactly right. The children ran outside into the white sunlight and looked at the monkey in the lacy chinaberry tree. He was busy catching fleas on himself and biting each one carefully between his teeth as if it were a delicacy.

They drove off again into the hot afternoon. The grandmother took cat naps and woke up every few minutes with her own snoring. Outside of Toombsboro she woke up and recalled an old plantation that she had visited in this neighborhood once when she was a young lady. She said the house had six white columns across the front and that there was an avenue of oaks leading up to it and two little wooden trellis arbors on either side in front where you sat down with your suitor after a stroll in the garden. She recalled exactly which road to turn off to get to it. She knew that Bailey would not be willing to lose any time looking at an old house, but the more she talked about it, the more she wanted to see it once again and find out if the little twin arbors were still standing. "There was a secret panel in this house," she said craftily, not telling the truth but wishing that she were, "and the story went that all the family silver was hidden in it when Sherman came through but it was never found . . ."

"Hey!" John Wesley said. "Let's go see it! We'll find it! We'll poke all the woodwork and find it! Who lives there? Where do you turn off at? Hey Pop, can't we turn off there?"

"We never have seen a house with a secret panel!" June Star shrieked. "Let's go to the house with the secret panel! Hey Pop, can't we go see the house with the secret panel!"

"It's not far from here, I know," the grandmother said. "It wouldn't take over twenty minutes."

Bailey was looking straight ahead. His jaw was as rigid as a horseshoe. "No," he said.

The children began to yell and scream that they wanted to see the house with the secret panel. John Wesley kicked the back of the front seat and June Star hung over her mother's shoulder and whined desperately into her ear that they never had any fun even on their vacation, that they could never do what THEY wanted to do. The baby began to scream and John Wesley kicked the back of the seat so hard that his father could feel the blows in his kidney.

"All right!" he shouted and drew the car to a stop at the side of the road. "Will you all shut up? Will you all just shut up for one second? If you don't shut up, we won't go anywhere."

"It would be very educational for them," the grandmother murmured.

"All right," Bailey said, "but get this: this is the only time we're going to stop for anything like this. This is the one and only time."

"The dirt road that you have to turn down is about a mile back," the grandmother directed. "I marked it when we passed."

"A dirt road," Bailey groaned.

After they had turned around and were headed toward the dirt road, the grandmother recalled other points about the house, the beautiful glass over the front doorway and the candle-lamp in the hall. John Wesley said that the secret panel was probably in the fireplace.

"You can't go inside this house," Bailey said. "You don't know who lives there."

"While you all talk to the people in front, I'll run around behind and get in a window," John Wesley suggested.

"We'll all stay in the car," his mother said.

They turned onto the dirt road and the car raced roughly along in a swirl of pink dust. The grandmother recalled the times when there were no paved roads and thirty miles was a day's journey. The dirt road was hilly and there were sudden washes in it and sharp curves on dangerous embankments. All at once they would be on a hill, looking down over the blue tops of trees for miles around, then the next minute, they would be in a red depression with the dust-coated trees looking down on them.

"This place had better turn up in a minute," Bailey said, "or I'm going to turn around."

The road looked as if no one had traveled on it in months.

"It's not much farther," the grandmother said and just as she said it, a horrible thought came to her. The thought was so embarrassing that she turned red in the face and her eyes dilated and her feet jumped up, upsetting her valise in the corner. The instant the valise moved, the newspaper top she had over the basket under it rose with a snarl and Pitty Sing, the cat, sprang onto Bailey's shoulder.

The children were thrown to the floor and their mother, clutching the baby, was thrown out the door onto the ground; the old lady was thrown into the front seat. The car turned over once and landed right-side-up in a gulch on the side of the road. Bailey remained in the driver's seat with the cat—gray-striped with a broad white face and an orange nose—clinging to his neck like a caterpillar.

As soon as the children saw they could move their arms and legs, they scrambled out of the car, shouting, "We've had an ACCIDENT!" The grandmother was curled up under the dashboard, hoping she was injured so that Bailey's wrath would not come down on her all at once. The horrible thought she had had before the accident was that the house she had remembered so vividly was not in Georgia but in Tennessee.

Bailey removed the cat from his neck with both hands and flung it out the window against the side of a pine tree. Then he got out of the car and started looking for the children's mother. She was sitting against the side of the red gutted ditch, holding the screaming baby, but she only had a cut down her face and a broken shoulder. "We've had an ACCIDENT!" the children screamed in a frenzy of delight.

"But nobody's killed," June Star said with disappointment as the grandmother limped out of the car, her hat still pinned to her head but the broken brim standing up at a jaunty angle and the violet spray hanging off the side. They all sat down in the ditch, except the children, to recover from the shock. They were all shaking.

"Maybe a car will come along," said the children's mother hoarsely.

"I believe I have an injured organ," said the grandmother, pressing her side, but no one answered her. Bailey's teeth were clattering. He had on a yellow sport shirt with bright blue parrots designed on it and his face was as yellow as the shirt. The grandmother decided that she would not mention that the house was in Tennessee.

The road was about ten feet above and they could see only the tops of the trees on the other side of it. Behind the ditch they were sitting in there were more woods, tall and dark and deep. In a few minutes they saw a car some distance away on top of a hill, coming slowly as if the occupants were watching them. The grandmother stood up and waved both arms dramatically to attract their attention. The car continued to come on slowly, disappeared around a bend and appeared again, moving even slower, on top of the hill they had gone over. It was a big black battered hearse-like automobile. There were three men in it.

It came to a stop just over them and for some minutes, the driver looked down with a steady expressionless gaze to where they were sitting, and didn't speak. Then he turned his head and muttered something to the other two and they got out. One was a fat boy in black trousers and a red sweat shirt with a silver stallion embossed on the front of it. He moved around on the right side of them and stood staring, his mouth partly open in a kind of loose grin. The other had on khaki pants and a blue striped coat and a gray hat pulled down very low, hiding most of his face. He came around slowly on the left side. Neither spoke.

The driver got out of the car and stood by the side of it, looking down at them. He was an older man than the other two. His hair was just beginning to gray and he wore silver-rimmed spectacles that gave him a scholarly look. He had a long creased face and didn't have on any shirt or undershirt. He had on blue jeans that were too tight for him and was holding a black hat and a gun. The two boys also had guns.

"We've had an ACCIDENT!" the children screamed.

The grandmother had the peculiar feeling that the bespectacled man was someone she knew. His face was as familiar to her as if she had known him all her life but she could not recall who he was. He moved away from the car and began to come down the embankment, placing his feet carefully so that he wouldn't slip. He had on tan and white shoes and no socks, and his ankles were red and thin. "Good afternoon," he said. "I see you all had you a little spill."

"We turned over twice!" said the grandmother.

"Oncet," he corrected. "We seen it happen. Try their car and see will it run, Hiram," he said quietly to the boy with the gray hat.

"What you got that gun for?" John Wesley asked. "Whatcha gonna do with that gun?"

"Lady," the man said to the children's mother, "would you mind calling them children to sit down by you? Children make me nervous. I want all you all to sit down right together there where you're at."

"What are you telling US what to do for?" June Star asked.

Behind them the line of woods gaped like a dark open mouth. "Come here," said their mother.

"Look here now," Bailey began suddenly, "we're in a predicament! We're in . . ."

The grandmother shrieked. She scrambled to her feet and stood staring. "You're The Misfit!" she said. "I recognized you at once!"

"Yes'm," the man said, smiling slightly as if he were pleased in spite of himself to be known, "but it would have been better for all of you, lady, if you hadn't of reckernized me."

Bailey turned his head sharply and said something to his mother that shocked even the children. The old lady began to cry and The Misfit reddened.

"Lady," he said, "don't you get upset. Sometimes a man says things he don't mean. I don't reckon he meant to talk to you thataway."

"You wouldn't shoot a lady, would you?" the grandmother said and removed a clean handkerchief from her cuff and began to slap at her eyes with it.

The Misfit pointed the toe of his shoe into the ground and made a little hole and then covered it up again. "I would hate to have to," he said.

"Listen," the grandmother almost screamed, "I know you're a good man. You don't look a bit like you have common blood. I know you must come from nice people!"

"Yes mam," he said, "finest people in the world." When he smiled he showed a row of strong white teeth. "God never made a finer woman than my mother and my daddy's heart was pure gold," he said. The boy with the red sweat shirt had come around behind them and was standing with his gun at his hip. The Misfit squatted down on the ground. "Watch them children, Bobby Lee," he said. "You know they make me nervous." He looked at the six of them huddled together in front of him and he seemed to be embarrassed as if he couldn't think of anything to say. "Ain't a cloud in the sky," he remarked, looking up at it. "Don't see no sun but don't see no cloud neither."

"Yes, it's a beautiful day," said the grandmother. "Listen," she said, "you shouldn't call yourself The Misfit because I know you're a good man at heart. I can just look at you and tell."

"Hush!" Bailey yelled. "Hush! Everybody shut up and let me handle this!" He was squatting in the position of a runner about to sprint forward but he didn't move.

"I pre-chate that, lady," The Misfit said and drew a little circle in the ground with the butt of his gun.

"It'll take a half a hour to fix this here car," Hiram called, looking over the raised hood of it.

"Well, first you and Bobby Lee get him and that little boy to step over yonder with you," The Misfit said, pointing to Bailey and John Wesley. "The boys want to ask you something," he said to Bailey. "Would you mind stepping back in them woods there with them?"

"Listen," Bailey began, "we're in a terrible predicament! Nobody realizes what this is," and his voice cracked. His eyes were as blue and intense as the parrots on his shirt and he remained perfectly still.

The grandmother reached up to adjust her hat brim as if she were going to the woods with him but it came off in her hand. She stood staring at it and after a second she let it fall on the ground. Hiram pulled Bailey up by the arm as if he were assisting an old man. John Wesley caught hold of his father's hand and Bobby Lee followed. They went off toward the woods and just as they reached the dark edge, Bailey turned and supported himself against a gray naked pine trunk, he shouted, "I'll be back in a minute, Mamma, wait on me!"

"Come back this instant!" his mother shrilled but they all disappeared into the woods.

"Bailey Boy!" the grandmother called in a tragic voice but she found she was looking at The Misfit squatting on the ground in front of her. "I just know you're a good man," she said desperately. "You're not a bit common!"

"Nome, I ain't a good man," The Misfit said after a second as if he had considered her statement carefully, "but I ain't the worst in the world neither. My daddy said I was different breed of dog from my brothers and sisters. 'You know,' Daddy said, 'it's some that can live their whole life out without asking about it and it's others has to know why it is, and this boy is one of the latters. He's going to be into everything!'" He put on his black hat and looked up suddenly and then away deep into the woods as if he were embarrassed again. "I'm sorry I don't have on a shirt before you ladies," he said, hunching his shoulders slightly. "We buried our clothes that we had on when we escaped and we're just making do until we can get better. We borrowed these from some folks we met," he explained.

"That's perfectly all right," the grandmother said. "Maybe Bailey has an extra shirt in his suitcase."

"I'll look and see terrectly," The Misfit said.

"Where are they taking him?" the children's mother screamed.

"Daddy was a card himself," The Misfit said. "You couldn't put anything over on him. He never got in trouble with the Authorities though. Just had the knack of handling them."

"You could be honest too if you'd only try," said the grandmother. "Think how wonderful it would be to settle down and live a comfortable life and not have to think about somebody chasing you all the time."

The Misfit kept scratching in the ground with the butt of his gun as if he were thinking about it. "Yes'm, somebody is always after you," he murmured.

The grandmother noticed how thin his shoulder blades were just behind his hat because she was standing up looking down on him. "Do you ever pray?" she asked.

He shook his head. All she saw was the black hat wiggle between his shoulder blades. "Nome," he said.

There was a pistol shot from the woods, followed closely by another. Then silence. The old lady's head jerked around. She could hear the wind move through the tree tops like a long satisfied insuck of breath. "Bailey Boy!" she called.

"I was a gospel singer for a while," The Misfit said. "I been most everything. Been in the arm service, both land and sea, at home and abroad, been twict married, been an undertaker, been with the railroads, plowed Mother Earth, been in a tornado, seen a man burnt alive oncet," and he looked up at the children's mother and the little girl who were sitting close together, their faces white and their eyes glassy; "I even seen a woman flogged," he said.

"Pray, pray," the grandmother began, "pray, pray . . ."

"I never was a bad boy that I remember of," The Misfit said in an almost dreamy voice, "but somewheres along the line I done something wrong and got sent to the penitentiary. I was buried alive," and he looked up and held her attention to him by a steady stare.

"That's when you should have started to pray," she said. "What did you do to get sent to the penitentiary that first time?"

"Turn to the right, it was a wall," The Misfit said, looking up again at the cloudless sky. "Turn to the left, it was a wall. Look up it was a ceiling, look down it was a floor. I forgot what I done, lady. I set there and set there, trying to remember what it was I done and I ain't recalled it to this day. Oncet in a while, I would think it was coming to me, but it never come."

"Maybe they put you in by mistake," the old lady said vaguely.

"Nome," he said. "It wasn't no mistake. They had the papers on me."

"You must have stolen something," she said.

The Misfit sneered slightly. "Nobody had nothing I wanted," he said. "It was a head-doctor at the penitentiary said what I had done was kill my daddy but I known that for a lie. My daddy died in nineteen ought nineteen of the epidemic flu and I never had a thing to do with it. He was buried in the Mount Hopewell Baptist churchyard and you can go there and see for yourself."

"If you would pray," the old lady said, "Jesus would help you."

"That's right," The Misfit said.

"Well then, why don't you pray?" she asked trembling with delight suddenly.

"I don't want no hep," he said. "I'm doing all right by myself."

Bobby Lee and Hiram came ambling back from the woods. Bobby Lee was dragging a yellow shirt with bright blue parrots in it.

"Throw me that shirt, Bobby Lee," The Misfit said. The shirt came flying at him and landed on his shoulder and he put it on. The grandmother couldn't name what the shirt reminded her of. "No, lady," The Misfit said while he was buttoning it up, "I found out the crime don't matter. You can do one thing or you can do another, kill a man or take a tire off his car, because sooner or later you're going to forget what it was you done and just be punished for it."

The children's mother had begun to making heaving noises as if she couldn't get her breath. "Lady," he asked, "would you and that little girl like to step off yonder with Bobby Lee and Hiram and join your husband?"

"Yes, thank you," the mother said faintly. Her left arm dangled helplessly and she was holding the baby, who had gone to sleep, in the other. "Hep that lady up, Hiram," The Misfit said as she struggled to climb out of the ditch, "and Bobby Lee, you hold onto that little girl's hand."

"I don't want to hold hands with him," June Star said. "He reminds me of a pig."

The fat boy blushed and laughed and caught her by the arm and pulled her off into the woods after Hiram and her mother.

Alone with The Misfit, the grandmother found that she had lost her voice. There was not a cloud in the sky nor any sun. There was nothing around her but woods. She wanted to tell him that he must pray. She opened and closed her mouth several times before anything came out. Finally she found herself saying, "Jesus, Jesus," meaning Jesus will help you, but the way she was saying it, it sounded as if she might be cursing.

"Yes'm," The Misfit said as if he agreed. "Jesus thrown everything off balance. It was the same case with Him as with me except He hadn't committed any crime and they could prove I had committed one because they had the papers on me. Of course," he said, "they never shown me my papers. That's why I sign myself now. I said long ago, you get you a signature and sign everything you do and keep a copy of it. Then you'll know what you done and you can hold up the crime to the punishment and see do they match and in the end you'll have something to prove you ain't been treated right. I call myself The Misfit," he said, "because I can't make what all I done wrong fit what all I gone through in punishment."

There was a piercing scream from the woods, followed closely by a pistol report. "Does it seem right to you lady, that one is punished a heap and another ain't punished at all?"

"Jesus!" the old lady cried. "You've got good blood! I know you wouldn't shoot a lady! I know you come from nice people! Pray! Jesus, you ought not to shoot a lady. I'll give you all the money I've got!"

"Lady," The Misfit said, looking beyond her far into the woods, "there never was a body that give the undertaker a tip."

There were two more pistol reports and the grandmother raised her head like a parched old turkey hen crying for water and called, "Bailey Boy, Bailey Boy!" as if her heart would break.

"Jesus was the only One that ever raised the dead," The Misfit continued, "and He shouldn't have done it. He thrown everything off balance. If He did what He said, then it's nothing for you to do but thow away everything and follow Him, and if He didn't, then it's nothing for you to do but enjoy the few minutes you got left the best way you can—by killing somebody or burning down his house or doing some other meanness to him. No pleasure but meanness," he said and his voice had become almost a snarl.

"Maybe He didn't raise the dead," the old lady mumbled, not knowing what she was saying and feeling so dizzy that she sank down in the ditch with her legs twisted under her.

"I wasn't there so I can't say He didn't," The Misfit said. "I wisht I had of been there," he said, hitting the ground with his fist. "It ain't right I wasn't there because if I had of been there I would of known. Listen lady," he said in a high voice, "if I had of been there I would of known and I wouldn't be like I am now." His voice seemed about to crack and the grandmother's head cleared for an instant. She saw the man's face twisted close to her own as if he were going to cry and she murmured, "Why you're one of my babies. You're one of my own children!" She reached out and touched him on the shoulder. The Misfit sprang back as if a snake had bitten him and shot her three times through the chest. Then he put his gun down on the ground and took off his glasses and began to clean them.

Hiram and Bobby Lee returned from the woods and stood over the ditch, looking down at the grandmother who half sat and half lay in a puddle of blood with her legs crossed under her like a child's and her face smiling up at the cloudless sky.

Without his glasses, The Misfit's eyes were red-rimmed and pale and defenseless-looking. "Take her off and thow her where you thown the others," he said, picking up the cat that was rubbing itself against his leg.

"She was a talker, wasn't she?" Bobby Lee said, sliding down the ditch with a yodel.

"She would of been a good woman," The Misfit said, "if it had been somebody there to shoot her every minute of her life."

"Some fun!" Bobby Lee said.

"Shut up, Bobby Lee," The Misfit said. "It's no real pleasure in life."

FLANNERY O'CONNOR was born in Savannah, Georgia, in 1925 and grew up on a small farm outside Milledgeville, Georgia. She attended a Catholic high school and the Women's College of Georgia, where she received her B.A. in 1945. She studied in the writer's program at the State University of Iowa and received a Master of Fine Arts degree in 1947. In 1950 she began suffering from a disease that caused her to become an invalid until her death in 1964. Although she was only thirty-nine, she was praised at her death as one of America's most promising writers. In addition to two novels, *Wise Blood* and *The Violent Bear It Away,* she wrote a number of short stories that can be found in the collections *A Good Man Is Hard to Find* and *Everything That Rises Must Converge.*

Florence Engel Randall

*In societies of the future, will men be controlled by
an all-powerful state? Will man fear and distrust
every person around him?*

Will everyone be like

THE
WATCHERS

From the moment Althea awoke that morning, she knew
their building had been chosen. She knew it even before she saw
the excitement in her husband's eyes as he handed her the official
notice that had been put under their door.

"Well," he said, smiling at her while she read it, "what do
you think of that?"

"I had a feeling, George," she said, "even before I opened
my eyes, I had a feeling that this would happen today."

"We were due to be next," George said. "The setup here
is about perfect for it."

"Will you be home early?" She watched him while he
sipped his coffee.

"It won't start until late," he said. "It won't start until it
gets dark. You know how these things are."

"Just the same," she said, "I couldn't bear it just sitting

around and waiting for you. We have so much to do. We have to have dinner first and then change our clothes and find seats. We want to have good seats," she reminded him. "They won't reserve any for us, you know."

"Don't worry about it." He touched her cheek lightly with the back of his hand. "I'll be home in plenty of time."

"Do you have everything? I was never so scared in my life yesterday when I found your gun on the top of the dresser. I just couldn't believe my eyes. I wanted to run after you but I didn't know which route you had taken."

"I always carry a spare," he said. "You know that. I always keep a spare in my coat pocket. Why don't you trust me?"

"I know I'm being foolish," Althea said, kissing him good-bye. "Just be careful, that's all. I don't want you to be so sure of yourself that you'll get careless."

"You be careful," he said. "Do you have to go out today?"

She frowned. "I have to go marketing, and then I thought I'd go downtown and buy a new dress for tonight. All the women will be dressed up and I don't want to go looking like a frump."

"Watch out for the department stores," he reminded her. "They can be dangerous. Don't take any crowded elevators and check the dressing room before you try anything on."

She locked and double-locked the door after him, then fastened the chain before she had her own breakfast. Standing at the window while she drank her coffee, she thought how ridiculous it was the way they went through the same routine each morning as if the very fact that they had to take precautions was making them nervous. When they were first married two years ago, it would never have occurred to either of them that there was any reason for worry.

It must be because we're so much in love, she told herself, stacking the dishes in the washer. Love breeds its own vulnerability, its own fear.

When the signal flashed on the wall, Althea had just finished dressing. She watched it for a moment. It was their code, all right. Three lights in a row, the flickering pause, and then the slow, deliberate hold. She pressed the button that buzzed downstairs.

"Who is it?" she said, her mouth against the intercom.

"It's all right," said a woman's voice, clear and high and a bit too shrill. "I've already shown my identification to your doorman. I'm Sally Milford—Cary Milford's wife. My husband works in your husband's office."

"What do you want?" said Althea cautiously. "I'm much too busy to see anyone this morning. Besides, I'm on my way out." She bit her lip. George would be right if he scolded her for being careless. Why had she told this woman she was going out?

"I'll only take a moment of your time. It's important."

"Can't you tell me what it is over the intercom?"

"If I wanted to talk this way, I could have called you on the phone. I must see you. Please."

"All right," said Althea, reluctantly, knowing she was being foolish, "you can come up."

She checked her own gun even though she knew it was loaded and she palmed the small dagger—the one her mother had given her as a wedding present—the one with the jeweled handle.

"Things are so different now," her mother had said, sighing. She had lifted the dagger from the tissue paper and had studied it for a moment before she handed it to Althea. "In my day we could walk the streets without this sort of thing."

"That's not true," Althea reminded her. "You told me you used to wear stilt-like heels and you always carried a whistle in your purse."

"But that's not the same. It still wasn't like this," said her mother. "Did you know we weren't allowed to carry weapons?"

"You weren't?" said Althea, startled.

"That was before everyone realized that our laws were lagging behind our customs and public opinion. That was before the Citizen's Defense Act was passed."

"There is only one crime," Althea said firmly, "and that is to be a victim. Nothing makes sense otherwise."

"I suppose not." Her mother shook her head. "I guess I'm just being sentimental," she added wistfully. "Sometimes I miss the policemen we used to have. They would wear blue uniforms and they would drive around with sirens blaring and lights flashing. It seems a shame they became obsolete. Why I can even remember the time when we could take a walk in the park."

"In the park?" said Althea, incredulous. "You could actually do that?"

Now Althea bit her lip. There was no point in daydreaming. She stationed herself at the oneway peephole. The woman who now came within her range of vision was thin of face and well-dressed. She blinked her eyes nervously and hesitated before she knocked.

"Just a moment," said Althea. She unfastened the chain and the two locks, and then stepped back so that when the door opened she would be behind it. "Come in," she said.

"Where are you?"

"Right behind you," said Althea, her hand on her gun. "You're not very smart to walk right in like that, are you?"

"But I know who you are," said Sally Milford, her eyes wide with fright. "My husband and your husband are good friends."

"The first thing you have to learn," said Althea, "is not to trust anyone." She kicked the door shut. "Hold up your hands." She found a small acid gun in Sally's purse and a knife in the pocket of her jacket. "Just put them on the table," Althea directed, "and then sit down. Would you like some coffee?"

Sally shook her head, "Look," she said, her mouth trembling, "I wouldn't trouble you like this—I wouldn't have come at all if I didn't, in a way, know you. You see that, don't you?"

"No," said Althea firmly, "I don't see anything. Suppose you tell me what you want."

Sally clasped her hands on the edge of the table. "I have a brother-in-law who knows someone on the Board of Commissioners," she said, leaning forward in her eagerness, "and we heard that your apartment house has been chosen."

"These things are supposed to be a secret," Althea said sharply. "No one except the people involved is supposed to know. Don't you realize what can happen to you if they find out? And what can happen to me?"

"I'm sorry but I just couldn't help it. When I heard about

it—all I could think was that I simply had to go. I have never been to a performance and, the way things look, I'll never have a chance."

"Where do you live?" Althea asked, putting the gun away.

"On the East Side. You know how safe it's getting to be over there. We haven't had an incident in months."

"That doesn't mean they won't choose your building eventually."

"Do you really think they will?"

"Why not?" said Althea.

"Then, in that case, why can't you make believe that we're visiting you or something? They do have special passes for visitors and then, when we're finally chosen, we could reciprocate. Cary and I could invite you and George. That way we could each see two performances."

"It wouldn't work," said Althea. "In the first place, we have the perfect setting for this sort of thing. That's why we picked this particular apartment building. We could have had a much better place to live but both George and I agreed that our best chance was being here. We had to wait two years for this day, and if they ever suspect that was a put-up thing, you know what would happen to us."

"I suppose I was foolish to even hope." Sally stood up. "I thought it would work out."

"It won't," said Althea, feeling a sudden pity for her. "Believe me, Sally, it won't. I happen to know that Mrs. Tremont, who lives on the third floor, has her sister-in-law staying with her; that, of course, makes it possible for her sister-in-law to go tonight, but if she had just arrived today someone would be sure to report it and Mrs. Tremont would get into trouble."

"You said you were going out," said Sally. "Do you want a ride with me?"

"I'm going downtown," said Althea. "I thought I'd buy a new dress for tonight."

"I haven't been shopping in ages," said Sally. "Cary won't let me go without him and he's been much too busy on Saturdays. We could shop together and maybe have lunch."

"Just remember one thing," Althea warned as she reached for her coat and hat. "No matter what you say, I won't change my mind. You can spend the whole day with me if you like but I still won't change my mind."

"I know you're right," said Sally as they pressed the button for the elevator. "It's just that I'm glad to have some company on the subway."

"Are you still taking the subway?" Althea stared at her, amazed. "George insists that I take the bus. Not taxis—they're not too reliable anymore but a bus is still fine."

"It takes too long," said Sally. "The subway is much quicker. I have my own system. I never wait on a platform if I'm alone and I usually ride in the first car where the motorman is and, just in case anyone is following me, I change at every other stop."

"Now," said Althea, watching as the elevator stopped at their floor, "run!"

They pounded through the corridor and down one flight of steps. Then they rang for the elevator again. When it arrived, it was empty and they rode it the rest of the way down.

It turned out to be, Althea told George later, a rather pleasant day. With the two of them together, the shopping proved much easier. Sally stood watch while Althea tried on dresses and Althea stood guard while Sally shopped. When they finally parted, it was after four.

Althea took a bus uptown again and got off three blocks before her destination. She glanced behind to make sure she wasn't being followed; then she bought a steak at the meat market. Steak would be the quickest thing to cook for dinner and she didn't want to load her arms with too many packages. It was difficult enough carrying the dress, although she had insisted that the clerk put it in a shopping bag instead of a box. With a shopping bag she would feel less clumsy and have one hand free.

The doorman beamed at her when she entered the lobby.

"This is a great day for us," he said.

Althea nodded. "I bought a new dress," she told him happily, "a black sheath."

"I'll ride the elevator with you if you like," he offered generously. "Most of the tenants are home by now."

"You're not supposed to leave your post," Althea reminded him. "Anyone could come in while you were away. You know what happened to the last doorman we had?"

"You're right," he admitted. "For a moment I forgot."

"By the way," she whispered, "do you know who will be giving the performance?"

He shook his head. "No one knows," he said. "I've been asking but no one knows for sure. I think it's a young one. They usually are."

"You'd think those kids could learn," said Althea, ringing for the elevator. "My parents were pretty strict with me—I can tell you that."

"That's the best way," the doorman said. "You have to be firm with them. I always say that from the time they can walk, they can be taught. Now, you take that kid of Mrs. Hammond. You know the Hammonds on the fifth floor? He got his first slash today and was sent home from school in disgrace."

"Oh, no," said Althea, in horror. "He's only eleven. He's only allowed two more mistakes."

"The way Mrs. Hammond spanked him, he'll learn," the doorman said. "That'll never happen to him again, I can tell you that."

"Who was the other boy?"

"It was a girl," said the doorman. "A pretty little thing, I understand. Well, she'll get her first gold star for that."

"I got a gold star when I was twelve," said Althea, stepping into the elevator.

She rode it to the fourth floor and got out. She took the stairs the rest of the way, then stood before her own front door for a moment, listening. When she was positive it was safe, she inserted her key in the lock.

At precisely six o'clock George came home and, by seven thirty, they had finished dinner and were dressed.

"I'd like to go now," said Althea, impatiently.

"It won't get dark until eight," George said. "You know how it is this time of year. Even then, we'll have to wait a while."

"I can see the stands from here," said Althea, craning her neck as she peered out of the window. "People are beginning to arrive now. Please, darling, let's go."

"You're like a child," he said, hugging her. "Just an anxious little kid."

"I can't help it," she said. "I'm excited. Aren't you thrilled, George?"

"Come on," he said, indulgently. He looked at her, chic and lovely in her new black sheath. "No pockets," he said, shaking his head. "What made you buy a dress without any pockets? I didn't know they made them that way anymore."

"I'll only wear it when I'm with you," she said. "Besides, I have a knife in my purse."

"Just see that you keep it handy." He held the door for her. "I'm glad you used your head this morning."

"For a moment I was tempted," Althea confessed. "Sally seems like a sweet person and it might be fun if we could go there sometimes, but then I realized we'd be taking a chance."

"It doesn't pay to take chances," said George. "Otherwise you can end up giving the performance instead of watching it."

"The doorman told me it was a young one. Probably a girl."

"It usually is," said George.

"Do you know what she did?" Althea asked as they walked through the back of the lobby and out into the courtyard. "No one seems to know what she did."

"Probably something stupid," said George, looking around and waving to their neighbors. "You know, honey, you were right. The stands are filling up."

The stands had been placed next to their building. They were permanent, sturdily built of brick and stone, and erected when the building itself had been new. Optimistically every building had its stands ready for the day when it would be chosen, and Althea looked around proudly as she and George found seats in the second row.

Mr. and Mrs. Hammond were there and seated between them was their son, Timmy. Timmy's right arm was bandaged and he huddled close to his mother.

"I heard about it," said Althea, with sympathy. "I'm sure Timmy will never let it happen again."

"Because she was pretty. Because it was a girl," said Mrs.

Hammond bitterly. "She called to him and he ran right over, leaving his knife in his pocket as if a knife ever did anybody any good in a pocket. Just because it was a little girl, he trusted her. But he's learned his lesson, haven't you, Timmy?" she said, slapping him across the face.

"No more," Timmy wept, putting his bandaged arm across his eyes. "Please, Mommy, don't hit me anymore."

He'll never amount to anything, Althea thought, staring at him in dismay. Only three chances and he's used up one already. He's too soft. When I have a child—

She thought about it for a moment, longing for a child but the apartment they were in was too small and they hadn't wanted to move until they had a chance at a performance. Maybe now—maybe now that they were finally spectators—perhaps now that the longed-for, dreamed-about moment had finally arrived, they could move to a larger place and she would have a child.

"You have to train them from the beginning," she whispered to George.

"Sure," he said, knowing what she meant. "It won't happen to us."

"It won't happen to us," she agreed, seeing the way George, even now, even at this moment of pleasure and relaxation, kept his hand in his pocket; George's hand curled over the bulge of his gun.

Althea leaned back. She had known, of course, what the stage setting would be but, just the same, sitting there, part of the expectant, eager audience, she had to admire its reality.

It represented a street scene. It could have been Althea's own street with its middle-class, red-brick buildings, the old-fashioned canopies extending from wide entrances to the edge of the curb. Behind the lighted windows of the buildings, Althea could see the people, all the families together, having dinner, watching television, reading, talking, laughing—all the people of the city settling down for the night.

In the center of the stage was a street lamp, still unlit although it was twilight now; on the far right, there was a fire hydrant. The first floor of the center building was occupied by a shop. The sign said, "ANTIQUES," and Althea could see the lovely things in the window—the paintings in the carved, ornate frames, the delicate crystal goblets, a curved brass bowl. Suddenly the street light went on, dominating the center of the stage with its soft, gentle glow.

The curtain is rising, thought Althea, taking a deep breath. She always loved that moment in the theatre, that magic moment when all the murmuring and the movement and the whispering stopped, the hush and wonder when the curtain rose and the stage lay there before them, the play ready to begin.

Someone somewhere in the back coughed and Althea drew a deep, sighing gasp of impatience.

The stage became alive. From the center building a man emerged, a nondescript man walking his dog at night. The dog tugged and the man whistled softly between his teeth as the two of them walked down the street. The stage became empty again and Althea clasped her hands in her lap, amazed to discover that they were shaking.

At the far right two shadows blurred, moved, took form. Now a girl and a boy strolled down the street. His arm was flung around her shoulders and, from the way she smiled at him, Althea knew they were in love. They moved slowly across the stage. They stopped before the antique shop and the girl pointed to the brass bowl and the boy nodded and gestured expansively showing her there was nothing in the world he wouldn't get for her. They disappeared on the far left and the stage was empty again.

Althea unclasped her hands and, because her palms were wet, she rubbed them furtively together. Beside her she could hear the sound of George's breathing, slow, heavy, as if each breath were an effort.

Onstage, in the lighted backdrop, in the center building, some of the windows began to darken as if the occupants were retiring for the night.

It's getting late, thought Althea, watching. The lights are dimming all over the city. People are yawning and stretching and getting into bed and even the sounds of the distant traffic seem muted as if someone had muffled all the rolling wheels.

A shadow, part of the shadow of the building, almost part of the square shape of the center building, took on form, and Althea saw that it was a man, a man who had been there all the time, hiding there without her being conscious of his presence.

From the far right she could hear the clicking of high heels on the pavement. Someone else, she thought, will walk down this street this night.

There was a rustle and a stir in the stands.

"Please, Mommy," Timmy whispered. "I don't want to stay here."

"Oh, you'll stay all right," said Mrs. Hammond grimly. "You just open your eyes wide. You watch everything, Timmy Hammond, if you know what's good for you."

"Be quiet down there," someone hissed. "Do you want to spoil everything?"

Althea gripped George's arm.

The footsteps grew louder and a girl came into view, entering downstage from the right. The shadow that was the man moved, and then became very still, waiting.

The girl moved across the stage. She paused under the street light. She touched the lamppost as if the feel of it under her fingers gave her some sort of reassurance. She hesitated, reluctant to leave the light.

Althea could see her clearly now. She was very young. She could be no more than nineteen—perhaps twenty. She wore a red suit and a little red beret with a feather stuck jauntily in it and her handbag was tucked under her arm. Her hair was blond and it tumbled loose over her shoulders.

Althea watched absorbed as the second figure moved again, the man crouching and then straightening as he ran toward the light, toward the girl in the red suit. At the clear view of his black-jacketed, black-clad figure, there was a sudden roar of applause. Althea clapped until her hands ached.

Out of the dark, into the light, he moved. The girl had her back toward him, not seeing him as the watchers saw him—sinuous, beautiful in his grace, tall, broad of shoulder, his hair allowed to grow long in back and his black cap set on the back of his head. The knife in his hand caught the light and sparkled.

He ran and then stopped. Deliberately, he stalked her. Professional that he was, he began to move slowly, coming down light on the balls of his feet.

The girl whirled around and, at the sight of him, she made a little whimpering sound in her throat. Her back now to the audience, she darted to the left and, as if they were part of a rigid dance pattern, the man stepped after her. She turned and ran to the right, her heels clicking frantically but he was there before her.

"Please," said the girl in the red suit. She darted back to the lamppost, back where the light was the brightest, where she could be seen most clearly. She turned and faced the backdrop, faced the buildings, the windows where the people were. Her right hand still clutched her purse, her left was now at her throat.

"Oh, please." Her voice rose to a keening wail of terror and anguish.

"Please," she screamed, her voice begging, her body begging. Then blindly she turned again and ran.

This cry in the night had awakened the sleepers. It had roused the dreamers. The darkened windows in the backdrop were illuminated again. Figures moved; there were silhouettes framed in the windows. The sleepers were awake. The dreamers had stopped dreaming and the city was alert and watching.

"Help me."

The city held its breath and listened.

"Please, help me."

But, Althea saw, she couldn't run far enough. She couldn't run fast enough. The man had her pinned against the wall now, pinned against the lighted, listening backdrop of the building and her handbag fell to the ground.

"I beg you." She was almost hidden by the man's bulk as he bent over her. "Won't someone help me?"

The man in the black jacket raised his arm and the knife flashed. The girl screamed in agony, her cheek now as crimson as her suit. Dodging under his arm, she ran again, the slowing rhythm of her clicking heels the only sound to be heard.

The man watched her for a moment. The quiet, lighted windows watched and the filled stands watched. The man stood very still as if he were resting and then, gracefully, quickly, easily, he caught her again.

That does it, thought Althea, her heart pounding; that does it.

The knife gleamed and Althea held her breath. The arm lifted. The black-draped arm lifted and fell, lifted and fell. The red suit crumpled, falling as if it were empty, the red suit only a splotch now on the pavement. Then the man moved toward the hushed, absorbed watchers.

And there he stood, bowing and smiling, the knife dripping red at his side. Over and over again he took his bow while they all gave him the ultimate, the supreme tribute of their silence.

FLORENCE ENGEL RANDALL was born in the Flatbush section of Brooklyn, New York, and she sold her first story at the age of eighteen. In addition to being a writer, she has raised three children and kept a home in Great Neck, Long Island. Her well-written short stories have appeared in many magazines, such as *Harper's, Redbook,* and *Seventeen.* Her novels include *Hedgerow* and *The Place of Sapphires.*

Ray Bradbury

Why do crowds always gather at automobile accidents?

What would you do if someone at the scene of an accident tried to move an injured victim?

Here is a story in which one man discovers a deadly secret about

THE CROWD

Mr. Spallner put his hands over his face.

There was the feeling of movement in space, the beautifully tortured scream, the impact and tumbling of the car with wall, through wall, over and down like a toy, and him hurled out of it. Then—silence.

The crowd came running. Faintly, where he lay, he heard them running. He could tell their ages and their sizes by the sound of their numerous feet over the summer grass and on the lined pavement, and over the asphalt street, and picking through the cluttered bricks to where his car hung half into the night sky, still spinning its wheels with a senseless centrifuge.

Where the crowd came from he didn't know. He struggled to remain aware and then the crowd faces hemmed in upon him, hung over him like the large glowing leaves of down-bent trees. They were a ring of shifting, compressing, changing faces over him, looking down, looking down, reading the time of his life or death by his face, making his face into a moon-dial, where the moon cast a shadow from his nose out upon his cheek to tell the time of breathing or not breathing any more ever.

How swiftly a crowd comes, he thought, like the iris of an eye compressing in out of nowhere.

A siren. A police voice. Movement. Blood trickled from his lips and he was being moved into an ambulance. Someone said, "Is he dead?" And someone else said, "No, he's not dead." And a third person said, "He won't die, he's not going to die." And he saw the faces of the crowd beyond him in the night, and he knew by their expressions that he wouldn't die. And that was strange. He saw a man's face, thin, bright, pale; the man swallowed and bit his lips, very sick. There was a small woman, too, with red hair and too much red on her cheeks and lips. And a little boy with a freckled face. Others' faces. An old man with a wrinkled upper lip, an old woman, with a mole upon her chin. They had all come from—where? Houses, cars, alleys, from the immediate and the accident-shocked world. Out of alleys and out of hotels and out of streetcars and seemingly out of nothing they came.

The crowd looked at him and he looked back at them and did not like them at all. There was a vast wrongness to them. He couldn't put his finger on it. They were far worse than this machine-made thing that happened to him now.

The ambulance doors slammed. Through the windows he saw the crowd looking in, looking in. That crowd that always came so fast, so strangely fast, to form a circle, to peer down, to probe, to gawk, to question, to point, to disturb, to spoil the privacy of a man's agony by their frank curiosity.

The ambulance drove off. He sank back and their faces still stared into his face, even with his eyes shut.

The car wheels spun in his mind for days. One wheel, four wheels, spinning, spinning, and whirring, around and around.

He knew it was wrong. Something wrong with the wheels and the whole accident and the running of feet and the curiosity. The crowd faces mixed and spun into the wild rotation of the wheels.

He awoke.

Sunlight, a hospital room, a hand taking his pulse.

"How do you feel?" asked the doctor.

The wheels faded away. Mr. Spallner looked around.

"Fine—I guess."

He tried to find words. About the accident. "Doctor?"

"Yes?"

"That crowd—was it last night?"

"Two days ago. You've been here since Thursday. You're all right, though. You're doing fine. Don't try and get up."

"That crowd. Something about wheels, too. Do accidents make people, well, a—little off?"

"Temporarily, sometimes."

He lay staring at the doctor. "Does it hurt your time sense?"

"Panic sometimes does."

"Makes a minute seem like an hour, or maybe an hour seem like a minute?"

"Yes."

"Let me tell you then." He felt the bed under him, the sunlight on his face. "You'll think I'm crazy. I was driving too fast, I know. I'm sorry now. I jumped the curb and hit that wall. I was hurt and numb, I know, but I still remember things. Mostly—the crowd." He waited a moment and then decided to go on, for he suddenly knew what it was that bothered him. "The crowd got there too quickly. Thirty seconds after the smash they were all standing over me and staring at me . . . it's not right they should run that fast, so late at night . . ."

"You only think it was thirty seconds," said the doctor. "It was probably three or four minutes. Your senses—"

"Yeah, I know—my senses, the accident. But I was conscious! I remember one thing that puts it all together and makes it funny, God, so damned funny. The wheels of my car, upside down. The wheels were still spinning when the crowd got there!"

The doctor smiled.

The man in bed went on. "I'm positive! The wheels were spinning and spinning fast—the front wheels! Wheels don't spin very long, friction cuts them down. And these were really spinning!"

"You're confused," said the doctor.

"I'm not confused. That street was empty. Not a soul in sight. And then the accident and the wheels still spinning and all those faces over me, quick, in no time. And the way they looked down at me, I *knew* I wouldn't die . . ."

"Simple shock," said the doctor, walking away into the sunlight.

They released him from the hospital two weeks later. He rode home in a taxi. People had come to visit him during his two weeks on his back, and to all of them he had told his story, the accident, the spinning wheels, the crowd. They had all laughed with him concerning it, and passed it off.

He leaned forward and tapped on the taxi window.

"What's wrong?"

The cabbie looked back. "Sorry, boss. This is one helluva town to drive in. Got an accident up ahead. Want me to detour?"

"Yes. No. no! Wait. Go ahead. Let's—let's take a look."

The cab moved forward, honking.

"Funny damn thing," said the cabbie. "Hey, *you*! Get that fleatrap out of the way!" Quieter, "Funny thing—more damn people. Nosey people."

Mr. Spallner looked down and watched his fingers tremble on his knee. "You noticed that, too?"

"Sure," said the cabbie. "All the time. There's always a crowd. You'd think it was their own mother got killed."

"They come running awfully fast," said the man in the back of the cab.

"Same way with a fire or an explosion. Nobody around. Boom. Lotsa people around. I dunno."

"Ever seen an accident—at night?"

The cabbie nodded. "Sure. Don't make no difference. There's always a crowd."

The wreck came in view. A body lay on the pavement. You knew there was a body even if you couldn't see it. Because of the crowd. The crowd with its back toward him as he sat in the rear of the cab. With its back toward him. He opened the window and almost started to yell. But he didn't have the nerve. If he yelled they might turn around.

And he was afraid to see their faces.

"I seem to have a penchant for accidents,' he said, in his office. It was late afternoon. His friend sat across the desk from him, listening. "I got out of the hospital this morning and first thing on the way home, we detoured around a wreck."

"Things run in cycles," said Morgan.

"Let me tell you about my accident."

"I've heard it. Heard it all."

"But it was funny, you must admit."

"I must admit. Now how about a drink?"

They talked on for half an hour or more. All the while they talked, at the back of Spallner's brain a small watch ticked, a watch that never needed winding. It was the memory of a few little things. Wheels and faces.

At about five-thirty there was a hard metal noise in the street. Morgan nodded and looked out and down. "What'd I tell you? Cycles. A truck and a cream-colored Cadillac. Yes, yes."

Spallner walked to the window. He was very cold and as he stood there, he looked at his watch, at the small minute hand. One two three four five seconds—people running—eight nine ten eleven twelve—from all over, people came running—fifteen sixteen seventeen eighteen seconds—more people, more cars, more horns blowing. Curiously distant, Spallner looked upon the scene as an explosion in reverse, the fragments of the detonation sucked back to the point of impulsion. Nineteen, twenty, twenty-one seconds and the crowd was there. Spallner made a gesture down at them, wordless.

The crowd gathered so fast.

He saw a woman's body a moment before the crowd swallowed it up.

Morgan said. "You look lousy. Here. Finish your drink."

"I'm all right, I'm all right. Let me alone. I'm all right. Can you see those people? Can you see any of them? I wish we could see them closer."

Morgan cried out, "Where in hell are you going?"

Spallner was out the door, Morgan after him, and down the stairs as rapidly as possible. "Come along, and hurry."

"Take it easy, you're not a well man!"

They walked out on to the street. Spallner pushed his way forward. He thought he saw a red-haired woman with too much red color on her cheeks and lips.

"There!" He turned wildly to Morgan. "Did you see her?"

"See *who?*"

"Damn it; she's gone. The crowd closed in!"

The crowd was all around, breathing and looking and shuffling and mixing and mumbling and getting in the way when he tried to shove through. Evidently the red-haired woman had seen him coming and run off.

He saw another familiar face! A little freckled boy. But there are many freckled boys in the world. And, anyway, it was no use, before Spallner reached him, this little boy ran away and vanished among the people.

"Is she dead?" a voice asked. "Is she dead?"

"She's dying," someone else replied. "She'll be dead before the ambulance arrives. They shouldn't have moved her. They shouldn't have moved her."

All the crowd faces—familiar, yet unfamiliar, bending over, looking down, looking down.

"Hey, mister, stop pushing."

"Who you shovin', buddy?"

Spallner came back out, and Morgan caught hold of him before he fell. "You damned fool. You're still sick. Why in hell'd you have to come down here?" Morgan demanded.

"I don't know, I really don't. They moved her, Morgan, someone moved her. You should never move a traffic victim. It kills them. It kills them."

"Yeah. That's the way with people. The idiots."

Spallner arranged the newspaper clippings carefully.

Morgan looked at them. "What's the idea? Ever since your accident you think every traffic scramble is part of you. What are these?"

"Clippings of motor-car crackups, and photos. Look at them. Not at the cars," said Spallner, "but at the crowds around the cars." He pointed. "Here. Compare this photo of a wreck in the Wilshire District with one in Westwood. No resemblance.

But now take this Westwood picture and align it with one taken in the Westwood District ten years ago." Again he motioned. "This woman is in both pictures."

"Coincidence. The woman happened to be there once in 1936, again in 1946."

"A coincidence once, maybe. But twelve times over a period of ten years, when the accidents occurred as much as three miles from one another, no. Here." He dealt out a dozen photographs. "She's in *all* of these!"

"Maybe she's perverted."

"She's more than that. How does she *happen* to be there so quickly after each accident? And why does she wear the same clothes in pictures taken over a period of a decade?"

"I'll be damned, so she does."

"And, last of all, why was she standing over *me* the night of my accident, two weeks ago!"

They had a drink. Morgan went over the files. "What'd you do, hire a clipping service while you were in the hospital to go back through the newspapers for you?" Spallner nodded. Morgan sipped his drink. It was getting late. The street lights were coming on in the streets below the office. "What does all this add up to?"

"I don't know," said Spallner, "except that there's a universal law about accidents. *Crowds gather.* They always gather. And like you and me, people have wondered year after year, why they gathered so quickly, and how? I know the answer. Here it is!"

He flung the clippings down. "It frightens me."

"These people—mightn't they be thrill-hunters, perverted sensationalists with a carnal lust for blood and morbidity?"

Spallner shrugged. "Does that explain their being at all the accidents? Notice, they stick to certain territories. A Brentwood accident will bring out one group. A Huntington Park another. But there's a norm for faces, a certain percentage appear at each wreck."

Morgan said, "They're not *all* the same faces, are they?"

"Naturally not. Accidents draw normal people, too, in

the course of time. But these, I find, are always the *first* ones there."

"Who are they? What do they want? You keep hinting and never telling. Good Lord, you must have some idea. You've scared yourself and now you've got me jumping."

"I've tried getting to them, but someone always trips me up, I'm always too late. They slip into the crowd and vanish. The crowd seems to offer protection to some of its members. They see me coming."

"Sounds like some sort of clique."

"They have one thing in common, they always show up together. At a fire or an explosion or on the sidelines of a war, at any public demonstration of this thing called death. Vultures, hyenas or saints, I don't know which they are, I just don't know. But I'm going to the police with it, this evening. It's gone on long enough. One of them shifted that woman's body today. They shouldn't have touched her. It killed her."

He placed the clippings in a briefcase. Morgan got up and clipped into his coat. Spallner clicked the briefcase shut. "Or, I just happened to think . . ."

"What?"

"Maybe they *wanted* her dead."

"Why?"

"Who knows. Come along?"

"Sorry. It's late. See you tomorrow. Luck." They went out together. "Give my regards to the cops. Think they'll believe you?"

"Oh, they'll believe me all right. Good night."

Spallner took it slow driving downtown.

"I want to get there," he told himself, "alive."

He was rather shocked, but not surprised, somehow, when the truck came rolling out of an alley straight at him. He was just congratulating himself on his keen sense of observation and talking out what he would say to the police in his mind, when the truck smashed into his car. It wasn't really his car, that was the disheartening thing about it. In a preoccupied mood he was tossed first this way and then that way, while he thought, what a shame, Morgan has gone and lent me his extra car for a few days until my other car is fixed, and now here I go again. The windshield hammered back into his face. He was forced back and forth in several lightning jerks. Then all motion stopped and all noise stopped and only pain filled him up.

He heard their feet running and running and running. He fumbled with the car door. It clicked. He fell out upon the pavement drunkenly and lay, ear to the asphalt, listening to them coming. It was like a great rainstorm, with many drops, heavy and light and medium, touching the earth. He waited a few seconds and listened to their coming and their arrival. Then, weakly, expectantly, he rolled his head up and looked.

The crowd was there.

He could smell their breaths, the mingled odors of many people sucking and sucking on the air a man needs to live by. They crowded and jostled and sucked and sucked all the air up from around his gasping face until he tried to tell them to move back, they were making him live in a vacuum. His head was bleeding very badly. He tried to move and realized something was wrong with his spine. He hadn't felt much at the impact, but his spine was hurt. He didn't dare move.

He couldn't speak. Opening his mouth, nothing came out but a gagging.

Someone said, "Give me a hand. We'll roll him over and lift him into a more comfortable position."

Spallner's brain burst apart.

No! Don't move me!

"We'll move him," said the voice, casually.

You idiots, you'll kill me, don't!

But he could not say any of this aloud. He could only think it.

Hands took hold of him. They started to lift him. He cried out and nausea choked him up. They straightened him out into a ramrod of agony. Two men did it. One of them was thin, bright, pale, alert, a young man. The other man was very old and had a wrinkled upper lip.

He had seen their faces before.

A familiar voice said, "Is—is he dead?"

Another voice, a memorable voice, responded, "No. Not yet. But he will be dead before the ambulance arrives."

It was all a very silly, mad plot. Like every accident. He squealed hysterically at the solid wall of faces. They were all around him, these judges and jurors with the faces he had seen before. Through his pain he counted their faces.

The freckled boy. The old man with the wrinkled upper lip.

The red-haired, red-cheeked woman. An old woman with a mole on her chin.

I know what you're here for, he thought. You're here just as you're at all accidents. To make certain the right ones live and the right ones die. That's why you lifted me. You knew it would kill. You knew I'd live if you left me alone.

And that's the way it had been since time began, when crowds gather. You murder much easier, this way. Your alibi is very simple; you didn't know it was dangerous to move a hurt man. You didn't mean to hurt him.

He looked at them, above him, and he was curious as a man under deep water looking up at the people on a bridge. Who are you? Where do you come from and how do you get here so soon? You're the crowd that's always in the way, using up good air that a dying man's lungs are in need of, using up space he should be using to lie in, alone. Tramping on people to make sure they die, that's you. I know *all* of you.

It was like a polite monologue. They said nothing. Faces. The old man. The red-haired woman.

Someone picked up his briefcase. "Whose is this?" they asked.

It's mine! It's evidence against you!

Eyes, inverted over him. Shiny eyes under tousled hair or under hats.

Faces.

Somewhere—a siren. The ambulance was coming.

But, looking at the faces, the construction, the cast, the form of the faces, Spallner saw it was too late. He read it in their faces. They *knew*.

He tried to speak. A little bit got out:

"It—looks like I'll—be joining up with you. I—guess I'll be a member of your—group—now."

He closed his eyes then, and waited for the coroner.

RAY BRADBURY, who has written strange and wonderful stories of other times and other planets, is one of America's most popular science-fiction and fantasy writers. He was born in Waukegan, Illinois, in 1920 and began his writing career while he was still in high school. He sold his first story in 1941, and in 1943 he became a full-time writer. Since then he has written more than a thousand stories, some of them for movies, television, and the stage. Although he lives in metropolitan Los Angeles, he does not drive a car, and he avoids flying. His books include *The Martian Chronicles, The Illustrated Man,* and *Dandelion Wine.*

Ambrose Bierce

Should an occupying military force have the right to execute civilians accused of sabotage?

What thoughts would flash through your mind at the moment you were being hanged?

During the U.S. Civil War strange events resulted in

AN OCCURRENCE AT OWL CREEK BRIDGE

I

A man stood upon a railroad bridge in northern Alabama, looking down into the swift water twenty feet below. The man's hands were behind his back, the wrists bound with a cord. A rope loosely encircled his neck. It was attached to a stout cross-timber above his head, and the slack fell to the level of his knees. Some loose boards laid upon the sleepers supporting the metals of the railway supplied a footing for him and his executioners—two private soldiers of the Federal army, directed by a sergeant who in civil life may have been a deputy sheriff. At a short remove upon the same temporary platform was an officer in the uniform of his rank, armed. He was a captain. A sentinel at each end of the bridge stood with his rifle in the position known as "support," that is to say, vertical in front of the left shoulder, the hammer resting on the forearm thrown straight across the chest—a formal and unnatural position, enforcing an erect carriage of the body. It did not appear to be the duty of these two men to know what was occurring at the center of the bridge; they merely blockaded the two ends of the foot plank which traversed it.

Beyond one of the sentinels, nobody was in sight; the railroad ran straight away into a forest for a hundred yards, then, curving, was lost to view. Doubtless there was an outpost farther along. The other bank of the stream was open ground—a gentle acclivity topped with a stockade of vertical tree trunks, loopholed for rifles, with a single embrasure through which protruded the muzzle of a brass cannon commanding the bridge. Midway of the slope between bridge and fort were the spectators—a single company of infantry in line, at "parade rest," the butts of the rifles on the ground, the barrels inclining slightly backward against the right shoulder, the hands crossed upon the stock. A lieutenant stood at the right of the line, the point of his sword upon the ground, his left hand resting upon his right. Excepting the group of four at the center of the bridge, not a man moved. The company faced the bridge, staring stonily, motionless. The sentinels, facing the banks of the stream, might have been statues to adorn the bridge. The captain stood with folded arms, silent, observing the work of his subordinates, but making no sign. Death is a dignitary who when he comes announced is to be received with formal manifestations of respect, even by those most familiar with him. In the code of military etiquette silence and fixity are forms of deference.

The man who was engaged in being hanged was apparently about thirty-five years of age. He was a civilian, if one might judge from his habit, which was that of a planter. His features were good—a straight nose, firm mouth, broad forehead, from which his long, dark hair was combed straight back, falling behind his ears to the collar of his well-fitting frock coat. He wore a mustache and pointed beard, but no whiskers; his eyes were large and dark gray, and had a kindly expression which one would hardly have expected in one whose neck was in the hemp. Evidently this was no vulgar assassin. The liberal military code makes provision for hanging many kinds of persons, and gentlemen are not excluded.

The preparation being complete, the two private soldiers stepped aside and each drew away the plank upon which he had been standing. The sergeant turned to the captain, saluted, and placed himself immediately behind that officer, who in turn moved apart one pace. These movements left the condemned man and the sergeant standing on the two ends of the same plank, which spanned three of the crossties of the bridge. The end upon which the civilian stood almost, but not quite, reached a fourth. This plank had been held in place by the weight of the captain; it was now held by that of the sergeant. At a signal from the former, the latter would step aside, the plank would tilt, and the condemned man go down between two ties. The arrangement commended itself to his judgment as simple and effective. His face had not been covered nor his eyes bandaged. He looked a moment at his "unsteadfast footing," then let his gaze wander to the swirling water of the stream racing madly beneath his feet. A piece of dancing driftwood caught his attention and his eyes followed it down the current. How slowly it appeared to move! What a sluggish stream!

He closed his eyes in order to fix his last thoughts upon his wife and children. The water, touched to gold by the early sun, the brooding mists under the banks at some distance down the stream, the fort, the soldiers, the piece of drift—all had distracted him. And now he became conscious of a new disturbance. Striking through the thought of his dear ones was a sound which he could neither ignore nor understand, a sharp, distinct, metallic percussion like the stroke of a blacksmith's hammer upon the anvil; it had the same ringing quality. He wondered what it was, and whether immeasurably distant or near by—it seemed both. Its recurrence was regular, but as slow as the tolling of a death knell. He awaited each stroke with impatience and—he knew not why—apprehension. The intervals of silence grew progressively longer; the delays became maddening. With their greater infrequency the sounds increased in strength and sharpness. They hurt his ear like the thrust of a knife; he feared he would shriek. What he heard was the ticking of his watch.

He unclosed his eyes and saw again the water below him. "If I could free my hands," he thought, "I might throw off the noose and spring into the stream. By diving I could evade the bullets and, swimming vigorously, reach the bank, take to the woods, and get away home. My home, thank God, is as yet outside their lines; my wife and little ones are still beyond the invader's farthest advance."

As these thoughts, which have here to be set down in words, were flashed into the doomed man's brain rather than evolved from it, the captain nodded to the sergeant. The sergeant stepped aside.

II

Peyton Farquhar was a well-to-do planter of an old and highly respected Alabama family. Being a slave owner and like other slave owners a politician, he was naturally an original secessionist and ardently devoted to the Southern cause. Circumstances of an imperious nature, which it is unnecessary to relate here, had prevented him from taking service with the gallant army which had fought the disastrous campaigns ending with the fall of Corinth, and he chafed under the inglorious restraint, longing for the release of his energies, the larger life of the soldier, the opportunity for distinction. That opportunity, he felt, would come, as it comes to all in war time. Meanwhile he did what he could. No service was too humble for him to perform in aid of the South, no adventure too perilous for him to undertake if consistent with the character of a civilian who was at heart a soldier, and who in good faith and without too much qualification assented to at least a part of the frankly villainous dictum that all is fair in love and war.

One evening while Farquhar and his wife were sitting on a rustic bench near the entrance to his grounds, a gray-clad soldier rode up to the gate and asked for a drink of water. Mrs. Farquhar was only too happy to serve him with her own white hands. While she was fetching the water her husband approached the dusty horseman and inquired eagerly for news from the front.

"The Yanks are repairing the railroads," said the man, "and are getting ready for another advance. They have reached the Owl Creek bridge, put it in order, and built a stockade on the north bank. The commandant has issued an order, which is posted everywhere, declaring that any civilian caught interfering with the railroad, its bridges, tunnels, or trains will be summarily hanged. I saw the order."

"How far is it to the Owl Creek bridge?" Farquhar asked.

"About thirty miles."

"Is there no force on this side the creek?"

"Only a picket post half a mile out, on the railroad, and a single sentinel at this end of the bridge."

"Suppose a man—a civilian and student of hanging—should elude the picket post and perhaps get the better of the sentinel," said Farquhar, smiling, "what could he accomplish?"

The soldier reflected. "I was there a month ago," he replied. "I observed that the flood of last winter had lodged a great quantity of driftwood against the wooden pier at this end of the bridge. It is now dry and would burn like tow."

The lady had now brought the water, which the soldier drank. He thanked her ceremoniously, bowed to her husband, and rode away. An hour later, after nightfall, he repassed the plantation, going northward in the direction from which he had come. He was a Federal scout.

III

As Peyton Farquhar fell straight downward through the bridge he lost consciousness and was as one already dead. From this state he was awakened—ages later, it seemed to him—by the pain of a sharp pressure upon his throat, followed by a sense of suffocation. Keen, poignant agonies seemed to shoot from his neck downward through every fiber of his body and limbs. These pains appeared to flash along well-defined lines of ramification and to beat with an inconceivably rapid periodicity. They seemed like streams of pulsating fire heating him to an intolerable temperature. As to his head, he was conscious of nothing but a feeling of fullness—of congestion. These sensations were unaccompanied by thought. The intellectual part of his nature was already effaced; he had power only to feel, and feeling was torment. He was conscious of motion. Encompassed in a luminous cloud, of which he was now merely the fiery heart, without material substance, he swung through unthinkable arcs of oscillation, like a vast pendulum. Then all at once, with terrible suddenness, the light about him shot upward with the noise of a loud plash; a frightful roaring was in his ears, and all was cold and dark. The power of thought was restored; he knew that the rope had broken and he had fallen into the stream. There was no additional strangulation; the noose about his neck was already suffocating him and kept the water from his lungs. To die of hanging at the bottom of a river!—the idea seemed to him ludicrous. He opened his eyes in the darkness and saw above him a gleam of light, but how distant, how inaccessible! He was still sinking, for the light became fainter and fainter until it was a mere glimmer. Then it began to grow and brighten, and he knew that he was rising toward the surface—knew it with reluctance, for he was now very comfortable. "To be hanged and drowned," he thought, "that is not so bad; but I do not wish to be shot. No; I will not be shot; that is not fair."

He was not conscious of an effort, but a sharp pain in his wrist apprised him that he was trying to free his hands. He gave the struggle his attention, as an idler might observe the feat of a juggler, without interest in the outcome. What splendid effort!— what magnificent, what superhuman strength! Ah, that was a fine endeavor! Bravo! The cord fell away; his arms parted and floated upward, the hands dimly seen on each side in the growing light. He watched them with a new interest as first one and then the other pounced upon the noose at his neck. They tore it away and thrust it fiercely aside, its undulations resembling those of a water snake. "Put it back, put it back!" He thought he shouted these words to his hands, for the undoing of the noose had been succeeded by the direst pang that he had yet experienced. His neck ached horribly; his brain was on fire; his heart, which had been fluttering faintly, gave a great leap, trying to force itself out at his mouth. His whole body was racked and wrenched with an insupportable anguish! But his disobedient hands gave no heed to the command. They beat the water vigorously with quick, downward strokes, forcing him to the surface. He felt his head emerge; his eyes were blinded by the sunlight; his chest expanded convulsively, and with a supreme and crowning agony his lungs engulfed a great draught of air, which instantly he expelled in a shriek!

He was now in full possession of his physical senses. They were, indeed, preternaturally keen and alert. Something in the awful disturbance of his organic system had so exalted and refined them that they made record of things never before perceived. He felt the ripples upon his face and heard their separate sounds as they struck. He looked at the forest on the bank of the stream, saw the individual trees, the leaves and the veining of each leaf—saw the very insects upon them: the locusts, the brilliant-bodied flies, the gray spiders stretching their webs from twig to twig. He noted the prismatic colors in all the dew-drops upon a million blades of grass. The humming of the gnats that danced above the eddies of the stream, the beating of the dragonflies' wings, the strokes of the water spiders' legs, like oars which had lifted their boat—all these made audible music. A fish slid along beneath his eyes and he heard the rush of its body parting the water.

He had come to the surface facing down the stream; in a moment the visible world seemed to wheel slowly round, himself the pivotal point, and he saw the bridge, the fort, the two soldiers upon the bridge, the captain, the sergeant, the two privates, his executioners. They were in silhouette against the blue sky. They shouted and gesticulated, pointing at him. The captain had drawn his pistol, but did not fire; the others were unarmed. Their movements were grotesque and horrible, their forms gigantic.

Suddenly he heard a sharp report and something struck the water smartly within a few inches of his head, spattering his face with spray. He heard a second report, and saw one of the sentinels with his rifle at his shoulder, a light cloud of blue smoke rising from the muzzle. The man in the water saw the eye of the man on the bridge gazing into his own through the sights of the rifle. He observed that it was a gray eye and remembered having read that gray eyes were keenest, and that all famous marksmen had them. Nevertheless, this one had missed.

A counterswirl had caught Farquhar and turned him half round; he was again looking into the forest on the bank opposite the fort. The sound of a clear, high voice in a monotonous sing-song now rang out behind him and came across the water with a distinctness that pierced and subdued all other sounds, even the beating of the ripples in his ears. Although no soldier, he had frequented camps enough to know the dread significance of that deliberate, drawling, aspirated chant; the lieutenant on shore was taking a part in the morning's work. How coldly and pitilessly—with what an even, calm intonation, presaging and enforcing tranquillity in the men—with what accurately measured intervals fell those cruel words:

"Attention, company! . . . Shoulder arms! . . . Ready! . . .
Aim! . . . Fire!"

Farquhar dived—dived as deeply as he could. The water
roared in his ears like the voice of Niagara, yet he heard the
dulled thunder of the volley and, rising again toward the surface,
met shining bits of metal, singularly flattened, oscillating slowly
downward. Some of them touched him on the face and hands,
then fell away, continuing their descent. One lodged between his
collar and neck; it was uncomfortably warm and he snatched
it out.

As he rose to the surface, gasping for breath, he saw that
he had been a long time under water; he was perceptibly farther
downstream—nearer to safety. The soldiers had almost finished
reloading; the metal ramrods flashed all at once in the sunshine
as they were drawn from the barrels, turned in the air, and thrust
into their sockets. The two sentinels fired again, independently
and ineffectually.

The hunted man saw all this over his shoulder; he was now
swimming vigorously with the current. His brain was as energetic
as his arms and legs; he thought with the rapidity of lightning.

"The officer," he reasoned, "will not make that martinet's
error a second time. It is as easy to dodge a volley as a single shot.
He has probably already given the command to fire at will. God
help me, I cannot dodge them all!"

An appalling plash within two yards of him was followed
by a loud, rushing sound, *diminuendo,* which seemed to travel
back through the air to the fort and died in an explosion which
stirred the very river to its deeps! A rising sheet of water, which
curved over him, fell down upon him, blinded him, strangled him!
The cannon had taken a hand in the game. As he shook his head
free from the commotion of the smitten water, he heard the de-
flected shot humming through the air ahead, and in an instant it
was cracking and smashing the branches in the forest beyond.

"They will not do that again," he thought; "the next time
they will use a charge of grape. I must keep my eye upon the
gun; the smoke will apprise me—the report arrives too late; it lags
behind the missile. That is a good gun."

Suddenly he felt himself whirled round and round—spinning like a top. The water, the banks, the forests, the now distant

bridge, fort, and men—all were commingled and blurred. Objects were represented by their colors only; circular horizontal streaks of color—that was all he saw. He had been caught in a vortex and was being whirled on with a velocity of advance and gyration which made him giddy and sick. In a few moments he was flung upon the gravel at the foot of the left bank of the stream—the southern bank—and behind a projecting point which concealed him from his enemies. The sudden arrest of his motion, the abrasion of one of his hands on the gravel, restored him, and he wept with delight. He dug his fingers into the sand, threw it over himself in handfuls, and audibly blessed it. It looked like diamonds, rubies, emeralds; he could think of nothing beautiful which it did not resemble. The trees upon the bank were giant garden plants; he noted a definite order in their arrangement, inhaled the fragrance of their blooms. A strange, roseate light shone through the spaces among their trunks and the wind made in their branches the music of aeolian harps. He had no wish to perfect his escape—was content to remain in that enchanting spot until retaken.

A whiz and rattle of grapeshot among the branches high above his head roused him from his dream. The baffled cannoneer had fired him a random farewell. He sprang to his feet, rushed up the sloping bank, and plunged into the forest.

All that day he traveled, laying his course by the rounding sun. The forest seemed interminable; nowhere did he discover a break in it, not even a woodman's road. He had not known that he lived in so wild a region. There was something uncanny in the revelation.

By nightfall he was fatigued, footsore, famishing. The thought of his wife and children urged him on. At last he found a road which led him in what he knew to be the right direction. It was as wide and straight as a city street, yet it seemed untraveled. No fields bordered it, no dwelling anywhere. Not so much as the barking of a dog suggested human habitation. The black bodies of the trees formed a straight wall on both sides, terminating on the horizon in a point, like a diagram in a lesson in perspective. Overhead, as he looked up through this rift in the wood, shone great golden stars looking unfamiliar and grouped in strange constellations. He was sure they were arranged in some order which had a secret and malign significance. The wood on either side was full of singular noises, among which—once, twice, and again—he distinctly heard whispers in an unknown tongue.

His neck was in pain and lifting his hand to it he found it horribly swollen. He knew that it had a circle of black where the rope had bruised it. His eyes felt congested; he could no longer close them. His tongue was swollen with thirst; he relieved its fever by thrusting it forward from between his teeth into the cold air. How softly the turf had carpeted the untraveled avenue—he could no longer feel the roadway beneath his feet!

Doubtless, despite his suffering, he had fallen asleep while walking, for now he sees another scene—perhaps he has merely recovered from a delirium. He stands at the gate of his own home. All is as he left it, and all bright and beautiful in the morning sunshine. He must have traveled the entire night. As he pushes open the gate and passes up the wide white walk, he sees a flutter of female garments; his wife, looking fresh and cool and sweet, steps down from the veranda to meet him. At the bottom of the steps she stands waiting, with a smile of ineffable joy, an attitude of matchless grace and dignity. Ah, how beautiful she is! He springs forward with extended arms. As he is about to clasp her, he feels a stunning blow upon the back of the neck; a blinding white light blazes all about him with a sound like the shock of a cannon—then all is darkness and silence!

Peyton Farquhar was dead; his body, with a broken neck, swung gently from side to side beneath the timbers of the Owl Creek bridge.

AMBROSE BIERCE was born in 1842 on a small farm in Meigs County, Ohio. He left home as a teen-ager and worked at numerous jobs before finally enlisting in the Union Army in 1861. He served honorably throughout the Civil War and, for his courage, received the rank of brevet major. After the war he went to San Francisco and became a journalist, eventually married, and then left for London. His stories and articles contain his own peculiar brand of acid humor and have earned him the name "Bitter Bierce." His most famous collection of caustic writings is entitled *The Devil's Dictionary*. In 1913 he disappeared into Mexico and was never seen again.

Maurice Ogden

What would you do if you found yourself driving on a strange freeway with no off-ramps and you didn't know where you were going? Would you keep driving to find out where the freeway ended?

One family did just that in

FREEWAY
TO WHEREVER

Rapid as spilled mercury, the freeway flowed west in a gay pattern of shifting pastels.

With easy motions Tom wove a brilliant way through the pattern, mildly intoxicated with power and combativeness. Beside him Mary lolled on the luxurious leather, breathing the rich new-car smell and trying hard to maintain a countenance of bored unconcern.

The children, momentarily subdued by the sweeping wallop Tom had aimed at Janey for bouncing on the rear cushion, had recovered enough to stand with arms braced on the back of the front seat.

No one knew where the freeway went—no one was curious.

"Will our car go faster than the Powers'?" Bobby demanded.

"Sure, I told you," Tom said.

"Is it a better car?"

"I told you twice. It cost a thousand dollars more, it's got fifty horsepower more, it's five inches longer, and it has an extra strip of chrome on the side."

"You children shouldn't worry about things like that," Mary put in mechanically.

"After the way Jim Powers lorded it over everybody when he bought that monstrosity?" Tom demanded. "You just tell Jimmy your folks wouldn't pay out good money for a car as cheap as theirs."

"We did get a prettier color combination," Mary said complacently. "It was the first thing I noticed."

Ahead of them, the traffic moved like a school of gaudy minnows, its common motion dramatically varied with angular darts and surges. A canary hardtop in the slower lane to their right challenged alertly as a brief opening appeared magically in front of them. Tom touched the accelerator, gratified at the smooth burst of power.

"Ah, you joker you!" he chuckled triumphantly.

Frustrated, the hardtop dropped back into its own lane.

A powder-blue convertible slid alongside and paced them on the right. The driver, a well-fed man with a large stone on the little finger of his near hand, grinned floridly around his cigar.

"Anybody know where this thing goes?" he asked across the few inches separating him from Mary. "I got on it by mistake."

Mary continued to stare ahead coldly, but her hands began a nervous fumbling in her purse for a cigarette. Tom leaned across her and called, "Search me, buddy. We made a wrong turn back there someplace, too."

Everybody laughed—even Mary, who had found a cigarette and recovered her composure now that Tom had taken the situation in hand.

"Who cares?" the man said, laughing. "Easiest-riding durn road I ever drove. Wonder where the eastbound is?"

"Probably on another level," Mary said, fumbling for a match.

"Be my guest..." The man extended a folder across the wind-whipped space. Mary took it and lit her cigarette.

"Look, Tom," she said, "real little sulphur matches!"

"Read the cover," their owner called over to her.

Obediently, she read:

DICK BLUE'S DRIVE-INS.
Matchless food wherever you are!

"That's me, Dick Blue," the man said. "Big blue signs, get it? And I do mean wherever. When we get to where this thing goes, I bet the first thing you recognize will be a big blue sign."

"I've seen them around," Tom said vaguely.

"Keep 'em," the man said expansively as Mary started to return the matches. "I got a ton of 'em."

A horn sounded impatiently behind him.

"Well, see you folks in wherever-it-is." He touched his hat jauntily and surged ahead.

"Character," Tom commented.

"Awfully common," Mary said.

"Worth a mint, though, I bet."

"I'm hungry," Janey announced from the back seat.

"Me too," Bobby seconded.

"We'll take the next turnoff and get a hot dog," Tom promised.

"There don't seem to be too many turnoffs."

"We passed one back there while you were talking to that man," Mary said.

"I saw it, but it would have caused a royal foulup if I'd tried to cut over."

"There must be plenty of turn-*ons*," Mary observed. "I don't think there's anybody in the world driving anyplace else."

"Maybe a few clowns in Model T's that can't make the speed," Tom said, and the children laughed. Cutting speed, he eased lane by lane to the slow-flowing file on the right.

"This is what I hate about the outside," he said. "Over here you always get stuck behind some clunk, and on the inside there's always some joker with two carburetors trying to blast you out of the way. The middle's easier on your nerves."

"Just an old middle-of-the-freewayer," Mary said, craning her neck to peer down the outside of the roadbed.

"I can't see a turnoff on this side," she announced, withdrawing behind the windshield. "Maybe there's one on the other side."

Whipping along at the furious pace of the inside lane, Tom leaned out with the wind beating at his hair. He retreated quickly, rubbing his eyes. No exit was visible.

"You'd think there'd be signs of some kind," Mary complained.

"There generally are," he said. "I guess they haven't got around to it yet."

The children had started a game, counting the lavender-flowering crests of jacaranda trees, rising from invisible landscaping below the roadbed, with points for the first to spy each one.

"Remember how we used to do that with white horses?" Mary said. Tom nodded absently.

"You'd of thought there'd be big headlines when they opened up a stretch this big," he said thoughtfully. "I can't figure out where it could go."

"Free ride to Fateville," Mary said in a singsong voice.

"What?"

"My sister," she explained, giggling a little. "I hadn't thought of it in years. Every Saturday we used to go into Fayetteville, and she'd be ready hours before anybody else, standing out by the car and yelling 'Free ride to Fateville!' every time anybody looked out the door."

"Your sister's a real cute kid," Tom said in a flat voice.

"You don't have to be snotty."

"Who's snotty?" Tom braked violently as a pert sports car whipped saucily in front of him. "Damn smart aleck!"

"Caught you napping, didn't he?"

"There's one too many drivers in this car," Tom said tightly.

As the traffic increased, the freeway's holiday mood slipped imperceptibly into irritable impatience. The current flowed slower and more tensely, and the fluid shifting of the pastel pattern became skittish and erratic. Now the greetings and laughter exchanged between strangers an hour earlier had become the grim silence between antagonists, broken by an occasional hysterical protest of rubber on cement or the momentary grate of metal against metal. From behind sun-glazed windows, faces peered out in attitudes of anxiety and hostility.

"We're finally coming to something," Tom said, pointing to a yellow pall of smog hanging along the horizon.

"I hope we can turn off before then," Mary protested. "It doesn't look very inviting."

"Oh, la-de-da!" Tom said in resigned disgust.

Suddenly he wrestled the wheel over frantically, shouting something incoherent at the driver on his left, who shouted back in flushed fury. Mary, thrown against Tom, pushed herself away and screamed as they caromed against the car on the right with a brief metallic screech. Tom and the other driver snarled at each other.

"There goes a hundred dollars' worth of paint," he groaned.

"Well, la-de-da!" Mary said viciously.

"Shut up!" he said. "Just shut up!"

"You too!" he added savagely as the children started to whimper chorally.

"I'm hungry!" Janey whined.

"I wanta get home before dark so Jimmy can see the car," Bobby complained.

"You two want another wallop?" Tom bellowed. They subsided resentfully.

"It beats me," he said, "why kids can't enjoy a ride without feeling mistreated if there's not a whole bunch of added attractions."

"They're only children," Mary said loftily.

"What kind of an alibi is that?"

"It's *so hot*." She ignored the question, passing her hands under her hair in a gesture he had always found particularly offensive. She touched the button, and the glass beside her slid down.

"It's just as hot out there," Tom grumbled.

"Maybe we should have got the one with the air-conditioners."

Ahead, the sun rested on the horizon, saffron and unreal behind the smog.

"I wonder." Mary stared fixedly through the windshield, half hypnotized by the sluggish shuttling of the traffic. "Is a new car really so much?"

"So much?" he demanded indignantly. "So much! I just wish I had a nickel for every time you've said, 'When we get the furniture paid for, and drive the best car on the block, we'll be fixed for life.' I just wish, that's all. What do you mean, 'so much'?"

"Oh, I don't know. But it seems like when what you want most is . . . is a *thing* . . . well, you always feel a little bit disappointed when you actually get it. Like a big part was just having something to want. Don't you ever feel that way?"

He concentrated stubbornly on his driving, refusing to commit himself. She sensed suddenly that he was bewildered and hurt, touched in some secret place. It was a new and unexpected insight, maliciously gratifying.

"Here we are, thirty years old, and we've got what we always said we wanted. It almost seems like we didn't have anything left to live for."

She was too tired to pursue it, too much caught up in a vague, critical uneasiness to relax.

"All those people out there." She glanced around at the montage of sullen and anxious faces behind their transparent shields. "What are they thinking about? I bet you could write an awful story about every one of them if you knew what they know about themselves."

"What are you all of a sudden?" he demanded irritably. "A philosopher or somebody?"

"I don't know." She stretched and yawned. "I guess I'm just tired and bored. How much longer do you think it will be before we can turn off?"

"How should I know?"

"I said how long do you *think*—but just skip it." Absently, she looked into the back seat. The children were asleep, their plump faces sullen and unattractive.

"Looks like an intersection up there."

Mary looked. The yellow smog had grown, reaching half-way up the evening sky now. Below it, she could make out the gray line of an elevation at right angles to the freeway, and what appeared to be a mammoth overpass.

"Well, thank heavens we're getting someplace finally," she breathed.

They drove for thirty minutes in blank silence.

"Tom!" Mary clutched his arm in sudden alarm. "That's not another freeway. It's some kind of a wall."

He nodded absently. "I've been watching it. Maybe it's a military setup or something."

Without warning, she began to cry weakly.

"Tom, couldn't we just pull over to the side and stop? We could climb down the embankment and find out where we are, or get directions or something. We could walk someplace if we had to."

"Are you crazy? One car stopped here would either get clobbered or jam things up clear back to the beginning. The one thing we can't do is stop."

The traffic moved slowly and orderly now, like a lava-flow. In the gathering twilight, like the sound of disturbed crickets, anxious voices and snatches of frightened questions floated to them from the surrounding automobiles.

Then, trapped and pressed forward in the relentless flow, they were crossing to the mighty gate, between the grim, smoke-blackened battlements reared against the black sky, and the scarred, ageless granite of ponderous walls.

Beyond, the indestructible city burned luridly.

The pastel pattern moved steadily into it, and all of a sudden nobody was very surprised, and nobody asked any more questions.

MAURICE OGDEN was born in Whizbang (now Denoya), Okla-homa. He received his education in Oklahoma and has since worked at a variety of jobs—steelworker, radio announcer, truck driver, and writer.

William Peden

Do you think carnival Ferris wheels, loop-the-loops, and other rides are dangerous for children to ride on?

What would you do if someone you knew disappeared while riding a Ferris wheel?

It might happen during a

NIGHT IN FUNLAND

They drove slowly down the highway that cut cleanly through the desert, past the glittering motels with their swimming pools of pale blue water, past the shops of pink or green or azure adobe. In the humming light of the mercury-vapor lamps, the child was a gnome in a pool of color, the shadows beneath her eyes sooty in the darkness that had overrun the mesa. The father reached over and patted her hand. She squeezed his and edged closer toward him.

"Are you sure this is the way, Daddy?"

"Of course it is, Amanda, don't you remember?"

"Well, yes, sort of, but I thought maybe it was the other way."

"The other way is east, goosie," he said; "we go west. Look, in a minute, at the next stop light, we'll see the wheel, and then you'll remember."

At the intersection he slowed down as the traffic light clicked from green to amber and then to red.

"Look..." He pointed at the rosy sky. "Over there; can't you see the top of the Ferris wheel?"

She squealed with delight; then the light changed and they left the shining highway, and in darkness that was like a sudden plunge into unknown waters turned onto a bumpy dirt road.

"Can we get there this way?" Amanda asked. "Does this road go through?"

"Don't worry; sure it does, honey. You just wait."

Then they were pulling into the tumbleweed-speckled parking lot. He switched off the motor and turned off the lights and went around and opened her door. Amanda came out slowly, and she smiled up at her spare, slightly stooped father.

"This is fun," she said. She reached for his hand and they walked beneath the arch that spelled out F-U-N-L-A-N-D in winking colored lights. It was a clean bright place, no leg shows, no wheels of fortune, no freak tents with greenish two-headed babies in discolored alcohol-filled jars; a clean bright place on the mesa, bounded by a miniature railroad with puffing steam engine and train of cars. They could hear the whistle now at the far dark end of the park, faraway and thin and clear, and Amanda tugged at his hand again. He wanted to pull her close to him and kiss her and pat her thin hair and tell her how glad he was that she was so much better and they could go on a spree together as they had in the old days, and he patted her hand and buttoned the top button of her sweater.

"Let's sit down a little," he said. His heart was thumping and the palms of his hands were damp.

"Oh, Daddy," she said, "not now."

"You must rest a minute," he insisted; "you must remember this is the first time...."

They sat down on the bench by the small depot, and the train with its bell clanging and its whistle shrilling and its headlight stabbing at the night swung around the turn and stopped quietly almost in front of them. The engineer, a teen-aged boy crouching precariously on the tender, got up to stretch his legs while the young passengers spilled from the coaches.

"What shall we do first?" the father asked. "Do you want to ride the train?"

"I'd like a snowball first," she said. Children were climbing on and off the train like monkeys and he thought there were too many of them and one of them might cough on her or something; it wouldn't help her, God knows, to catch a cold just now. She walked ahead of him slowly, a trace of her old jauntiness in the blue toreadors with the white bows tied neatly just below her knees and the white-trimmed cap on her dark head, past the pool with its boats floating in the oil-dark water, and the enclosure where the ponies awaited their riders, and the clanking fury of the scenic railway.

"This is the nicest park ever," he said, and squeezed her hand. "I've never been in a nicer park, have you, Amanda?"

"No," she said; "it's the nicest ever."

At the refreshment booth he ordered two snowballs with grape flavoring. The efficient girl in her starched white uniform pushed a button and there was a whirling sound, and ice as white and fine as snow poured through a vent, and the girl scooped it up and expertly without touching it by hand transferred it into paper cups, and then she squirted thick dark purple fluid onto the ice, and it was suddenly, magically, like a sunset transformed into a violet delight, and she smiled and passed the cups over the counter.

"Keep your fingers out of it," he said to Amanda.

They rested on a bench and tilted the cups to their lips, and the sweet ice gushed into their mouths.

"Isn't it good?" Amanda said. "It gets sweeter as it goes down."

"Yes," he said, and thought how few things were sweeter as they got down, and he squeezed his cup and the fluid was bright and clean in his mouth.

"This is the nicest park there is," he said again.

"Yes," she said, and drained at her snowball with a sucking, bubbling sound. She thrust her thin fingers into the cup to extract the last sweet dregs. Roughly he snatched out her hand and slapped her hard, and cried by God he had told her to keep her fingers out of it and did she want to get sick all over again. She flushed and he felt as if he had kicked her, and he pulled her close to him and kissed and stroked her hair; her thinness was like a blow.

"I'm so sorry, honey," he said, "but I've been worried

about you. You mustn't mind when I act like this. It's only because I love you so much, and I don't want you to get sick again,
ever."

She slowly turned her head towards him, and tried to
smile, and he took out his monogrammed handkerchief and
brushed at the corners of her eyes.

"Now how do you feel?" he asked, and when she said
she felt fine he wanted to shout and dance and sing. He held her
hand as they walked away from the refreshment booth while the
starched girl squinted at him, and they walked slowly over the
hard-packed grayish dirt. There was very little dust, he thought
with satisfaction; he had never known a place like Funland to be
so clean and orderly.

Amanda suddenly broke from his grasp.

"Oh," she cried, and ran towards a large brightly lighted
cage near an open place where baby tanks puffed and grunted.

"Look," she called; "oh, Daddy, look."

In the bright clean cage, littered with a scooter, a tricycle,
rubber balls, a trapeze, and a punching bag, a young chimpanzee
sat in a baby's high chair, munching at a banana.

"Rollo," the sign atop the cage read, "Just Recently
Arrived from the Belgian Congo Region of West Africa. A two-
year-old chimpanzee . . . just four and a half months in captivity."

Daintily Rollo nibbled, breaking off small chunks with his
long-haired, tiny-nailed hands and placing the fruit meticulously
in a mouth like the furnace door or the small train emerging from
its tunnel with a triumphant toot and jangle. The chimpanzee
finished his treat, placed the parachute of limp skin on the tray of
his chair, and wiped his hands on scarlet trousers. Amanda
screamed with delight and Rollo swung with dedicated grace to
land noiselessly on the floor with flat tennis-shoe-clad feet. With
beautiful, strong, pink-palmed hands he grasped the bars of his
cage and gazed at the child, stone-dark eyes in his clean tan face,
and he opened his great lips and smiled.

Amanda clapped her hands and Rollo whirled and leaped
to the rope which spanned the cage; hand over hand, he swung
from one end of the cage to the other. By ones and twos people
approached, laughing and chatting, and Rollo again dropped like
a sunbeam to the floor. His trainer, a gentle, patient man with a
limp and a face too much like Rollo's to be a coincidence, reached

for the roller skates hanging on the wall and attached them to the chimpanzee's high-topped tennis shoes. He held his hand, and Rollo glided noiselessly on his well-oiled skates, skating surely and competently and enjoying himself.

When the man climbed clumsily over the low iron railing in front of the cage and tossed a few pieces of popcorn between the bars, Rollo stumbled and almost fell. The attendant reached quickly for the chimpanzee's hand, and frowned at the intruder. Amanda turned upon the popcorn thrower, a fat man whose hairy black nipples stared blankly beneath a bilge-colored nylon sport shirt.

"You've frightened him," she said in sudden fury. "You've frightened him."

In anger the fat man threw another handful of popcorn between the bars, and the trainer sadly shook his head. Still holding Rollo by the hand, he led him to the high chair and swung him up to the seat, and removed the skates. Then he pulled a switch, and all the lights in the cage went out. Rollo sat alone, his yellow shirt and scarlet trousers and sneakered feet now gray in the darkness.

"Christ," the fat man said. "Who does that guy think he is, anyways? Christ, it's only a monkey."

He grabbed his fat child, a child with a face like a rutabaga, and disappeared.

"What a horrid, nasty man," Amanda said. "Can't we see Rollo again? Won't he come out again?"

"Maybe later," the father said; "maybe later."

"Besides," she said, "he's not a monkey. He's a chimpanzee, an anth . . . anthropoid, isn't he, Daddy?"

"That's right," he said. "He's not a monkey, he's an anthropoid, and maybe he'll come out later anyhow."

Amanda walked away, but soon stopped at the foot of the Ferris wheel. She gazed upwards at its swift smoothness, sparkling, a small circle of lights winking near the hub, and a larger circle glowing in the middle, and the whole great machine alive with an outline of red and blue and green neon tubing, flashing as the twelve carriages, one red then one black and then another red and another black, swam miraculously into the cool dry blackness of the starless night, some carriages swinging empty, in another two teen-age girls singing *Oklahoma*, in others a father and a white-faced, pop-eyed infant, a young man and a girl, their arms locked around each other as they soared from the light to the darkness, and two boys clowning and roaring. The operator squeezed the grip-handle of the lever and pushed it and the engine slowed down, and the wheel came to a silent stop. There was a sudden, almost reverent hush, and a squeal of terrified delight from the occupants of the carriage at the very top of the wheel swinging coldly in the dark, and then the voices of the girls singing *Oklahoma* clear and far away and miles and miles away in the thin cold air at the top of the wheel, and miles and miles away from the hard gray ground and the prancing merry-go-round horses with their flaring orange nostrils and white champing cannibal teeth and the refreshment stand with the efficient girl in her starched white uniform. The operator stepped on a pedal, and a landing platform slid close to the carriage; the attendant lifted the bar and the occupants stepped gingerly down, the father glad to deposit the child into the mother's arms.

"Must we ride this now, Amanda?" the father asked.

"Oh, yes," she said and edged her way towards the entrance. "Can I," she said, and squeezed his hand, and her dark eyes glistened, "oh, can I go all alone like you promised when I was sick?"

"Let me go with you," he said.

"Don't be a meanie," she said. "Please, Daddy, remember you promised."

"All right," he said. "All right, but you must be very, very careful. You must promise to sit right in the middle of the seat, and you must keep your hands tight on the bar all the time. Do you promise?"

"Brownie's honor," she said and held up her hand, palm outwards and two fingers aloft in a half salute. She hugged him, and he lowered his head and she brushed his cheek with a quick kiss.

The wheel stopped again, and he gave her the money and said loudly, "Give it to the man." He looked at the operator like a fellow-conspirator suddenly catching in a great crowd the long-anticipated signal, and again he said loudly, "If you don't sit right in the middle and hold the bar tightly I shall ask the attendant to stop the wheel."

"Oh, Daddy," she said. The operator smiled when she

gave him the money, and placed her firmly in the very middle of the carriage, clicking the protective bar into place with special emphasis as though to say: I understand the way you feel; don't worry.

Amanda sat very straight in her seat and gripped the iron bar. The operator pushed the lever slowly forward, and the wheel rose noiselessly. Amanda smiled from her perch as the operator again pulled back the lever, and the wheel stopped and an aged man and wife emerged from their carriage as though from the floor of the ocean.

Again the operator pushed the lever, and the wheel began to turn. The father ran back a few feet; he could see Amanda tiny, disappearing into the darkness. He hoped the operator would not halt the wheel with Amanda's carriage at the summit. His scrotum tightened as he thought of her, up there alone in the dark. He saw the crouching mountains, a ragged darkness palpable against the blue-black of the night, and the city swimming in a blob of red and blue and green and orange and white lights, while to the west naked and blue the desert scattered its bones to the ends of the vanished watershed. Then Amanda in a black carriage outlined with green neon swept past him and smiled and was gone. He started to wave, but checked his arm, not wanting her to take her hands from the iron bar to reply. Then in what seemed an instant she came by him again, and he winked at her reassuringly before her carriage swam upwards into the darkness. He looked at the sturdy iron wheel and the concrete foundation. This was no fly-by-night carnival, but a permanent operation, thank God, he thought; thousands of people rode the safe, sturdy wheel each season. Again Amanda was smiling when her carriage flashed by, and he lighted a cigarette and smiled conspiratorially at the operator in his white overalls, a sensible man with one foot resting nonchalantly near the fly-wheel of the generator.

He counted the carriages as they glided before his line of vision, one red then one black, then another red and another black. He awaited the passage of Amanda's carriage which he must have missed while he was lighting his cigarette. Suddenly, painfully, a hard ball of fear exploded in his throat.

This is absurd, he thought. He forced himself to stand still and look with studied calm at the swiftly turning wheel. What had been the color of the tubing which outlined Amanda's carriage? Green? No, red. Surely not red on a red, or was it a black, carriage?

The wheel made several more swift, noiseless circuits, and still he could not see the pale smiling face of Amanda. His hands shook and sweat drenched his back and upper legs. With an effort as conscious and deliberate as holding his breath under water he controlled himself. This is ridiculous, he thought. This is an optical illusion. He said to himself, I will count each carriage very carefully as it goes past, and then I'll see her, and soon the wheel will stop, and she'll get out, and we'll have a very good laugh about this.

He counted the carriages as they glided swiftly before his eyes. First a red with an old man, then two empties, then a black with two grinning nobheaded boys, then a red with the girls now singing *Oh, What a Beautiful Morning*, then an empty, then another red, and his heart suddenly soared like a geyser only to sink hideously; it was not Amanda, but a much older child. Then a man and a child and two more empties, then a red with a mother and a baby followed by a black with a soldier and a girl, then another red with an old.man, the same hideous old man he'd begun counting with, and with a cry like an animal's he leaped over the low steel railing and clutched at the attendant's arm.

"Stop it," he said, "for God's sake, stop the wheel."

The attendant frowned, then smiled, and squeezed the handle of the lever, and pulled back the lever, and an empty black carriage swung like a dry leaf above his head.

"My daughter," he gasped, "the little one with the black hair," but two dirty-nosed boys pushed their way between him and the operator, poking out their hands with the money in them, and climbed into the carriage snickering and guffawing and wolfing popcorn.

"For the love of God!" he cried, and the popcorn-eaters looked at him as though he were an ape in a straw hat. "For the love of God, where is my daughter? I think it's time you let the little girl off. The one with the black hair. She has on a blue suit and a cap. You remember?"

"Yes sir," the attendant said, and smiled.

Relief flowed through him; he slapped the operator heartily on the back. "I lost sight of her for a moment," he said. "In the dark. My eyes. It gave me a turn, for a moment."

The operator nodded, and pushed the lever, and the next carriage, empty, swung past, and he stopped the wheel at the next to let the mother and baby out. The baby had wet its diaper and a black stain overspread the mother's breast like a wound. Then there was the carriage with the soldier and the girl, and they leaned out and yelled whatsthematterwhyduhyuhkeepstoppinthewheel? Then another empty and one in red with the old man, and he lost count.

"Amanda," he screamed. His voice was like a ship sinking darkly. "Amanda," he screamed again, and the attendant stopped the wheel and came towards him and he was no longer smiling. People converged upon him, he was the center of a whirling funnel of blank paper faces.

"Good God, good God," he cried. "Where are you, baby?"

The children in the toy train again making its sliding halt before the depot leaned over the edges of the coaches and looked questioningly at the Ferris wheel glowing in the distance.

"Amanda," the father cried, and the sound tore and twisted its way above the clanking of the scenic railway and the put-put-put of the miniature tractors and the wheezing of the merry-go-round. Noiselessly the curtains of the clean cage parted, and the lights flowed on, and Rollo climbed quietly down from his high chair. He listened intently to the wild broken cries in the night. Then he pressed his tan face against the bars and gazed with comprehending eyes at the dark figure with uplifted head outlined like a corpse against the spokes of the great wheel blazing in the night.

WILLIAM PEDEN was born in 1913 and educated at the University of Virginia, where he received his bachelor's, master's, and Ph.D. degrees by 1942. He has taught at the Universities of Virginia, Maryland, New Mexico, and Missouri. In addition, he has served as a staff member at several writers' conferences, received a Guggenheim Fellowship, and worked as an editor of *Story* magazine. His books include *The American Short Story*, *29 Stories* (a critical anthology), and *Night in Funland and Other Stories*.

STUDY GUIDE

THE SUPERMEN

What Facts Do You Remember?

1. When the three young men came into George Summers' lunch-room, the first thing one of them asked for was (a) money, (b) cigarettes, (c) liquor, (d) food.

2. George Summers remembered the store owner at Turner Corners who (a) sold out in disgust, (b) arrested three young men, (c) bought a pistol, (d) was found dead.

3. George was backed up tight against the (a) wall, (b) shelves, (c) counter, (d) telephone booth.

4. George had seen combat in (a) World War I, (b) World War II, (c) the Korean War, (d) Vietnam.

5. When Joe took the money out of the cash register, he announced the amount as (a) two hundred and ten smacks, (b) a hundred and eighty clams, (c) seventy-five beans, (d) sixty bucks.

6. When the leader said "Hit him a couple, Joe," Joe stepped forward and (a) took out a piece of lead pipe, (b) raised his fists threateningly, (c) slugged George in the stomach, (d) refused to do anything.

7. When George pulled out his hand in front of him, he held a (a) sword, (b) hand grenade, (c) Colt revolver, (d) Luger pistol.

8. When George asked "Was it you boys at Turner Corners?" the young man (a) laughed, (b) nodded yes, (c) ran out the door, (d) fired his gun.

What Ideas Did You Find?

1. The title of this story, "The Supermen," refers to (a) vigilante citizens like George, (b) the young people of today, (c) young hoodlums who resemble Hitler's Nazis, (d) members of the Hell's Angels motorcycle club or some similar organization.

2. The "terrible need" in the last sentence of the story refers to the need for (a) worldwide peace, (b) better law enforcement, (c) a man to kill in self-defense, (d) everyone to own a gun.

Composition Exercises

1. You are the police officer investigating the shooting at George Summers' lunchroom. Describe in detail (with dimensions, etc.) what you find there. Mention the layout of the lunchroom, positions of the participants, locations of the bodies, the bullet holes, and anything else you notice.

2. You are George Summers on the witness stand at the coroner's inquest. In your own words, give your testimony of what happened in the lunchroom and why you shot the three young men.

Language Exercise

Prefixes: Many words in the English language are made up of two words hooked together, such as *supermen* in the title of this story. In this example *super* is called a *prefix* because it "fixes" on "before." In the same way the word *hinterlands* (p. 2) is made up of two words—*hinter* and *lands*. Here the prefix comes from a German preposition meaning *behind*. Therefore the word *hinterlands* means "behind lands" or "back country." See if you can discover five more words using the prefix *super* and a root word, as in *supermarket*. Also try to find five words that include the word *land*, either as a root word with a prefix word attached (*highland*) or as a prefix word with a root word attached (*landlady*).

MARIHUANA AND A PISTOL

What Facts Do You Remember?

1. "Red" Caldwell's girlfriend had quit him because (a) she caught him with another woman, (b) he didn't have any more money to spend on her, (c) he was shiftless and lazy, (d) she thought he drank too much.

2. Caldwell's first idea after the marihuana began to take effect was to turn on the (a) radio, (b) television, (c) heater, (d) light bulb.

3. His second idea was to (a) call the gang for a party, (b) stick up the Cleveland Trust Company, (c) go rob a movie house, (d) play Russian roulette.

4. As he walked down the street, he found himself in front of a (a) confectionery store, (b) liquor store, (c) hardware store, (d) department store.

5. When he got inside the store, he found that (a) he was afraid, (b) there were too many people in the store, (c) he had forgotten what he had come in for, (d) the owner ignored him.

6. When the owner asked him what he wanted, Red (a) began to laugh uncontrollably, (b) sat down in the middle of the floor, (c) told the owner to shut up, (d) pulled the trigger five times.

7. After a fit of laughter, Red ate some (a) peanuts, (b) sunflower seeds, (c) peppermint candy, (d) potato chips.

8. When Red bent over to vomit, he saw (a) two five-dollar bills, (b) his name written in blood, (c) a dead man, (d) a joint of marihuana.

What Ideas Did You Find?

1. The main idea the author is trying to describe for the reader is (a) the result of a murder, (b) what happens during a robbery, (c) the effect of marihuana on a person's thinking, (d) the consequences of falling in love.

2. Because he brings together a pistol and marihuana, the author is perhaps expressing his own (a) disapproval of marihuana, (b) interest in violent murder, (c) fear of marihuana smokers, (d) hatred of store owners.

Composition Exercises

Select *one* of the following:

1. (a) You are the defense attorney at Red Caldwell's trial. Explain to the jury why Red was not responsible for his actions during the robbery and murder. Make your argument convincing, and try to obtain a "not guilty" verdict.

   (b) You are the prosecuting attorney at Red's trial. Argue that the defendant should be judged guilty of armed robbery and murder, even though he was on drugs. Try to convince the jury to bring in a "guilty" verdict.

2. Relate an incident involving drugs or liquor that you know about in which a person committed a crime or almost committed a crime.

3. Write a letter to the editor of your local newspaper in which you defend or reject the proposition that marihuana be legalized and controlled like liquor.

Language Exercise

Match each word on the left with its correct definition on the right.

1. despondency (p. 7)
2. grotesque (p. 7)
3. excruciatingly (p. 8)
4. livid (p. 8)
5. eluded (p. 8)
6. sinister (p. 8)
7. essence (p. 9)
8. engulfed (p. 9)
9. sheer (p. 9)
10. reveling (p. 9)
11. gorged (p. 9)
12. brackish (p. 9)

a. true substance
b. end-over-end
c. wicked, evil, ominous
d. dejection
e. salty and distasteful
f. agonizingly, painfully
g. changed beyond recognition
h. distorted, fantastic, bizarre
i. escaped, evaded
j. grayish-blue or lead-colored
k. merrymaking
l. absolute, pure
m. overwhelmed, swallowed up
n. ate gluttonously

THE SNIPER

What Facts Do You Remember?

1. This story takes place in what city? (a) London, (b) Dublin, (c) Paris, (d) Madrid.

2. The civil war in this story was between the Irish Free Staters and the (a) Anarchists, (b) Democrats, (c) Republicans, (d) Loyalists.

3. The sniper in this story is on (a) a window ledge, (b) O'Connell Bridge, (c) a stairway, (d) a rooftop.

4. The sniper soon discovered that the man opposite him was (a) dead, (b) firing a machine gun, (c) shooting at troops in the street, (d) shooting at him.

5. The sniper shot at the woman in the street and (a) missed her, (b) killed her, (c) wounded her, (d) scared her.

6. The sniper was wounded in his (a) hand, (b) neck, (c) shoulder, (d) arm.

7. The sniper managed to kill the enemy sniper with his (a) revolver, (b) rifle, (c) knife, (d) hands.

8. When the sniper examined the body of his enemy, he saw (a) his best friend, (b) his father, (c) his brother, (d) his cousin.

What Ideas Did You Find?

1. The sniper killed the old woman in the street because (a) he hated her for telling on him, (b) she was a threat to his security, (c) he wanted revenge, (d) she was an enemy agent.

2. The author wants us to believe that (a) snipers are vicious, (b) war is exciting, (c) killing in war is ironic, (d) men should all become brothers.

Composition Exercises

1. You are the sniper, but you refuse to accept another assignment. Write to your commander to explain your reasons.

2. Draw a word picture of the sniper lying in wait on the rooftop. Visualize your description as a telephoto snapshot in color. Start with the frame or edge of the snapshot, and work toward the center with the man as the focal point. Provide as many details of the picture as possible.

Language Exercise

Look up each of the following words in a dictionary, and decide which alternative word (synonym) provides almost the same meaning.

1. *beleaguered*: "Around the *beleaguered* Four Courts the heavy guns roared." (p. 11)
   (a) bedazzled, (b) bewildered, (c) beguiled, (d) besieged.

2. *ascetic*: "His face was the face of a student—thin and *ascetic*." (p. 11)
   (a) severe, (b) painful, (c) germicidal, (d) colorless.

3. *paroxysm*: "A *paroxysm* of pain swept through him." (p. 13)
   (a) intensity, (b) fear, (c) quantity, (d) spasm.

4. *ruse*: "His *ruse* had succeeded." (p. 13)
   (a) activity, (b) development, (c) stratagem, (d) changeover.

5. *gibber*: ". . . he began to *gibber* to himself." (p. 14)
   (a) complain, (b) argue, (c) chatter, (d) swear.

JUST LATHER, THAT'S ALL

What Facts Do You Remember?

1. When the man sat down in the barber chair, he asked for a (a) haircut, (b) shave, (c) shampoo, (d) shave and shampoo.

2. When the barber asked him how many he had caught on his expedition, Captain Torres said (a) forty, (b) thirty-four, (c) twenty, (d) fourteen.

3. The barber thought of Captain Torres as a (a) man of imagination, (b) conscientious policeman, (c) stupid military officer, (d) strange and villainous madman.

4. The barber wanted to give Captain Torres a good shave because (a) the barber feared for his life, (b) Captain Torres was a handsome man, (c) the barber was a conscientious professional, (d) Captain Torres would praise his skill.

5. Captain Torres asked the barber to come to the school at (a) twelve noon, (b) two o'clock, (c) four o'clock, (d) six o'clock.

6. As the beard disappeared, the barber thought Captain Torres looked (a) older and wearied, (b) younger and rejuvenated, (c) sadder and wiser, (d) meaner and more cunning.

7. The barber finally decided against killing Captain Torres because (a) he didn't want blood on his hands, (b) murder would not satisfy his hatred, (c) he wanted to confuse his enemy, (d) someone might see him do it.

8. When Captain Torres left the shop, he said, (a) "They told me you are the best barber in the village," (b) "They said I need have no fear of you," (c) "They told me that you'd kill me," (d) "They said you believe killing is easy."

What Ideas Did You Find?

1. The barber didn't kill his enemy because he (a) was sure he'd be caught, (b) didn't know what to do with the body, (c) was not an executioner—just a barber, (d) was afraid of the sight of blood.

2. One of the main ideas in this story is that (a) killing isn't easy, (b) anyone could be a murderer, (c) revolutionaries are always caught, (d) the more a person delays, the less likely he is to act.

Composition Exercises

1. Continue the story and tell what happens to the barber. Now that Torres knows the barber is a revolutionary, will he arrest him and have him executed? Or will he allow the barber to remain frightened, never knowing what to expect?

2. You are an investigating officer in the barber's revolutionary army, and you are assigned to find out about this incident. Write a report to your commander, Captain Gonzales, arguing as follows: (a) the barber could have and should have killed Captain Torres while he had the opportunity; or (b) the barber could not and should not have killed Captain Torres. Use as many arguments as you can to prove your point.

Language Exercise

Select the letter of the definition that best fits the meaning of the word used in the sentence.

1. *gesture*: "with a *gesture* of fatigue" (p. 17)
   (a) angry expression, (b) a movement of the body, (c) a gushing eruption, (d) an attitude or belief.

2. *feigned*: "with a *feigned* lack of interest" (p. 18)
   (a) pretended, (b) loosened, (c) faint-hearted, (d) concentrated.

3. *emitted*: "no single pore *emitted* a drop of blood" (p. 18)
   (a) elongated, (b) regulated, (c) formulated, (d) gave forth.

4. *faction*: "many of our *faction* had seen him enter" (p. 18)
   (a) observers, (b) fractional parts, (c) party or group, (d) factory workers.

5. *inflexible*: "His beard was *inflexible* and hard" (p. 18)
   (a) not acceptable, (b) stiff and rigid, (c) not fashionable, (d) hateful.

6. *poised*: "with the razor *poised*" (p. 18)
   (a) ignored, (b) moved, (c) suspended, (d) pointed.

7. *excursion*: "a rebel-hunting *excursion*" (p. 19)
   (a) existence, (b) activity, (c) production, (d) trip.

8. *rejuvenated*: "Torres was being *rejuvenated*" (p. 19)
   (a) renewed, (b) regulated, (c) reinforced, (d) dominated.

9. *ineradicable*: "inching along the floor, warm, *ineradicable*, uncontainable" (p. 20)
   (a) not visible, (b) not removable, (c) not containable, (d) unrecognizable.

10. *strop*: "the skin would give way . . . like the *strop*" (p. 20) (a) fluffs of lather, (b) pearls of blood, (c) strap of leather, (d) growth of beard.

THE UPTURNED FACE

What Facts Do You Remember?

1. While the officers were burying their dead comrade, (a) the wind howled in the trees, (b) the rain kept falling, (c) bombs continued to fall, (d) bullets snapped overhead.

2. The burial service was incomplete because the two officers (a) couldn't remember the lines, (b) refused to participate, (c) gave up in disgust, (d) were wounded by artillery.

3. When the first private threw dirt into the grave, (a) he swore aloud, (b) the sound was terrifying, (c) the dirt fell on the corpse's feet, (d) the adjutant laughed.

4. When the private ducked and grabbed his own arm, Lean ordered him to (a) keep on shoveling, (b) go to the rear, (c) hand his shovel to the other private, (d) get out of the way.

5. Lean told the other private to (a) keep on shoveling, (b) hurry as fast as he could, (c) dig a new grave, (d) get under cover.

6. The officer who took the shovel and filled it with dirt was (a) the adjutant, (b) Spitzbergen, (c) Lean, (d) the commanding officer.

7. As the grave was filled with dirt, the face of the corpse (a) became quickly covered, (b) changed its color, (c) remained in full view, (d) seemed to grow larger.

8. The sound—plop—that the dirt made when it hit (a) was ignored by the men, (b) made the men nervous, (c) seemed to relax the men, (d) was accepted as necessary by the men.

What Ideas Did You Find?

1. The men in this story are frightened by (a) the bullets and artillery, (b) the dead comrade's body, (c) their desire to run away, (d) the possibility of making a mistake.

2. The men were nervous about putting dirt on the dead man's face because they (a) thought of him as still alive, (b) didn't want to hurt him, (c) had lost their sanity, (d) wouldn't want dirt on their own faces.

Composition Exercises

1. You are the officer, Lean, in this story. Write a brief, factual military report to your commanding officer, Major General Harold P. Morgan, First Regiment, Rostina Sharpshooters, describing the circumstances of the young officer's death (which you will have to imagine) and burial under fire. Include a recommendation that the dead officer, Lieutenant William C. Campbell, receive a posthumous medal for heroism.

2. Consider carefully why the men in this story were afraid to throw dirt on the corpse's face. Did they perhaps think the man was still alive? What difference would it have made if the corpse were face down? What would you have done in the same circumstances? Explain.

Language Exercise

A. Adjectives that Describe People. Although many adjectives can be used to describe things, people, or ideas, the following adjectives, taken from the story, describe the appearance of people. Look up each adjective in the dictionary, write out its meaning, and provide another word that might fit the sense of the sentence.

   1. *gleaming* eyes (p. 22)

   2. *prostrate* company (p. 22)

3. *ghastly* face (p. 23)

4. *academic* expression (p. 24)

5. *aggrieved* privates (p. 25)

B. Adjectives that Describe Things. The following adjectives, taken from the story, describe things or ideas. Look up each adjective in the dictionary, write out its meaning, and provide another word that might fit the sense of the sentence.

1. *entrenching* tools (p. 23)

2. *curious* abstraction (p. 23)

3. *grisly* business (p. 23)

4. *inexplicable* hesitation (p. 25)

5. *pendulum* curve (p. 26)

A MYSTERY OF HEROISM

What Facts Do You Remember?

1. At the beginning of the story, everything is confusion because the regiment is engaged in (a) retreating, (b) attacking, (c) artillery dueling, (d) putting out fires.

2. Collins of A Company wanted (a) some food, (b) a drink, (c) extra ammunition, (d) a horse.

3. The other men in A Company treated Collins with (a) laughter and jeers, (b) polite respect, (c) quiet consideration, (d) amazed wonder.

4. When Collins asked permission to go into the meadow, the colonel (a) ignored him, (b) refused permission, (c) became angry, (d) granted permission.

5. Collins took with him on his trip to the well several (a) pistols, (b) drinking cups, (c) hand grenades, (d) canteens.

6. Collins ran back across the meadow with (a) a full canteen, (b) a filled bucket, (c) an empty drinking cup, (d) a wounded officer.

7. Halfway back to his own lines, Collins returned to the (a) well, (b) house, (c) dying officer, (d) stone fence.

8. When the two young lieutenants took Collins' bucket, one of them (a) dropped it on the ground, (b) hit the other officers with it, (c) passed it on to the men, (d) gave it back to the captain.

What Ideas Did You Find?

1. Collins was as surprised as everyone else at (a) the artillery barrage, (b) the fear of the men, (c) his own courage, (d) the distance he had run.

2. The author wants the reader to believe that the two lieutenants (a) deliberately emptied the bucket, (b) accidentally dropped the bucket, (c) were getting even with Collins, (d) did not care what happened.

Composition Exercises

1. Personal courage can be exhibited not only in war but under many circumstances of everyday life. Relate an incident that you know about in which someone performed a courageous act. Describe the person's thoughts and feelings, and give as many vivid details as possible.

2. Did you ever try to do something to impress someone and have it backfire? Describe a personal experience that turned out differently than you had planned.

Language Exercise

Many military words in English are of French origin. Look up in the dictionary each of the words below (which were taken from the story) and do the following: (a) write the *military* definition of the word; (b) record the derivation—that is, the language(s) the word comes from; (c) write a sentence of your own using the *military* meaning.

1. battery (p. 27)
2. canteen (p. 34)
3. caissons (p. 27)
4. carnage (p. 30)
5. colonel (p. 31)
6. lieutenant (p. 30)
7. maneuver (manoeuver, p. 32)
8. regiment (p. 36)
9. sergeant (p. 33)
10. volleys (p. 28)

THE SEA DEVIL

What Facts Do You Remember?

1. This story takes place in Florida during the month of (a) August, (b) June, (c) September, (d) May.
2. What fish were jumping in the bay? (a) sharks, (b) porpoises, (c) manta rays, (d) mullet.
3. The man in the story was (a) in his twenties, (b) in his thirties, (c) almost forty-two, (d) past fifty.
4. The man's first catch that night was (a) a giant ray, (b) a mullet and an angel fish, (c) a porpoise, (d) a small school of sardines.

5. The *Manta birostris* that the man ensnared with his net was (a) four feet in width and weighed some five hundred pounds, (b) nine feet from tip to tip and weighed over a thousand pounds, (c) fifteen feet in width and weighed almost two thousand pounds, (d) of unknown size and weight.

6. When the giant ray was dragging the man toward the open channel of the bay, it was stopped and turned back by (a) a wooden stake, (b) the man's thrashing and lunging in the water, (c) a porpoise coming into the bay, (d) the incoming tide.

7. After he was finally free from the giant ray, the man heard a noise and realized that (a) the mullet was still in the skiff, (b) the ray had slapped the water, (c) he was sobbing, (d) he was laughing happily.

8. After his frightening experience, the man decided that in the future he would (a) not go fishing again, (b) not cast alone at night, (c) fish only with fishing tackle, (d) never harm a porpoise.

What Ideas Did You Find?

1. If you had to say that this story is about just one thing, would you say it is about (a) fishing with a net? (b) a fisherman making a mistake? (c) porpoises being helpful to man? (d) man's struggle for self-preservation against nature?

2. The drone of the airplane overhead at the end of the story means that (a) mankind has conquered at least some part of nature—the sky, (b) other men are nearby, so the man is not alone, (c) the plane is similar in shape to a fish, (d) the man's ordeal is over and he is still alive.

Composition Exercises

1. To visualize the action in a story, a reader must see mental pictures—images—of what is happening. In this story a person must form a mental map of the setting—the bay, the dock, the

posts, and so forth. Check your mental map by trying to draw an accurate setting map for this story. Make certain that you include everything that was important to the action of the story.

2. Write a brief newspaper account of how the man in the story escaped death in his fight with the huge ray.

Language Exercise

A. *Words in Context.* The meanings of many words can often be guessed from their context—all the words that surround them. A person must be alert to find these clues to the meaning of a word.

Directions: The page numbers after the definitions below indicate where you can find the word in context. Select the *one* word on the given page that is closest to the definition provided for the word.

1. Confused and tumultuous (p. 38)
   (a) orderly, (b) weltering, (c) sullen.
2. Spreading out from a center (p. 39)
   (a) radical, (b) diameter, (c) coiled.
3. Marked with blotches and streaks (p. 41)
   (a) mottled, (b) impending, (c) sluggish.
4. Bound up tightly or held fast (p. 42)
   (a) projecting, (b) unyielding, (c) pinioned.
5. Likely to occur at any moment (p. 45)
   (a) lacerated, (b) placid, (c) imminent.

B. *Multiple Meanings.* Often a word may have more than one meaning. The way it is used in the sentence determines which meaning it has. Try to guess the meaning given in the sentence for each word below.

1. *skirt* (p. 40) "He raised the skirt to his mouth. . . ." (a) the bottom of a lady's dress, (b) the edge, fringe, or border of something, (c) a hanging flap or cover.

2. *monstrous* (p. 41) "... a monstrous survival ..." (a) un-
   usually large or enormous, (b) unnatural or unusual, (c)
   horrible, hideous, or shocking.
3. *sullen* (p. 43) "... and pushing a sullen wave ..." (a) slow-
   moving and sluggish, (b) in bad humor or sulky, (c) gloomy,
   sad, or depressing.

THE TIGER'S HEART

What Facts Do You Remember?

1. This story takes place in (a) Africa, (b) India, (c) Persia, (d) Latin
   America.
2. In Pepe's world a man was king who owned a (a) machete, (b)
   rifle, (c) herd of goats, (d) dagger.
3. Juan Aria wanted Pepe to (a) kill his goat, (b) attack a devil,
   (c) murder a man, (d) hunt a tiger.
4. Pepe drove a hard bargain and made Juan Aria pay him (a) two
   hundred pesos, (b) two goats and one kid, (c) three cows, (d)
   twenty-nine goats.
5. Pepe trailed the animal into the jungle by using his skillfully
   trained (a) eyes, (b) sense of smell, (c) hearing, (d) bloodhound.
6. When Pepe pulled the trigger of the rifle the first time, it (a) did
   nothing, (b) only hissed, (c) exploded, (d) fired perfectly.
7. When the big cat attacked him, Pepe killed it using only his
   (a) bare hands, (b) hunting knife, (c) machete, (d) rifle.
8. Pepe fired into the dead tiger's body to (a) make sure it was
   dead, (b) test his rifle, (c) signal other hunters, (d) convince the
   villagers he had shot it.

What Ideas Did You Find?

1. If Pepe had told the villagers how he really killed the tiger, he
   would have been (a) considered a hero, (b) thought of as just

another villager, (c) laughed out of the village, (d) made the chieftain of the village.

2. This story is about a young man's (a) search for courage, (b) desire to own a rifle, (c) wish to be considered an important person, (d) cunning and skill as a hunter.

Composition Exercises

1. Continue the story where it ended, and tell what happens to Pepe as he brings the tiger back to the village. Do you think Pepe got away with his pretense that he shot the tiger?

2. Describe a personal experience you have had or know about that involves hunting or killing animals.

Language Exercise

For each of the following sentences, find another word that means almost the same (synonym) as the word in italics.

1. "There was a *pattering* rush of small hoofs. . . ." (p. 48)
2. "Juan Aria gestured with *eloquent* hands. . . ." (p. 49)
3. "Only death would end his *forays*." (p. 49)
4. "Only Pepe dared and, because he did, he must be *revered*." (p. 49)
5. ". . . Pepe underwent a *transformation*." (p. 51)
6. ". . . his nostrils could not be *assailed* by its unwelcome scents. . . ." (p. 51)
7. "It did not snarl or *grimace*. . . ." (p. 52)
8. ". . . and no puff of black powder smoke *wafting* away from the muzzle." (p. 52)
9. "His *flailing* left paw flashed at Pepe." (p. 53)
10. "Red blood *welled* out." (p. 53)

THE RAIN HORSE

What Facts Do You Remember?

1. At the beginning of the story, the young man stopped (a) in a field, (b) on a hill, (c) beside a farmhouse, (d) under a tree.

2. While the man stood there, (a) clouds appeared, (b) the sun came out, (c) the stars appeared, (d) the rain came down.

3. When the man first saw the horse, he was most attracted by (a) the way it ran, (b) its jet-black color, (c) its vivid eyes, (d) its huge size.

4. While the man was crouching in the wood, the horse (a) disappeared over the hill, (b) neighed and shook his mane, (c) tried to attack him, (d) went back to the farmhouse.

5. Because the horse always seemed to be waiting for the man, he thought perhaps it was (a) just lonely, (b) terribly frightened, (c) reading his mind, (d) completely insane.

6. To protect himself, the man picked up (a) an old fence post, (b) two stones, (c) some goose eggs, (d) an iron bar.

7. When the horse attacked again, the man (a) shouted and threw stones, (b) yelled and waved the stick, (c) ran at the horse, (d) jumped behind a tree.

8. After the man had gotten free of the horse and was on the other side of the fence, he sat down and (a) cried happily, (b) counted his blessings, (c) swore at the horse, (d) began taking off his clothes.

What Ideas Did You Find?

1. The man in this story had returned to the area to (a) do some hiking, (b) find the village again, (c) visit where he had grown up, (d) keep from getting lost.

2. The man's nightmare experience with the horse troubled him deeply because (a) the horse obviously was a trained killer,

(b) the physical exertion had weakened the man's heart, (c) the horse never really existed, except in the man's mind, (d) the horse's actions were unexplainable.

Composition Exercises

1. Explain why you think the horse attacked the man. Was the animal crazy? Was it just feeling frisky in the rain? How did it always know where the man was? Did it represent some evil force?

2. Describe some encounter of your own with an animal—dog, cat, horse, etc. Carefully describe the animal, giving as many details as you can. Then relate the events of your encounter.

Language Exercise

Match each of the words on the left with its correct definition on the right.

1. *clairvoyant* (p. 60)
   "Was it *clairvoyant?*"

2. *squelching* (p. 60)
   "The water was... *squelching in his shoes.*"

3. *antagonist* (p. 61)
   "... whether the horse was his *antagonist.*"

4. *supple* (p. 62)
   "... an immensely *supple* ... motion."

5. *careering* (p. 63)
   ". . . and went *careering* down."

a. an opponent

b. running at full speed

c. a wet, slushing sound

d. one who sees things that are not in sight

e. beyond human powers

f. lithe and limber movement

THE NEW DEAL

What Facts Do You Remember?

1. Rafferty was gambling at the (a) crap table, (b) poker table, (c) roulette wheel, (d) blackjack table.
2. Rafferty complained about the (a) house percentage, (b) deck of cards, (c) roulette wheel, (d) dice.
3. Seemingly out of nowhere (a) the manager arrived, (b) two policemen entered, (c) the pit boss appeared, (d) the owner came in.
4. Rafferty offered to (a) buy a new deck of cards, (b) double his bets, (c) buy everyone a drink, (d) wait his turn.
5. The pit boss and the dealer thought Rafferty was (a) out of his mind, (b) trying to make trouble, (c) a professional gambler, (d) a plainclothes detective.
6. Rafferty finally got them to agree to give him a fresh start and to let him play (a) as long as he wished, (b) until closing time, (c) until midnight, (d) for one hour.
7. When Rafferty finished and stood up, he (a) had lost $1000, (b) had won $18,000, (c) had broken even, (d) was out of money.
8. Up in his room afterward, Rafferty (a) took a shower, (b) phoned the police, (c) met the cigar-counter girl, (d) counted his winnings.

What Ideas Did You Find?

1. At the end of the story we realize that Rafferty and the girl had (a) never met before, (b) been sweethearts, (c) swindled the club, (d) wasted their time.
2. The reader is supposed to believe that Rafferty and the girl

were going to Reno to (a) get married, (b) get a divorce, (c) hide from the gamblers, (d) swindle another club.

Composition Exercises

1. Do you believe that the gambling club was fair game for Rafferty to swindle? Was it wrong for him to take the money after winning it dishonestly, or should he be entitled to outsmart professional gamblers in any way possible? Present arguments in favor of one side or the other.

2. Describe a gambling experience you have had or know about. Give as many details as you can.

Language Exercise

Criminal slang. Almost all criminals use slang connected with their specialties, but the most colorful and imaginative variety is that of the swindler or confidence man. Many of his slang words and expressions remain unknown to outsiders—*cush* for money, *bumblebee* for a one-dollar bill, *hopscotching* for operating a con game, *twist* for a woman or girl. Others, however, come into general use and become permanent parts of the language. Such words as *fin* for a five-dollar bill, *heat* for trouble, *mark* for a victim, *stool pigeon*, and *sucker* are just a few of the more common words that have come into the language from criminal slang.

Look up each of the following words, which were originally the slang of confidence men. Write the definition, and try to use the word in a sentence.

1. bilk
2. boodle
3. grifter
4. moniker
5. shill

HOW MR. HOGAN ROBBED A BANK

What Facts Do You Remember?

1. Mr. Hogan did not plan an elaborate and complicated robbery because he (a) believed bank robbers usually went to too much trouble, (b) did not have enough time to plan ahead, (c) was the only one involved in the robbery, (d) robbed the bank by accident.

2. Mr. Hogan worked (a) in the bank, (b) for an armored-car company, (c) for a janitorial service, (d) in a grocery store.

3. The best day of all for the robbery, Mr. Hogan decided, was (a) the Thursday payday at the American Can Company, (b) the Monday after a holiday, (c) the Saturday before a long weekend in the summer, (d) Wednesday just after the noon rush.

4. Mr. Hogan thought about robbing the bank for (a) five years, (b) one year, (c) four months, (d) six weeks.

5. The Hogan family received an inheritance from Mrs. Hogan's brother Larry of (a) $5000, (b) $2500, (c) $1200, (d) $600.

6. Mr. Hogan's children had entered (a) a popularity contest, (b) a dancing competition, (c) a give-away game contest, (d) an essay-writing contest.

7. The gun Mr. Hogan used in the robbery was (a) a child's toy, (b) a silver-colored Iver Johnson, (c) a black snub-nosed Colt, (d) an old-fashioned derringer.

8. The amount of money Mr. Hogan got away with was (a) $1200, (b) $2500, (c) $5280, (d) $8320.

What Ideas Did You Find?

1. The author of this story seems to say that he (a) disapproves of bank robbery, (b) approves of bank robbery, (c) neither approves nor disapproves of bank robbery.

2. John Steinbeck allows Mr. Hogan to get away with the robbery

because (a) it actually happened that way, (b) he wants to point out something about Mr. Hogan's character, (c) the story is more exciting that way, (d) the Hogan family really needs the money.

Composition Exercises

1. You are the bank teller, Will Cup, reporting to the police on the events of the bank robbery. Tell them what you saw and thought about during and after the robbery.

2. Select one of the following propositions and argue for or against it. Bring in as much specific evidence from the story as you can to support your argument. (a) It was wrong for Mr. Hogan to get away with the robbery. (b) Americans regard bank robbers as heroes. (c) Bank robbery is a particularly American kind of thievery. (d) In this story Steinbeck is judging the American attitude of "getting something for nothing."

Language Exercise

Echoic and Rhyming Compound Words. The word *hulla-baloo* (on p. 72) is called an echoic duplication in which part of the word duplicates (echoes) the sound of another part of the word or of a separate compound word, as in the slang expression *hanky-panky* (which follows *hullabaloo* on p. 72).

Listed below are ten echoic or rhyming compound words that you may know. See if you can match each word on the left with its definition on the right.

1. heyday	a. a disorderly mixture or jumble
2. hobnob	
3. hoodoo	b. reckless and wild
4. hubbub	c. headlong, disorderly haste
5. humdrum	d. sleight of hand
6. hocus-pocus	e. to chatter unwisely

7. hodge-podge
8. harum-scarum
9. helter-skelter
10. higgledy-piggledy

f. topsy-turvy, end-over-end
g. time of ones greatest vigor
h. a foolish person
i. loud noises, as of many voices
j. dull or monotonous
k. to associate familiarly with
l. that which brings bad luck

THE CATBIRD SEAT

What Facts Do You Remember?

1. Mr. Martin worked at F & S as head of the (a) production department, (b) accounting department, (c) filing department, (d) shipping department.

2. Mrs. Ulgine Barrows had been baiting Mr. Martin now for almost (a) two years, (b) one year, (c) six months, (d) three weeks.

3. Mr. Martin had decided that Mrs. Barrows should be (a) transferred, (b) fired, (c) asked to resign, (d) murdered.

4. After buying the pack of Camels, Mr. Martin got to Mrs. Barrows' apartment by (a) cab, (b) walking, (c) his car, (d) the subway.

5. Even though he did not drink, Mr. Martin agreed when Mrs. Barrows offered to fix him a (a) bourbon and water, (b) scotch and soda, (c) old-fashioned, (d) whiskey sour.

6. Mr. Martin told Mrs. Barrows that he was preparing a bomb with which to kill (a) his wife, Margaret, (b) his assistant, Joey Hart, (c) his employer, Mr. Fitweiler, (d) his sweetheart, Miss Paird.

7. One of the last things Mr. Martin said to Mrs. Barrows as he left her apartment was (a) "I love you, Ulgine," (b) "I'm sitting in the catbird seat," (c) "I drink and smoke all the time," (d) "I'm tearing up the pea patch."

8. Mr. Fitweiler fired Mrs. Barrows because he thought she had (a) overstepped her authority, (b) lied about the other employees, (c) wasted company money, (d) become insane.

What Ideas Did You Find?

1. Mr. Martin changed his plan to kill Mrs. Barrows because he (a) couldn't find a murder weapon, (b) was afraid he would get caught, (c) thought of a better idea, (d) was afraid of her.

2. When a person is sitting in the catbird seat, he is (a) about to be caught, (b) sitting pretty, (c) on his best behavior, (d) living on borrowed time.

Composition Exercises

1. You are the editor of the office newsletter for F & S, and you are writing a humorous article about the events leading up to the firing of Mrs. Barrows. Remember that you know only what went on in the office—not about Mr. Martin's murder plan.

2. Describe in detail how you "got even" with someone much as Mr. Martin did. Or, if you have never pulled off the "perfect squelch," write a fictional account in which your hero concocts a plan that works on the evildoer.

Language Exercise

Without looking at a dictionary, see if you can guess the meaning of each of the following words from the clues around the word. After you have written down your own definition, compare it with that of the dictionary.

1. *peccadillos:* "He must keep his mind on her crimes as a special adviser, not on her *peccadillos* as a personality." (p. 82)

2. *blatant:* "Mrs. Ulgine Barrows stood charged with willful, *blatant,* and persistent attempts to destroy the efficiency and system of F & S." (p. 83)

3. *wrought:* "When Mrs. Barrows appeared . . . Mr. Martin . . . became acutely conscious of the fantasy he had *wrought.*" (p. 86)

4. *grimace:* "The stuff tasted awful, but he made no *grimace.*" (p. 87)

5. *lay:* "These matters are not for the *lay* mind to grasp." (p. 89)

THE BIG IT

What Facts Do You Remember?

1. Two Plumes was an Indian (a) squaw, (b) brave, (c) chief, (d) witch doctor.

2. This story takes place in (a) Wyoming, (b) Colorado, (c) Texas, (d) Montana.

3. The big IT in this story was a (a) wagon train, (b) brass cannon, (c) mule, (d) steamboat.

4. The white men were afraid of the Indians because (a) they were on the warpath, (b) they had surrounded the town, (c) the trappers were selling them liquor, (d) there were so many of them.

5. The men decided to fire the "mountain howitzer" to (a) impress the Indians, (b) signal the cavalry, (c) kill as many Indians as possible, (d) set fire to the Indian tepees.

6. The "mountain howitzer" was mounted on a (a) wagon, (b) mule, (c) platform, (d) pile of logs.

7. When the cannon began moving around and pointing to the people, everyone (a) laughed, (b) said they knew it would happen, (c) ran away or lay on the ground, (d) went home disgusted.

8. Two Plumes said he thought the white men were like a (a) jackass, (b) thunderbolt in the sky, (c) crazy fox, (d) child with a toy.

What Ideas Did You Find?

1. This story expects the reader to laugh at the antics of (a) mule drivers, (b) white man, (c) Indians, (d) all men.

2. If you had to say that this story is about one thing only, would you say it is about (a) Indians and Westerners? (b) plans that backfire humorously? (c) the fear of death? (d) the wisdom of Indians?

Composition Exercises

1. Describe a real-life situation you know about that backfired in a humorous way. Give as many details as possible.

2. Write a humorous account for the local newspaper at Fort Benton in which you describe the actions down by the river. Give a humorous title to your newspaper story (such as "Mule Joins Indians and Palefaces in Jackass Dance"), and describe not only the event but what happened after it was over.

Language Exercise

Word Borrowings. Many American words originally were adopted into the English language because colonists and pioneers borrowed a word from an Indian language to name something that had had no name in English. For example, when the Europeans first encountered an odorous little animal with a stripe down its back, they had no name for such a creature and adopted the Abnaki Indian word *segonku*, which eventually became *skunk*.

Look up in the dictionary each of the words below and find the word's derivation, or language the word is taken from (the information enclosed in brackets with "derived from" symbols < indicating the origin of the word). Copy down (a) the word; (b) the derivation, including the Indian language or tribe (if given) and the Indian word; and (3) the common definition.

Example: (a) *skunk*, n.; (b) [contr. < Am. Ind. (Abnaki) segonku]; (c) a bushy-tailed mammal about the size of a cat that has a white stripe down its back and ejects an offensive-smelling liquid when molested.

1. raccoon
2. squash (noun)
3. hominy
4. toboggan
5. persimmon
6. terrapin

7. opossum
8. pone
9. hickory
10. succotash
11. moccasin
12. totem

THE LIGHTNING-ROD MAN

What Facts Do You Remember?

1. The house in this story is located (a) on the plain, (b) in a valley, (c) in some hills, (d) in a forest.

2. The lightning rod carried by the lightning-rod man was made from (a) copper and brass, (b) aluminum and wood, (c) iron and aluminum, (d) copper and wood.

3. The lightning-rod man believed the safest place to be in a storm was (a) next to the walls, (b) in the center of the room, (c) on the hearth, (d) in the cellar.

4. The narrator says he thinks the lightning-rod man's name is (a) Zeus of Olympus, (b) Jupiter Pluvius, (c) Neptune Uranus, (d) Jupiter Tonans.

5. The price of the lightning rod was (a) $20, (b) $15, (c) $10 per foot, (d) $5 per foot.

6. The lightning-rod man travels during (a) the nighttime, (b) rainstorms, (c) thunderstorms, (d) the winter.

7. The lightning-rod man wanted a rug to stand on because (a) his clothes were dripping, (b) rugs are nonconductors, (c) he was cold, (d) lightning avoids rugs.

8. When the lightning-rod man sprang at the narrator with the tri-forked staff, the narrator (a) killed the man, (b) fled from the house, (c) laughed out loud, (d) threw the man outside.

What Ideas Did You Find?

1. The lightning-rod man in this story might represent man's (a) interest in money, (b) fear of nature, (c) superstitious fears, (d) scientific knowledge.

2. The narrator of the story was not afraid of the lightning because he (a) had faith in God, (b) knew the lightning-rod man was a fake, (c) was filled with courage, (d) did not care if he died.

Composition Exercises

1. This story presents a number of beliefs man has held about lightning. Go back through the story and make a list of all the things the lightning-rod man says about lightning. Can you add any other superstitious beliefs you have heard about lightning? Make as complete a list as you can of superstitions concerning lightning.

2. Describe a personal experience you have had during a violent storm of some kind—a hurricane, thunderstorm, blizzard, tornado, etc. Where and when did it happen? What were your feelings at the time? What did you do? Try to make the reader see, hear, and feel the storm along with you.

Language Exercise

Words from Mythology. The author of this story, Herman Melville, makes several references to *Jupiter* and *Jupiter Tonans* from classical mythology. Jupiter was the most powerful of the Roman gods (he was called Zeus in Greek mythology) and was always associated with the thunderbolt, which he used as a weapon. A number of the words that we use today come originally from classical mythology. The word *vulcanize*, for instance, comes from the name of the god Vulcan, blacksmith and keeper of the forge; the word *panic* is derived from the nature god Pan, who could cause men to run from him in fear and panic. Look up each of the following words, and try to find out the identity of the god or goddess connected with the word.

1. chaotic
2. geology
3. erotic
4. uranium
5. Saturday

6. jovial
7. cereal
8. martial
9. January
10. venereal

WET SATURDAY

What Facts Do You Remember?

1. This story takes place in what month of the year? (a) May, (b) July, (c) August, (d) January.

2. Mr. Princey's son George had been thrown out of (a) medical school, (b) law school, (c) a military academy, (d) dental college.

3. Millicent was in love with a (a) farmer, (b) soldier, (c) clergyman, (d) policeman.

4. Millicent hit Withers with (a) an iron bar, (b) a heavy shovel, (c) a claw hammer, (d) a croquet post.

5. Because Captain Smollett overheard their conversation, Mr. Princey decided to (a) turn him over to the police, (b) implicate him in the murder, (c) kill him at once, (d) ask his cooperation.

6. Mr. Princey had Withers' body put into (a) a coffin, (b) the deep well, (c) the sewer, (d) the wet cement.

7. After getting rid of the body, they went back into the house and (a) phoned the police, (b) scolded Millicent, (c) had supper, (d) had tea.

8. The last thing Mr. Princey did after Captain Smollett left was (a) write a letter to Ella Brangwyn-Davies, (b) take a stroll around the yard, (c) telephone the Bass Hill police station, (d) breathe a deep sigh of relief.

What Ideas Did You Find?

1. The author intends the reader to believe that Mr. Princey (a) double-crossed Captain Smollett, (b) turned Millicent in to the police, (c) kept his word to Captain Smollett, (d) never revealed that there was a murder.

2. We can assume that Captain Smollett (a) escaped being charged with the murder when he revealed the plot to the authorities, (b) was convicted of murdering Withers, (c) left the country at once, (d) kept quiet about the murder.

Composition Exercises

1. Visualize the courtroom scene in which Captain Smollett is tried for the murder of Withers. Present the case against Smollett as if you were the prosecuting attorney. List the "proofs" you have of his guilt.

2. The author of this story has taken a very serious affair—murder— and written about it in a matter-of-fact and humorous way. See if you can do the same thing in describing a local crime, scan-

dal, or public disaster. Have a character, much like Mr. Princey, handle the situation in a very casual manner.

Language Exercise

Latin Roots. Captain Smollett coins a word, *parsonicide* (p. 107), after he overhears of the clergyman Withers' murder. His word literally means *parson-killing*, using the prefix *parson* and the Latin root *-cide* (from the verb *caedere*, to cut or kill). A number of words contain this root and a different prefix. Two examples are *suicide* and *homicide*. The prefix *sui* means *self* and the prefix *homo* means *man*. Therefore, these words mean *self-killing* and *man-killing*, respectively.

Look up each of the following words with the *-cide* root. Find the meaning of the prefix, and write the definition of the word.

1. fratricide
2. infanticide
3. matricide
4. parricide
5. patricide

THE SNAKE

What Facts Do You Remember?

1. When he first came across the snake, the man in this story was (a) digging a well, (b) cutting firewood, (c) repairing fences, (d) plowing a field.
2. The man thought the snake was (a) ugly, (b) beautiful, (c) frightening, (d) harmful.

3. When the snake would not get out of his way, the man (a) killed it quickly, (b) ignored it completely, (c) moved it aside, (d) watched it suspiciously.

4. The boy who brought the water out to the man was the man's (a) nephew, (b) cousin, (c) son, (d) neighbor.

5. The boy thought the snake was (a) very beautiful, (b) just interesting to watch, (c) ugly and bad, (d) quite unimportant.

6. The man finally hit the snake with a (a) rock, (b) shovel, (c) stick, (d) wrench.

7. Because of the boy's attitude, the man became (a) angry, (b) fearful, (c) pleased, (d) sad.

8. Suddenly the man grabbed the snake and (a) threw it into the field, (b) put it around the boy's neck, (c) dropped it into the well, (d) carried it back to the house.

What Ideas Did You Find?

1. If you had to select another title for this story, which of the following would best describe the main idea? (a) The Generation Gap, (b) Live and Let Live, (c) Nature's Threat to Man, (d) Beauty and the Beast.

2. At the end of the story the man recognized that he, like the boy, was (a) afraid of the snake, (b) glad the snake was killed, (c) brutal to nature's beauty, (d) relieved that no one was hurt.

Composition Exercises

1. You are the man in this story, and you are explaining to the boy's father, your brother, why you scared the boy with the snake. Explain what happened and why you did what you did.

2. Describe the beauty of an animal you have observed, such as a dog, cat, horse, etc. Relate its physical appearance, size, color, shape, and proportions through a selection of as many specific details as you can. Then try to describe how the animal moves

by using verbs and adverbs (e.g., "The cat *flows smoothly* and *silently* as he *stalks* a bird on the grass").

Language Exercise

Parts of Speech. Every word in a sentence has a job to do. Nouns name things or ideas (*frustration, automobile*); verbs express some kind of action or condition (*jump, to be*); adjectives modify or describe people, things, and ideas (*sloppy, dull*); adverbs modify verbs, adjectives, or even other adverbs (*rapidly, suddenly*).

A. Noun   C. Adjective

B. Verb   D. Adverb

Match each of the following words taken from the story with the letter of the part of speech above that best fits the word.

1. hideous (p. 116)   9. caressed (p. 114)

2. ferocity (p. 114)   10. effeminate (p. 115)

3. cringed (p. 117)   11. remnant (p. 115)

4. frenetic (p. 115)   12. splayed (p. 116)

5. stubble (p. 112)   13. innocently (p. 117)

6. pirouette (p. 114)   14. gasped (p. 117)

7. already (p. 115)   15. wrenched (p. 116)

8. radiant.(p. 113)

DE MORTUIS

What Facts Do You Remember?

1. Dr. Rankin was a (a) lawyer, (b) veterinarian, (c) physician, (d) professor.

2. Buck and Bud were friends who came to ask Doc to (a) go hunting, (b) go fishing, (c) buy real estate, (d) sell his house.

3. When his friends arrived, Doc was in his cellar (a) cementing the floor, (b) repairing a chair, (c) building some shelves, (d) burying his wife.

4. When Doc moved to the small town to live, he was (a) married, (b) broke, (c) too trusting, (d) hard to get along with.

5. Bud and Buck jumped to the conclusion that Doc had (a) stolen some wine, (b) gotten drunk, (c) killed his sister, (d) murdered his wife.

6. Doc admitted that Irene was (a) stupid, (b) religious, (c) murdered, (d) a good housekeeper.

7. Bud and Buck agreed to (a) wait for Doc in town, (b) go and look for Irene, (c) go to the police at once, (d) keep Doc's grisly secret.

8. After Bud and Buck left the house, (a) Irene returned, (b) Irene telephoned, (c) Doc cried, (d) Doc wrote a letter.

What Ideas Did You Find?

1. In this story we are led to believe that, before Doc met his wife, she was the town's (a) most gabby woman, (b) religious leader, (c) well-known whore, (d) most respected citizen.

2. At the end of the story we are led to believe that Doc (a) showed Irene his handiwork, (b) drove Irene to catch the train, (c) reported Irene to the police, (d) buried Irene beneath the concrete.

Composition Exercises

1. Complete the ending of the story, and describe what you think happens. Does Doc kill his wife, or does he change his mind? If he does not kill her, how can he continue to live with her, knowing what he does about her past? If he does kill her,

how does he do it? What does he do with the body? Does he get away with the murder, or is he caught?

2. Consider what might happen if Doc decides to confess his crime after several years. His friends Buck and Bud have sworn not to tell anyone what they know (or think they know). Describe the confusion of the courtroom scene as Doc is brought to trial, and then relate his confession to the murder.

Language Exercise

The title of the story, *De Mortuis*, is Latin meaning "Of Death" or "About Death." A writer often selects a title that reveals the theme or suggests what the story is about. Obviously, in this story the author could have used the English words "About Death" for an adequate title. But by using the Latin, as a doctor might do when writing a prescription, the author gives even greater meaning and depth to his story. Here the Latin title becomes a medical prescription of death, and our knowledge of that dimension in the story enhances our pleasure in reading it.

Using your dictionary, (a) look up the root word *mort* (from Middle English, Old French, and Latin *mors* or *mortis*) and copy its definition. (b) Make a list of ten common and useful words (such as *mortal*) using that root. Notice the suffixes attached to the root in some of the words (such as *-gage* in *mortgage*). How does the suffix change the meaning? (c) Break each of your ten words into its root and suffix, and then give the meaning for the suffix and the whole word.

BARGAIN

What Facts Do You Remember?

1. When they met on the street, Mr. Baumer tried to give Slade (a) money, (b) a bill, (c) advice, (d) a job.

2. Slade called Mr. Baumer (a) a coward, (b) an ugly name, (c) Dutchie, (d) boss.

3. The second time Mr. Baumer met Slade on the street, Slade knocked him down and (a) broke his hand, (b) knocked out his front teeth, (c) shot him, (d) knifed him.

4. Mr. Baumer owned the Moon Dance (a) Saloon, (b) Newspaper, (c) Hotel, (d) Mercantile Company.

5. Slade was (a) an outlaw, (b) a cowboy, (c) a freighter, (d) a bounty hunter.

6. Mr. Baumer knew that Slade liked to drink whiskey and (a) might shoot up the town, (b) could not read, (c) sometimes got into fights, (d) often gambled in the saloon.

7. Mr. Baumer hired Slade at Christmastime to (a) haul some freight, (b) kill a man, (c) be his bodyguard, (d) pretend he was Santa Claus.

8. Slade died on the trail from drinking (a) too much whiskey, (b) poisoned water, (c) polluted wine, (d) wood alcohol.

What Ideas Did You Find?

1. Mr. Baumer proved that an ordinary man could (a) turn the other cheek, (b) outsmart his enemies, (c) persuade a bully to be his friend, (d) forget wrongs done to him.

2. The "bargain" in this story was (a) Al's good deeds, (b) Slade's bill of $21.50, (c) Mr. Baumer's revenge on Slade, (d) the cheap price of the wood alcohol.

Composition Exercises

1. Describe Slade's last trip of hauling freight. Keep in mind that it is winter, almost Christmas, with the temperature somewhere around 42° below zero. Slade thinks he is pulling a fast one on Mr. Baumer by drinking from the barrel he believes is whiskey and blaming the loss on evaporation (in winter!). Relate his trip through the miles of snow and ice, and then tell about his final moments before death

2. Do you think revenge is sweet? Did Mr. Baumer deliberately set a trap for Slade, thereby indirectly murdering him? Or do you believe that Mr. Baumer is innocent in the whole affair—that Slade himself is the only one responsible for his death? Write a letter to the Moon Dance district attorney arguing your position.

Language Exercise

Each of the words below have a meaning connected with the idea of revenge. Look up each word in the dictionary to be sure of its meaning, and then write a sentence of your own using the word.

Example: *revenge*; used as a verb (*v.t.*) meaning to inflict damage, injury, or punishment in return for an injury, insult, etc., as in the sentence "He *revenged* himself on his enemy." Also used as a noun (*n.*) meaning a revenging, desire to revenge, etc., as in the sentence "His *revenge* was complete."

1. avenge
2. revengeful
3. vendetta

4. vengeance
5. vindictive

A & P

What Facts Do You Remember?

1. This story takes place entirely in a (a) department store, (b) supermarket, (c) drugstore, (d) clothing store.
2. The narrator of the story admires (a) two young girls in slacks, (b) an oldish lady of fifty, (c) a mature woman in shorts, (d) three girls in bathing suits.
3. The narrator of the story was (a) nineteen, (b) twenty-two, (c) twenty-seven, (d) thirty.

4. The location of this story is (a) at the beach in New Jersey, (b) just outside Miami, (c) north of Boston, (d) south of Los Angeles.

5. Queenie took a dollar bill out of (a) her purse, (b) her pocket, (c) her wallet, (d) her bra top.

6. After the scene at the checkout counter, the narrator said to the manager (a) "I quit," (b) "I'm sorry," (c) "I wanted to act that way," (d) "I won't do it again."

7. The narrator's name was (a) Sandy, (b) Stokesie, (c) Sammy, (d) McMahon.

8. When the narrator left the store, he saw that the man working his checkout slot was (a) Stokesie, (b) McMahon, (c) the butcher, (d) the manager.

What Ideas Did You Find?

1. The narrator thinks his impulsive action concerning his job was (a) regrettable, (b) not so sad, (c) stupid, (d) very clever.

2. The author of this story no doubt believes that the boy's act is (a) just the ill-considered action of a kid, (b) poorly timed and badly carried out, (c) something that will hurt the boy's future, (d) a necessary act of rejection by a questioning young adult.

Composition Exercises

1. Do you think Sammy's act of impulsively quitting his job was admirable or not? Could he have handled the situation in any other way and still felt satisfied about the result? How would you have reacted in this same situation? Praise or criticize Sammy's action, and tell what you think he could or should have done.

2. Relate an incident from your own life in which you bumped against the policies of the adult establishment and then suffered the consequences. Describe what happened, what punishment you suffered, and how you felt about it. Give as

many details as possible, and try to decide whether your action and the result were right.

Language Exercise

Body English. The narrator, Sammy, admires the bodies of the three girls in bathing suits and uses descriptions such as "chunky," "chubby berry faces," "prima-donna legs," "clean bare plain of the top of her chest," "two smoothest scoops of vanilla," and "really sweet can." Many words in English contain the name of a part of the body. For example, a pendant that hangs from the neck is a *neck*lace. See if you can fill in the missing part of the body for the words below by studying the definitions.

1. mo — — — —	a cloth made from the fleece of an angora goat
2. — — — — flint	a mean, miserly person
3. mistle — — —	a parasitic plant used as a Christmas decoration
4. s — — — shape	in good order, tidy
5. — — — — — screw	an instrument of torture
6. s — — — shod	careless, untidy, or slovenly
7. bare — — — —	to ride without a saddle
8. — — — — chilla	a rodent fur used for coats
9. — — — — long	rash, hasty, impetus
10. ro — — — —	strong, healthy, vigorous

DEBUT

What Facts Do You Remember?

1. Mrs. Simmons wanted Judy's dress to be perfect because

(a) Mrs. Simmons had a good reputation as a seamstress, (b) Judy was underdeveloped and needed a beautiful dress for improvement, (c) Mrs. Simmons insisted on Judy being the *best* at the dance, (d) Judy was queen of the dance and would be in the limelight.

2. Judy's father was a (a) carpenter, (b) mailman, (c) janitor, (d) postal clerk.

3. Judy overheard some boys in the alley talking to (a) Betty Jo Hamilton, (b) Linda Sue Williams, (c) Mary Ann Handley, (d) Lucy Mae Watkins.

4. The boys in the alley were outsmarted by the girl who took from them (a) a five-dollar bill, (b) a pack of cigarettes, (c) a pocket knife, (d) some books.

5. To keep her away from low-class kids, Judy's parents sent her to (a) a finishing school for girls, (b) the best public high school, (c) a Catholic high school, (d) a private tutor.

6. While she was dancing in her room, the boys in the alley (a) spied on her, (b) smoked cigarettes, (c) made lots of noise, (d) got into a fight.

7. Judy intended to ditch Ernest Lee at the dance and (a) refuse to dance with the other boys, (b) make a play for the Gay Charmer's sons, (c) dance with all the boys, (d) come home with one of the college boys.

8. After Judy left with Ernest Lee, Mrs. Simmons told her husband she believed that Judy (a) was still a baby in many ways, (b) would have to grow up one of these days, (c) had learned what she'd been trying to teach her, (d) was in love with Ernest Lee.

What Ideas Did You Find?

1. As a result of her experience of overhearing the boys talking in the alley, Judy had become more (a) frightened of boys, (b) confident and sure of herself, (c) disgusted at the cruelty of boys, (d) uncertain as to what she would do around boys.

2. Mrs. Simmons decided she wasn't worried about Judy anymore because she recognized that her daughter was quite suddenly (a) mature, (b) boy crazy, (c) aware of Ernest Lee, (d) getting some common sense.

Composition Exercises

1. What happens while Judy is at the dance? Continue the story until she arrives home that night. Does she ditch Ernest Lee and come home with a college boy? Is she the hit of the ball or just a faded wallflower sitting on the sidelines?

2. What did Judy mean when she said that "she knew better than to settle for a mere pack of cigarettes"? What does she intend to do? Write a letter to Judy in which you advise her on the best way to get along with boys. If you are a girl, give her a friend's advice, girl-to-girl. If you are a boy, give her brotherly advice for her own good.

Language Exercise

   Listed below are ten words and ten phrases taken from the story. See if you can insert into each phrase the word used in the story.

precipitate	cascaded
ritual	guffaws
tartly	mannequin
tapestry	ingratiated
diffidence	sophisticated

1. a wide sash that _____ in a butterfly effect behind

2. "You would," Mrs. Simmons said _____

3. who had _____ her way into the Gay Charmers

4. might _____ her into the battle

5. Judy recognized the familiar _____

6. a low indistinct murmur punctuated by _____

7. and began to weave her _____ to its music

8. with her hair in a _____ upsweep

9. and that there would be awe and _____ in his manner

10. stood there motionless as a _____

SUCKER

What Facts Do You Remember?

1. Sucker's relationship to the narrator was that of (a) brother, (b) cousin, (c) nephew, (d) friend.

2. The narrator's name was (a) Richard, (b) William, (c) Dave, (d) Pete.

3. The girl, Maybelle Watts, was a high school (a) senior, (b) junior, (c) sophomore, (d) freshman.

4. When the narrator first went to Maybelle's house to visit her, he took her (a) a ring, (b) some flowers, (c) a carton of cigarettes, (d) a box of candy.

5. When Maybelle began to change and treat the narrator nicely, he began to (a) ignore Sucker a lot, (b) treat Sucker as a friend and brother, (c) complain about Sucker's attentions, (d) hate Sucker's guts.

6. At the movie, the narrator felt good because he was there (a) with Maybelle alone, (b) with Sucker only, (c) with Maybelle and Sucker both, (d) by himself.

7. After Maybelle started running around with the fellow in the yellow roadster, the narrator (a) felt very relieved that she was gone, (b) found another girlfriend, (c) tried to be friendlier with Sucker, (d) became more and more irritated with Sucker.

8. When Sucker became hard and tough, the narrator felt that Sucker (a) would kill him if he could, (b) was like a big brother to him, (c) was acting like a phony, (d) would get into trouble some day.

What Ideas Did You Find?

1. According to this story, one strange thing about friendship and love is that you are often attracted to those people who (a) have an opposite personality to your own, (b) ignore you and treat you badly, (c) try to be kind to you, (d) are willing to meet you halfway.
2. The real "sucker" in this story is the narrator, who (a) should have known better than to chase girls, (b) hangs out at the drugstore smoking and loafing, (c) threw away a genuine friendship, (d) was fooled into believing Sucker was his friend.

Composition Exercises

1. Relate the history of a friendship or love affair of yours that went sour and died. Describe the other person, your first meeting, the events in the friendship, and what happened to end it all. Try to determine just what went wrong and whose fault it was.
2. Living with another person—whether with a friend in a dorm, a relative at home, or a spouse in marriage—is at best difficult. There are so many possibilities for misunderstanding and conflict that it is a wonder any two people can live together at all. What do you think is the secret for harmonious living with another person? Give what you believe to be a workable plan that people who are living together can follow for a successful friendship or marriage.

Language Exercise

Personality Words. Certain words in English designate personality types we see around us every day. See if you can match each word on the left with its correct definition on the right.

1. altruist	a. is a conceited braggart
2. egoist	b. is shy and inward-turning
3. egotist	c. lives a life of self-denial and simplicity
4. egocentric	
5. introvert	d. is both inwardly and outwardly directed
6. extrovert	
7. ambivert	e. hates women
8. misanthrope	f. hates his fellow man
9. misogamist	g. regards himself as the center of all things
10. misogynist	h. is interested in the welfare of other people
	i. hates marriage
	j. is insanely wrapped up in himself
	k. is outwardly friendly and directed toward other people
	l. is self-centered and selfish

ON THE ROAD

What Facts Do You Remember?

1. When the Reverend Mr. Dorset opened the door and saw Sargeant, he told him to go (a) around to the back door, (b) to the church rectory, (c) to a neighbor's house, (d) to the relief shelter.

2. After leaving the parsonage, Sargeant went to the church, where he found that (a) the doors were locked, (b) the congregation was singing, (c) the people were friendly, (d) he would be treated kindly.

3. Sargeant knew that the church was (a) for Negroes only, (b) a white folks' church, (c) for anyone to use, (d) the last place he should go.

4. Sargeant held on to a stone pillar of the church and the people (a) thought he was sick or drunk, (b) praised his fantastic strength, (c) tried to pull him loose from the pillar, (d) completely ignored him.

5. After Sargeant left the church, he heard someone walking behind him and turned to see (a) the Reverend Mr. Dorset, (b) many people following him, (c) two policemen hurrying forward, (d) Jesus Christ walking beside him.

6. Sargeant tried to jump aboard a freight train the next morning, but he found that (a) the boxcar doors were sealed, (b) the coal car was filled with police, (c) his strength had vanished during the night, (d) the train was moving too fast.

7. Instead of winding up on the freight train, Sargeant found himself (a) back at the church, (b) walking down the tracks, (c) locked in jail, (d) sitting in the hobo jungle.

8. The last thing Sargeant wondered about was whether (a) Mr. Dorset knew his whereabouts, (b) the church was still standing, (c) Christ had gone to Kansas City, (d) he would get a good hot meal.

What Ideas Did You Find?

1. Langston Hughes wants the reader to believe that Sargeant merely dreamed or imagined (a) the whole story from beginning to end, (b) that he pulled down the church and talked with Christ, (c) the conversation with the Reverend Mr. Dorset, (d) that he was in jail and shouting at the cop.

2. The biblical figure that Sargeant much resembles is (a) Samson, (b) David, (c) Jesus, (d) Joseph.

Composition Exercises

1. Continue the story beyond the ending. Tell what happens to Sargeant as a result of his run-in with the law. Is he tried and convicted for what he did? What sentence does he receive? Or is he allowed to leave town, as many bums were allowed to do in those days? Do you think Sargeant will ever find work and some measure of happiness in this life? Why or why not?

2. Describe an incident that you know of in which someone was discriminated against because of his race, color, or religion. Give as many specific details as you can to make the reader see very clearly the injustice of the situation.

Language Exercise

Word Curiosities. Many common words in English begin and end with the same letter, such as *blab* (to chatter unwisely) or *tract* (a pamphlet or a housing development). Listed below are ten words beginning and ending with the letter *d*. See if you can fill in the missing letters after you have studied the definitions.

Example: d e *l i g h t* e d = joyful

1. d — d	head of the house
2. d — — d	inanimate
3. d — — — d	old-fashioned
4. d — — — — d	protect
5. d — — — — — d	determined
6. d — — — — — d	cheat
7. d — — — — — d	faithful
8. d — — — — — — d	contorted
9. d — — — — — — d	melancholy
10. d — — — — — — — — — d	separated

THE BITTER BREAD

What Facts Do You Remember?

1. This story takes place in the (a) spring, (b) summer, (c) fall, (d) winter.

2. Robert was bringing home what person to see his wife, Jeannie? (a) doctor, (b) midwife, (c) preacher, (d) nurse.

3. Robert took Jeannie to the hospital in (a) his car, (b) a pickup truck, (c) his wagon, (d) an ambulance.

4. Before Jeannie could be admitted into the hospital, Robert was asked to pay in advance, (a) $100, (b) $75, (c) $50, (d) $15.

5. Robert first went to borrow the money from (a) his father, (b) the cotton company, (c) Joe-Thell, (d) Mama Lavorn.

6. When Robert finally borrowed the money, the interest on it was (a) eight percent, (b) $20 per month, (c) $1 a day, (d) $12.50 per week.

7. When Robert got back to the hospital, he discovered that (a) he needed more money, (b) his wife was dead, (c) he was the father of a baby boy, (d) a misunderstanding had occurred.

8. Robert left the hospital and went (a) to his home, (b) back to Joe-Thell's, (c) out of town and into the fields, (d) on down the road to the next town.

What Ideas Did You Find?

1. The hospital in this story was (a) County, (b) Memorial, (c) Presbyterian, (d) Catholic.

2. The author of this story might be criticizing (a) Negroes who accept the white man's injustice, (b) people and institutions that value money over human life, (c) the way Negroes are treated in white society, (d) people who make a living off the poor and ignorant.

Composition Exercises

1. Write a letter to the administrator of the hospital in this story, and complain about the treatment given to Robert and his wife by the hospital staff. Explain in detail just what happened from start to finish.
2. This story might serve as an example of man's inhumanity to man. Describe and explain in detail another example that you know about.

Language Exercise

Medical terminology—the words used by doctors, nurses, and others of the medical profession—consists of a specialized set of words that often seem confusing to people outside medicine. Everyone should learn certain basic medical words, particularly the names for specialized doctors. See if you can identify the different kinds of doctors by matching the names on the left with their descriptions on the right.

1. neurologist
2. pediatrician
3. optometrist
4. dermatologist
5. obstetrician
6. ophthalmologist
7. internist
8. gynecologist
9. psychiatrist
10. orthodontist

a. delivers babies and cares for pregnant women

b. specializes in the mentally disturbed and the insane

c. specializes in the expert diagnosis of internal ailments

d. treats improper functioning of the nervous system

e. is concerned with the treatment of eye disorders and diseases

f. specializes in the diagnosis and treatment of skin diseases

g. restricts his practice to females

h. specializes in the care and treatment of infant and childhood ailments

i. does not engage in medical activities but merely prescribes and fits glasses

j. specializes in the straightening of teeth

KING OF THE BINGO GAME

What Facts Do You Remember?

1. The two men sitting next to the main character were drinking (a) Cokes, (b) wine, (c) gin, (d) rye whiskey.

2. The main character's wife was named (a) Laura, (b) Louise, (c) Lana, (d) Lottie.

3. Although he knew the "guy at the door wouldn't like it," the main character (a) had sneaked into the theater, (b) had won at bingo last week, (c) had obtained five bingo cards, (d) had sat down in the expensive loge seats.

4. The bingo jackpot for that night was (a) $500, (b) $300, (c) $75.85, (d) $36.90.

5. The main character told the audience that he was from a town in the (a) North, (b) South, (c) East, (d) West.

6. To win, the contestant had to stop the wheel between (a) a red and a black number, (b) the double zero, (c) the single zero and the one, (d) the 500 and the 600.

7. The main character made the crowd angry because he (a) wouldn't stop the wheel, (b) sat down on the stage, (c) used obscene language, (d) ignored them completely.

8. When the wheel came slowly to a stop, the main character saw that it (a) indicated he could spin it again, (b) rested at the winning spot, (c) pointed to the consolation prize, (d) indicated that he had lost.

What Ideas Did You Find?

1. The author of this story, Ralph Ellison, does not give his main character a name because he (a) probably couldn't think of one, (b) wants the character to represent all men—to be the universal man, (c) knew that this character wouldn't have wanted his name known, (d) thought that if he gave a name to the character some of the readers would become angry.

2. The title, "King of the Bingo Game," means that the (a) main character was an excellent bingo player, (b) theater manager actually controlled the bingo game, (c) manager finally allowed the main character to win the bingo prize, (d) main character became a bingo king or god as long as he pressed the button.

Composition Exercises

1. What do you think happened to the man in this story? Was he killed, or did he survive? Was he thrown into jail, or was he simply thrown out of the theater? What happened to his sick wife, Laura? Assume you were sitting in the audience during this bingo game, and you became interested in finding out what happened after the curtain came down. Write a narrative describing the events and the fate of the man and his wife.

2. Games of chance such as bingo are banned in some communities because many people regard them as gambling games. However, other communities allow bingo games in churches, private clubs, and military installations. Examine your own feelings about bingo and take a position for or against allowing bingo games in your area. Write a letter to the editor of your newspaper arguing your point.

Language Exercise

Games: See how many of the twelve games listed below you can identify from your own experience. Then check your dictionary to match up the name with the game.

1. baccarat
2. backgammon
3. chess
4. cribbage
5. faro
6. loo
7. lotto
8. Mah-Jongg
9. pachisi
10. Patience
11. tarot
12. whist

a. card game in which the ten counts as zero

b. game using a special board in which two people throw dice for moves of pieces around the board

c. game of skill using a special board in which two people move "men" in different ways

d. card game in which two, three, or four players keep score on a small board with holes and pegs

e. card game in which players bet on the cards to be turned up from the dealer's pack

f. card game in which the players play for a pool or "pot" made up of stakes and forfeits

g. game of chance using cards in which players cover numbered squares to win

h. game using 136 or 144 pieces called titles in which four players build combinations of suits by drawing

i. game using a special board in which four players throw

dice or shells for moves of
pieces around the board

j. card game in which one
    player plays against an ima-
    ginary opponent

k. card game using 22 playing
    cards that depict vices and
    virtues

l. card game using 52 playing
    cards in which two pairs of
    players try to take "tricks"
    from each other

POISON

What Facts Do You Remember?

1. This story takes place in (a) Brazil, (b) South Africa, (c) Egypt,
    (d) India.

2. The character in the story who was lying on the bed was named
    (a) Timber, (b) Woods, (c) Harry, (d) Dr. Ganderbai.

3. The man on the bed was convinced that on his stomach lay a
    (a) krait, (b) cobra, (c) rattlesnake, (d) water moccasin.

4. Harry vetoed Timber's plans for removing the snake and told
    him to (a) call the police, (b) get a doctor, (c) call in a snake
    expert, (d) do nothing.

5. The serum injected into Harry's vein gave him (a) complete
    protection, (b) very little protection, (c) no protection at all.

6. It was decided that an anesthetic should be administered to
    (a) Harry, (b) Timber, (c) the snake.

7. The anesthetic they decided to use was (a) ether, (b) sodium
    pentathol, c) chloroform.

8. When they removed the sheet, what did they find on the man's stomach? (a) nothing, (b) two snakes, (c) a rope, (d) a mongoose.

What Ideas Did You Find?

1. The author of this story wanted the reader to (a) agree with Harry, (b) feel sorry for Harry, (c) condemn Harry for the things he said, (d) excuse Harry's actions because of his ordeal.
2. The "poison" in this story refers not only to snake venom but also to (a) tension, (b) racism, (c) fear, (d) death.

Composition Exercises

1. After Timber Woods came back into the house, what do you think he said to Harry Pope about Harry's treatment of Dr. Ganderbai? Describe the scene and relate the dialogue between these two friends.
2. You are Harry Pope the day after the krait incident, and you are now sorry for the things you said to Dr. Ganderbai. Write him a letter apologizing for your actions, and explain your feelings during the whole frightening episode. Don't try to excuse your bad manners, but do try to make the doctor understand why you did what you did.

Language Exercise

Match the medical words below, taken from the story, with their original meanings and origins.

1. intravenously
2. hypodermic
3. syringe
4. calibrations
5. anesthetic

a. Latin: one who suffers
b. Greek: without + feeling
c. Latin: a cylinder
d. Greek: hand + work
e. Latin: to make + lawful

6. chloroform
7. tourniquet
8. surgeon
9. patient
10. scalpel

f. Greek: under + skin
g. Latin: within + vein
h. Latin: knife
i. French: size of diameter
j. Greek: a pipe or tube
k. French: turning device
l. Greek: pale green + formic acid

THE BURNING

What Facts Do You Remember?

1. This story takes place in (a) California, (b) Missouri, (c) Pennsylvania, (d) Kentucky.

2. Gates, the driver who was killed, was driving a truck filled with (a) oil, (b) gasoline, (c) kerosine, (d) explosives.

3. The accident occurred when Gates swerved to avoid hitting (a) a family in a station wagon, (b) another truck, (c) two college girls in a small car, (d) a school bus.

4. The restaurant at the top of the hill was named (a) Manny's Place, (b) June's Stop, (c) Wakefield's Corner, (d) Pleasant Valley Inn.

5. The driver who was questioning the girls in the motel room was named (a) Johnny Manley, (b) Gates, (c) Singleton, (d) Wakefield.

6. The reason they couldn't get Gates out of his burning truck was that (a) the fire was too hot, (b) the truck was in a ditch, (c) they arrived too late, (d) Gates' leg was pinned.

7. The thing that killed Gates was (a) the fire, (b) the crash, (c) a bullet, (d) an explosion.

8. The driver really responsible for Gates' death was (a) Manny, (b) Arnie, (c) Singleton, (d) Wakefield.

What Ideas Did You Find?

1. The author of this story hopes to make the reader more sympathetic toward (a) highway accidents, (b) cruising policemen, (c) passenger-car drivers, (d) truck drivers.
2. The most important idea in this story is that sometimes (a) mercy killing is justified, (b) being burned to death is horrible, (c) women drivers are careless, (d) truck drivers stick together.

Composition Exercises

1. Draw an accurate setting map of the story, being careful to include the highway, the scene of the accident, the positions of the vehicles, the truck-stop restaurant, the motel, etc. Label the map accurately, and provide short descriptions and explanations of its main elements.
2. Because of their reputation for helping people on the highway, truck drivers have been called "knights of the road." Do you believe they deserve such a reputation, or do you think that the idea is a false one? Support your answer with examples from your own experience.

Language Exercise

Euthanasia, a word that means "mercy killing," comes from the Greek word for a painless and happy death. It is made up of a Greek prefix *eu*, meaning *well*, and a root word, *thanatos*, meaning *death*. English has several fairly common words taken from the Greek that utilize the prefix *eu*. Look up in your dictionary each of the following words, and write the meaning for the prefix and the root. Then write down the modern dictionary definition of the word.

1. euphoria   4. euphemism
2. eugenics   5. euphony
3. eulogy

THE LEDGE

What Facts Do You Remember?

1. The fisherman had promised to take the boys (a) to the city, (b) on a boat ride, (c) duck hunting, (d) deep-sea fishing.

2. The place where the fisherman and the two boys were headed in the skiff was named (a) Devil's Hump, (b) Ship-Trap Island, (c) Pirate's Ledge, (d) Finnegan's Reef.

3. The fisherman was dismayed when he learned he had left at home all of his (a) fishing gear, (b) stock of food, (c) foul-weather clothing, (d) pipe tobacco.

4. While waiting on the rock for some action, the boys became (a) sleepy, (b) nervous, (c) noisy, (d) seasick.

5. As the tide began to come in, the fisherman stood up and discovered (a) one of the boys was missing, (b) the skiff was gone, (c) the dog had vanished, (d) all their gear had washed away.

6. When the fisherman offered to buy the boys anything they wanted before school started, his son said he would like (a) a Remington shotgun, (b) some new fishing gear, (c) a sloop-rigged sailboat, (d) a thirty-horse outboard.

7. As the fisherman stared at the mainland, he noticed that it was beginning to (a) snow, (b) rain, (c) get warmer, (d) fog up.

8. To try and save his son as long as possible, the fisherman (a) gave the boy his coat, (b) tied the boy to the rock, (c) told the boy to run in place, (d) held the boy on his shoulders.

What Ideas Did You Find?

1. The reason the fisherman was so irritable on the trip was that (a) he hadn't wanted to go that day, (b) everything seemed to go wrong, (c) the boys were stupid and annoying, (d) he had a sour personality.

2. This story has an unhappy ending because the author (a) couldn't think up a solution to the fisherman's problem, (b) was reporting what happened to a real person, (c) wanted the story to end tragically in order to move the reader emotionally, (d) has a morbid interest in death and sadness.

Composition Exercises

1. Draw a setting map for this story showing the coastline, the bay, the fisherman's house, Brown Cow Island, and the ledge. Write a paragraph describing these items in detail for a movie director who intends to film the story.

2. Explain why this story is tragic. Could the tragedy have been prevented, or was what happened inevitable? Also, why doesn't the author give the names of the fisherman, the two boys, and the dog? Does this namelessness make the story more or less tragic? Why?

Language Exercise

Listed below are ten words and ten phrases taken from the story. See if you can insert into each phrase the word used in the story.

lolling	athwartships
iridescent	ashen
consternation	incredulous
attrition	averted
painter	indomitable

1. and though prices were high the storms made the rate of _____ high on gear

2. heaved the skiff and outboard onto the stern and secured it _____

3. [the deck was] _____ in the ray of the light shone through the windshield

4. anticipation of a day out with nothing to smoke made him _____

5. swirled as it had for eons round the _____ edges

6. gripping the _____ and balancing himself

7. feet upturned and necks _____

8. the sky was more _____, and the wind had freshened

9. [the boys were] gawking at him in _____

10. his face _____ in an effort neither to give nor show pain

A GOOD MAN IS HARD TO FIND

What Facts Do You Remember?

1. The family wanted to go to Florida, but the grandmother wanted to go to (a) California, (b) western Texas, (c) eastern Tennessee, (d) southern Arkansas.

2. On the trip the family stopped for lunch at Red Sammy Butts' restaurant, which was named (a) the Timothy Tavern, (b) Tall Trees Inn, (c) Sammy's Place, (d) the Tower.

3. The grandmother talked Bailey into turning off the highway to see (a) an old plantation mansion, (b) an abandoned castle, (c) a haunted house, (d) the house of wonders.

4. The accident was caused by (a) a tire blowing out, (b) Pitty Sing, the cat, (c) a drunk driver, (d) a ditch across the road.

5. The first car that came by after the accident was (a) a black and white police car, (b) a gray pickup truck, (c) a black hearselike car, (d) an old Model A Ford.

6. The leader of the three men was called (a) The Malformed, (b) The Malcontent, (c) The Misfit, (d) The Madman.

7. Hiram and Bobby Lee first shot (a) the grandmother and Pitty Sing, (b) the mother and June Star, (c) John Wesley and the baby, (d) Bailey and John Wesley.

8. The leader of the three men said that Jesus had (a) saved the world for all men, (b) thrown everything off balance, (c) never really helped anybody, (d) always been the light of his life.

What Ideas Did You Find?

1. One of the things the author of this story seems to be saying is that (a) Jesus caused all the trouble, (b) women talk too much, (c) killing is sometimes necessary, (d) some men are evil for no reason at all.

2. The grandmother as a person has an outlook on life that is (a) very praiseworthy, (b) quite shallow, (c) a pleasure to everyone, (d) her salvation.

Composition Exercises

1. Have you ever had a family outing turn into an unpleasant experience? Relate an incident involving a trip that turned into a complete mess or a disaster.

2. Do you accept violence as necessary, or are you outraged by the kind and amount of violence in the world? Write a letter to the editor of a newspaper either deploring violence and offering an alternative for it or explaining that violence is natural—and sometimes good—for man. Try to give as many examples as you can to support your argument.

Language Exercise

Descriptive Words. Nouns and verbs can often be turned into adjectives by adding a suffix onto the word. In this way we can expand the language almost limitlessly and at the same time make words perform multiple jobs. For example, the noun *lace* can be turned into a word describing something lacelike when we add the suffix *y* to form *lacy*. The verb *differ* can become the adjective *different* by adding *ent*. Notice that the spelling may change slightly when the suffix is added. Some of the most useful and frequently used adjective suffixes are as follows:

-able (ible)	*-ent (ant)*
-al	*-ive*
-ic	*-ful*
-ous	*-y*

For each word below, separate the base word (spelled correctly) from the adjective suffix, and then find another base word to form another adjective.

Example: *accident* + *al* = *accidental*
          occasion + *al* = *occasional*

1. irritable	11. memorable
2. original	12. pleasant
3. allergic	13. expensive
4. various	14. suitable
5. arrogant	15. decisive
6. restive	16. terrible
7. respectful	17. cautious
8. dreamy	18. imitative
9. dramatic	19. frightful
10. normal	20. populous

THE WATCHERS

What Facts Do You Remember?

1. When Althea awoke that morning, she knew that (a) her husband was returning, (b) she would be visited by a friend, (c) their building had been chosen, (d) they would have to move.

2. After Althea had finished dressing, the flickering signal lights on the wall indicated that (a) her husband was home, (b) the roast was done, (c) it was time to go out, (d) someone was downstairs.

3. When Sally Milford came into the apartment, Althea (a) hid behind the door, (b) ignored her, (c) refused to visit, (d) asked her to leave.

4. Althea and Sally decided (a) not to go to the performance, (b) to go downtown together, (c) not to be mad at each other, (d) to spy on each other.

5. When she got back to the apartment, Althea heard from the doorman that Timmy Hammond was slashed (a) in a fight, (b) with a razor, (c) by a girl, (d) during a gang war.

6. After she and her husband had eaten and dressed, Althea was eager to (a) see a movie, (b) go to a nightclub, (c) visit the Milfords, (d) attend the performance.

7. The age of the girl in the red suit and beret was approximately (a) fifteen, (b) twenty, (c) twenty-one, (d) twenty-five.

8. The man in the black jacket (a) loved the girl, (b) ran away, (c) stabbed the girl, (d) didn't want to be watched.

What Ideas Did You Find?

1. The author of this story is presenting here a new kind of society (a) in which the people feel more secure than they do today, (b) in which people are distrustful, watchful, and careful, (c) that could only develop in a country like Russia, (d) in which the people are trained to be just like everyone else.

2. In this story the writer's main purpose is to (a) expose and criticize an unpleasant aspect of human nature and life, (b) frighten the reader about a possible future society, (c) merely entertain the reader with an interesting story, (d) present the argument that everyone should carry a gun.

Composition Exercises

1. You are Althea or her husband. Write a short drama review (to be published in your local paper) of the "performance" you and your neighbors have seen. Describe the performance in detail, and point out its good and bad points (remember to judge it through the eyes of these people). Also describe the major characters, and evaluate how well each one performed. Finally, come to a decision as to its overall value for people living in your time.

2. You are either the victim or the attacker in this story. Write your thoughts and feelings during the attack. Describe what you think about and your emotions from the beginning of the attack until its end. Let the thoughts and feelings stream through your mind like dialogue in a story. Capture them on paper as they appear.

Language Exercise

Select the letter of the definition that best fits the meaning of the word used in the sentence.

1. *vulnerability:* "Love breeds its own *vulnerability*, its own fear." (p. 254)
   (a) quality of being wounded or injured, (b) transportability, (c) light-headedness, (d) quality of being afraid.

2. *incredulous:* " 'In the park?' said Althea, *incredulous*." (p. 256)
   (a) being fearful, (b) being inconsistent, (c) showing doubt or disbelief, (d) seeing humor in a situation.

3. *indulgently:* " 'Come on,' he said, *indulgently.*" (p. 260)
   (a) acting from influence, (b) being kindly and lenient, (c) explaining patiently, (d) being unhappy.

4. *nondescript:* "... a *nondescript* man was walking his dog...."
   (p. 262)
   (a) unrestrained, (b) nonexistent, (c) unrivaled (d) indescribable.

5. *expansively:* "... the boy nodded and gestured *expansively.*"
   (p. 262)
   (a) excitedly, (b) expectantly, (c) broadly, (d) happily.

6. *furtively:* "... she rubbed them *furtively* together." (p. 262)
   (a) stealthily, (b) strangely, (c) functionally, (d) forgetfully.

7. *muted:* ". . . the sounds of the distant traffic seemed
   muted...." (p. 262)
   (a) mixed, (b) distorted, (c) unreal, (d) softened.

8. *jauntily:* "... a feather stuck *jauntily* in it. . . ." (p. 263)
   (a) jerkily, (b) sprightly, (c) awkwardly, (d) haphazardly.

9. *sinuous:* [he was] "... *sinuous*, beautiful in his grace...."
   (p. 263)
   (a) snakelike, (b) mysterious, (c) quick, (d) light-footed.

10. *keening:* "Her voice rose to a *keening* wail of terror...."
    (p. 264)
    (a) unhappy, (b) awesome, (c) piercing, (d) terrifying.

THE CROWD

What Facts Do You Remember?

1. The thing that bothered Mr. Spallner after his first accident was
   that (a) he had driven too fast, (b) his car was totally demolished, (c) the crowd got there too quickly, (d) the ambulance took so long to arrive.

2. One of the faces Mr. Spallner remembered seeing in the crowd was that of a woman (a) with red hair and red on her cheeks and lips, (b) who was thin, gaunt, and beady-eyed, (c) who smiled through crooked teeth, (d) with fat cheeks and stringy black hair.

3. In his first accident Mr. Spallner knew by the look on the faces of the crowd that (a) they hated him, (b) he was a doomed man, (c) he was very badly injured, (d) he would not die.

4. On his way home from the hospital in the taxi, Mr. Spallner saw (a) one of the faces in the crowd, (b) an accident and a crowd, (c) wheels spinning in his mind, (d) the extent of the damage to his car.

5. While Mr. Spallner talked to his friend at the office, he remembered (a) seeing the faces, (b) wheels and faces, (c) the agony of the accident, (d) the odors of the wreck.

6. At about 5:30 during his conversation with Morgan, Mr. Spallner saw an accident out in the street that involved (a) a car and a motorcycle, (b) two passenger cars, (c) two delivery trucks, (d) a truck and a Cadillac.

7. While he was in the hospital, Mr. Spallner had an agency collect (a) names of people involved in accidents, (b) police reports of auto accidents, (c) clippings and photographs of accidents, (d) books on crowd behavior.

8. Mr. Spallner was taking his evidence to the police when he (a) was shot, (b) was run over in the street, (c) was smashed into by a truck, (d) lost control of his car and went off a bridge.

What Ideas Did You Find?

1. The reader is supposed to believe that Mr. Spallner was deliberately killed by "The Crowd" because he (a) had discovered the secret of the crowd's existence, (b) was no longer important to their plans, (c) ignored warnings to stay away, (d) was needed as a member of the crowd.

2. In this story Ray Bradbury is criticizing man's tendency to (a) become involved in accidents, (b) morbidly enjoy any scene containing blood and death, (c) ignore the desires of accident victims, (d) gather like vultures at any accident.

Composition Exercises

1. Relate a personal experience involving an automobile accident that drew a crowd. How did the accident happen? How fast did the people arrive on the scene? What did they look like? Were they helpful, or did they get in the way? Why do you think people gather at the scene of an accident?

2. You are Mr. Spallner's friend, Mr. Morgan, and you have discovered in his desk drawer a letter he wrote before he was killed. The letter concerns his discoveries about the crowd, and it points out all the evidence Mr. Spallner had collected. Write the letter with all its details, and then tell what you, Mr. Morgan, intend to do with it.

Language Exercise

Figurative Language: Many times in using language we find it necessary to say one thing and yet mean something else. For instance, when we say "You're pulling my leg," we actually mean "You're kidding me." When we say "He was stubborn as a mule" or "He was a workhorse," we mean he was stubborn in the same way a mule is stubborn and he could work as hard as a horse works. This kind of language is called figurative language (using a figure of speech)—that is, language that cannot be taken literally. Often figures of speech are comparisons—his stubbornness is compared to a mule's stubborness—and these comparisons are either *similes* or *metaphors*. A *simile* compares through the use of *as* or *like*; a metaphor compares directly. Thus "He was stubborn as a mule" is a simile and "He was a workhorse" is a metaphor.

Examine each of the following figures of speech, taken from the story, and see if you can identify each one as either a simile or a metaphor.

1. "[their faces] . . . hung over him like the large glowing leaves of down-bent trees." (p. 266)

2. "They were a ring of shifting, compressing, changing faces over him. . . ." (pp. 266–67)

3. ". . . making his face into a moon-dial." (p. 267)

4. "[a crowd comes] . . . like the iris of an eye compressing in out of nowhere." (p. 267)

5. [They—the crowd—are] "Vultures, hyenas or saints." (p. 273)

6. "It was like a great rainstorm. . . ." (p. 274)

7. "Curiously distant, Spallner looked upon the scene as an explosion in reverse. . . ." (p. 270)

8. "The windshield hammered back into his face." (p. 274)

9. "They straightened him into a ramrod of agony." (p. 274)

10. "He looked at them, above him, and he was curious as a man under deep water looking up at people on a bridge." (p. 275)

AN OCCURRENCE AT OWL CREEK BRIDGE

What Facts Do You Remember?

1. This story takes place in (a) Alabama, (b) Mississippi, (c) South Carolina, (d) Virginia.

2. The man being hanged was approximately (a) twenty, (b) twenty-five, (c) thirty-five, (d) forty.

3. Peyton Farquhar's occupation was that of (a) soldier, (b) planter, (c) spy, (d) informer.

4. Owl Creek Bridge was in the possession of the (a) civilian militia, (b) railroad company, (c) Confederate troops, (d) Union troops.

5. The soldier who told Farquhar about the bridge was a (a) deserter, (b) picket, (c) scout, (d) friend.

6. When Farquhar came to the surface of the stream, the soldiers on the bridge (a) shouted at him, (b) shot their pistols at him, (c) did not see him, (d) ran to the stockade.

7. After the cannon fired at him, Farquhar was caught (a) by a snag in the river, (b) by a ring of boulders, (c) by a rope from shore, (d) in a vortex of water.

8. At the end of the story Peyton Farquhar was (a) finally at home, (b) rescued by his friends, (c) dead from hanging, (d) a long distance downstream.

What Ideas Did You Find?

1. All the events of Farquhar's escape from the bridge occurred (a) only in his mind, (b) before he was captured, (c) after he was captured, (d) except for the reunion with his wife.

2. The main idea in this story is that (a) many soldiers hate civilians, (b) all civilians should stay out of war zones, (c) every man fears death, (d) each man creates reality in his own mind.

Composition Exercises

1. This story is based on the idea that scenes from a dying man's life flash suddenly through his mind and that these events seem real in much the same way that a dream seems real to a dreamer. Try to relate a "realistic" dream that you have had or that someone you know has had. Bring in as many concrete and realistic details from the dream as you can.

2. You are the Union Army captain in charge of the hanging of Peyton Farquhar. Write a complete military report describing your capture of the bridge, the attempt by a Southern civilian

(Farquhar) to destroy the bridge, and the ultimate capture and hanging of that civilian. Give as many details as possible.

Language Exercise

Look up in your dictionary each of the following words taken from the story. Then read the sentences and select the word from the list that fits into the blank space in each sentence.

a. traversed (p. 278)
b. embrasure (p. 278)
c. deference (p. 278)
d. imperious (p. 280)
e. dictum (p. 280)
f. poignant (p. 281)
g. ramification (p. 281)
h. inaccessible (p. 282)

i. gesticulated (p. 283)
j. commingled (p. 285)
k. vortex (p. 285)
l. interminable (p. 285)
m. rift (p. 285)
n. malign (p. 285)
o. ineffable (p. 286)

1. Both husband and wife had _____ their funds so that the original ownership was lost.

2. Circumstances of an _____ nature commanded his retirement from public office.

3. Her long ordeal seemed _____ to her.

4. She knew the mountain cabin was _____ from the road.

5. The old ladies were sure to gossip and to _____ the next unmarried woman they came across.

6. The runner had _____ a great distance.

7. A huge, swirling _____ caught the ship and dashed it to pieces.

8. He had shown a great amount of _____ to his superior officer.

9. It was a sad and _____ scene of tragedy.
10. He had _____ energetically with his arms.

FREEWAY TO WHEREVER

What Facts Do You Remember?

1. The members of the family in this story were proud of their car because it (a) cost a thousand dollars, (b) was brand new, (c) was the fastest car on the road, (d) was a convertible.

2. The man in the powder-blue convertible owned (a) two cars, (b) a repair shop, (c) a company that produced matches, (d) a string of drive-in restaurants.

3. After a while the family discovered that the freeway (a) had not been opened, (b) circled back to the city, (c) had no turnoff ramps, (d) was too narrowly built for three lanes.

4. Tom announced that they were coming to something when he saw on the horizon (a) a pall of smog, (b) a big blue sign, (c) some buildings, (d) many blinking lights.

5. Because it was so hot, Mary thought they should (a) stop and buy cold drinks, (b) roll down all the windows, (c) turn around and go home, (d) perhaps have bought an air-conditioned car.

6. Because they had gotten everything they wanted, it seemed to Mary that they (a) would be satisfied in the future, (b) had nothing left to live for, (c) were all spoiled, (d) didn't appreciate any of it.

7. When Mary absently looked into the back seat, the children were (a) playing a game, (b) arguing among themselves, (c) sound asleep, (d) looking out the windows.

8. As they approached the wall of the city ahead, they saw that they were crossing to a (a) huge overpass, (b) single turnoff ramp, (c) toll plaza, (d) mighty gate.

What Ideas Did You Find?

1. The "indestructible city" that the family arrived at was (a) a well-built modern city, (b) the city of dreams, (c) Heaven, (d) Hell.

2. The author of the story implies that the family deserves to die because they worshiped (a) things, (b) idols, (c) themselves, (d) status.

Composition Exercises

1. You are a visitor from a highly advanced planet that we shall name Arcturus. You have been assigned to investigate in your flying saucer a modern American city such as Los Angeles. Write a report for the commander of your mother ship describing what you see as you make hovering passes over the city. Give particular attention to the freeways, expressways, turnpikes, etc., that make up a complex pattern through the city.

2. Explain this story to a person from another country—say, India. He will know very little about many of the things in the story, such as freeways, drive-in restaurants, automobiles, etc. Tell him what the author was attempting to do in the story. What does the title mean? Who was Dick Blue? What was the indestructible city? What happened to the people? Why?

Language Exercise

See if you can match the words from the story on the left with their proper definitions on the right.

1. countenance (p. 287)   a. calm, self-possession

2. subdued (p. 287)   b. pale lime-green color

3. complacently (p. 288)   c. not noticeably

4. gratified (p. 288)

5. floridly (p. 288)

6. composure (p. 288)

7. imperceptibly (p. 290)

8. skittish (p. 291)

9. incoherent (p. 291)

10. caromed (p. 291)

11. saffron (p. 292)

12. maliciously (p. 292)

13. relentless (p. 293)

14. ponderous (p. 293)

15. luridly (p. 293)

d. ruddy; highly colored complexion

e. orange-yellow color

f. living within, or having to do with life within

g. not logically connected; rambling

h. conquered or vanquished

i. spitefully and vindictively

j. gradually increasing in loudness or intensity

k. flames glowing through smoke

l. heavy and massive

m. great luster or brightness

n. harsh and persistent

o. the expression of the face

p. to relate in detail

q. jumpy, easily frightened

r. very well pleased

s. self-satisfied, smug

t. hitting and rebounding

NIGHT IN FUNLAND

What Facts Do You Remember?

1. This story takes place (a) in a large Eastern city, (b) at the edge of a small Southern town, (c) on the outskirts of a desert city, (d) along the oceanfront of a coastal city.

2. The funland in this story was (a) a clean, bright place on the mesa, (b) ugly, dirty, and noisy, (c) a gyp joint for suckers, (d) a typical carnival, with wheels of fortune, leg shows, and freak tents.

3. Amanda had gone to the funland with her (a) brother, (b) mother, (c) uncle, (d) father.

4. Amanda was scolded because she (a) got too excited, (b) stuck her fingers into the grape snowball, (c) spent all her money, (d) ran away.

5. Rollo was (a) an elephant, (b) a fat man, (c) a chimpanzee, (d) the Ferris-wheel attendant.

6. Some girls on the Ferris wheel were singing (a) *Oklahoma,* (b) *Camelot,* (c) *California, Here I Come,* (d) *The Daring Young Man on the Flying Trapeze.*

7. Amanda was riding in a carriage that was (a) green, (b) black, (c) red, (d) orange.

8. The wild cries by Amanda's father attracted the attention of (a) the police, (b) Rollo, (c) the fat man, (d) the attendant.

What Ideas Did You Find?

1. At the end of the story we are led to believe that Amanda and her father were (a) playing a silly game, (b) reunited and went their happy way, (c) suffering from insanity, (d) separated from each other forever.

2. This story is trying to convince us that (a) funlands are dangerous, (b) children are not careful enough, (c) parents suffer greatly when children are taken by death, (d) parents should protect their children at all times.

Composition Exercises

1. Describe to someone who has never had the experience what it feels like to ride a Ferris wheel or other carnival ride. What

is the feeling that you get in the pit of your stomach? Do you experience fear or excitement or both? Try to make the person reading your paper experience all the feelings of the ride.

2. Using police language as much as you can, write a brief police report such as might have been written by the policeman investigating Amanda's disappearance from the Ferris wheel. Explain in detail what happened, and tell what the father did when his daughter could not be found.

Language Exercise

What's in a Name? The Ferris wheel in this story is one of the central elements. Have you ever thought about where such a machine got its name? It was invented by George W. G. Ferris, an American engineer who designed and constructed the first one of these amusement wheels for the Chicago World's Fair of 1893. Since that time the wheel has been one of the most popular rides in carnivals and fun zones. Many other words in our language have similarly interesting backgrounds, some of them connected with the names of persons. Look up each of the words below, and write down the word's (a) definition, and (b) connection with a person.

1. bloomers
2. chesterfield (sofa)
3. cesarean (operation)
4. daguerreotype
5. derringer
6. doberman pinscher
7. Fahrenheit
8. Levi's
9. malapropism
10. Pulitzer Prize
11. quisling
12. sadism
13. saxophone
14. silhouette
15. watt (electrical)